OUTSIDERS STILL

Why Women Journalists Love – and
Leave – Their Newspaper Careers

Despite years of dominating journalism school classrooms across North America, women remain vastly under-represented at the highest levels of newspaper leadership. Why do so many female journalists leave the industry and so few reach the top?

Interviewing female journalists at daily newspapers across Canada, Vivian Smith – who spent fourteen years at the *Globe and Mail* as a reporter, editor, and manager – finds that many of the obstacles that women face in the newspaper industry are the same now as they have been historically, indeed made worse by the challenging times in which the industry finds itself. The youngest fear they will have to choose between a career and a family; mid-career women madly juggle the pressures of work and family while worrying that they are not "good mothers"; and the most senior reflect on decades of accomplishments mixed with frustration at newsroom sexism that has held them back.

Listening carefully to the stories these journalists tell, both about themselves and about what they write, Smith reveals in *Outsiders Still* how overt hostility to women in the newsroom has been replaced by systemic inequality that limits or ends the careers of many female journalists. Despite decades of contributions to society's news agenda, women print journalists are outsiders still.

VIVIAN SMITH, PhD, is a journalist, media consultant, and sessional instructor in the Department of Writing at the University of Victoria. She is a former National Beats Editor at the *Globe and Mail* whose freelance work has appeared in the *Globe, National Post, Canadian Living, ROB Magazine,* and *Maclean's.*

Outsiders Still

Why Women Journalists Love – and Leave – Their Newspaper Careers

VIVIAN SMITH

UNIVERSITY OF TORONTO PRESS
Toronto Buffalo London

© University of Toronto Press 2015
Toronto Buffalo London
www.utppublishing.com
Printed in the U.S.A.

ISBN 978-1-4426-5001-5 (cloth)
ISBN 978-1-4426-2795-6 (paper)

Printed on acid-free, 100% post-consumer recycled paper

Library and Archives Canada Cataloguing in Publication

Smith, Vivian, 1953–, author
Outsiders still : why women journalists love – and leave – their newspaper
careers / Vivian Smith.

Includes bibliographical references and index.
ISBN 978-1-4426-5001-5 (bound). – ISBN 978-1-4426-2795-6 (pbk.)

1. Women journalists – Canada.   2. Women journalists – Canada –
Interviews.   3. Journalism – Canada.   I. Title.

PN4784.W7S65 2015   070.4082   C2014-907980-X

This book has been published with the help of a grant from the Federation
for the Humanities and Social Sciences, through the Awards to Scholarly
Publications Program, using funds provided by the Social Sciences and
Humanities Research Council of Canada.

University of Toronto Press acknowledges the financial assistance to its
publishing program of the Canada Council for the Arts and the Ontario
Arts Council, an agency of the Government of Ontario.

 Canada Council Conseil des Arts
for the Arts du Canada

ONTARIO ARTS COUNCIL
CONSEIL DES ARTS DE L'ONTARIO
an Ontario government agency
un organisme du gouvernement de l'Ontario

University of Toronto Press acknowledges the financial support of
the Government of Canada through the Canada Book Fund for its
publishing activities.

In memory of Shirley Sharzer, who made everything possible

Contents

Acknowledgments

I have spent far more of my working life as an editor rather than writer, but an examination of the careers of women print journalists was a book I could not resist undertaking myself. It was worth every moment.

The defining experience of working in the newspaper world for so long and the excitement of becoming a late-blooming academic pushed me forward. Pride and anxiety, in equal amounts, kept me from retreating. So did the trust placed in me by the journalists I interviewed, whose candour, wisdom, and passion give this project whatever value it may have. I am endlessly grateful to them.

My thanks go out to acquisitions editor Doug Hildebrand and the University of Toronto Press. Doug agreed to my nervous request for a dance, and swung me gently around the publication process, not complaining when I stepped on his feet. Newspapers Canada, the print industry's national group, readily provided detailed information about its member papers and leadership ranks. Beth McAuley of The Editing Company performed a generous, masterful edit. Whatever errors remain are mine alone.

I cajoled many people into contributing directly to this project; I drew on others for friendship, inspiration, and humour, whether they knew it or not. Enthusiastically and alphabetically, I thank Dr. Gene Allen, Janet Bagnall, Dr. David Black, Stevie Cameron, Dr. Sienna Caspar, Callie Cesarini, Dr. Darlene Clover, Mary Doyle, Dr. Barbara Freeman, Anita Girvan, Dr. Kelly Grindrod, Tom Hawthorn, Joyce Hookings, Deborah Irvine, Dr. Peter Keller, Lynn Kennedy, Paul Knox, Verna Laliberte, Dr. Annalee Lepp, Heather MacAndrew, Melinda Marks, Duncan McMonagle, Alanna Mitchell, Anne Mullens, Candy Porter, Ann Rauhala, Judy Robertson, Denise Rudnicki, Dr. Margaret Scaia, Susan

Schwartz, Dorelle Scott, Gwen Smith, Lisa Smith, Sylvia Stead, Geoffrey Stevens, Penny Stevens, Dr. Eileen van der Flier-Keller, Dr. Lynne Van Luven, Dr. Christopher Waddell, Jan Wong, and a cheering section of beloved family. I wish Kipper the Wonderdog could read, as she kept me company for a month on Hornby Island, BC, quietly waiting for walks while I combed through binders of interview transcripts and started to figure out what the lead was.

I also wish my *Globe and Mail* pal Nanci Lugsdin could have seen this book. She would have bought a caseload just to be supportive. June Callwood would have whooped with delight. My dad, a proud U of T engineering grad, would have made me a rye and Coke to celebrate.

They are not the only ones gone from my life whose influence I still appreciate. Shirley Sharzer, my teacher and mentor at graduate school and at the *Globe and Mail*, died in late summer of 2014. Fortunately, I had taken an early draft to her in Ottawa for her comments, and to thank her for all she has done for me and for so many others in Canadian journalism. She seemed pleased. This book is dedicated to her memory.

My mother, Ruth Smith, my husband, Craig McInnes, and our children, Will and Mary McInnes, deserve special mention for their enduring patience and affection. I love you.

OUTSIDERS STILL

Why Women Journalists Love – and
Leave – Their Newspaper Careers

Chapter One

Introduction: Are You Still *Here*?

The publisher of the *Globe and Mail* from 1978 to 1992 was a beaming Irish-born accountant with a reputation for solid financial management, back in the glory days when Canada's news barons had solid finances to manage. In press reports, Roy Megarry was invariably described as bold and as a publisher who, perhaps more than others, personified his paper. Inside the *Globe*'s Toronto newsroom at 444 Front Street West, editorial staffers on the second floor – reporters, columnists, photographers, editors, librarians, administrators, and managers – rarely saw him.

On a blistering hot afternoon in late August of 1987, I was surprised when I looked up to see him stride towards me in the newsroom. I had just come out of a meeting in the managing editor's office and was engrossed in a printout of a story. Without slowing, Megarry eyed my approaching midsection and asked with his broad grin, "Are you still *here*?"

"Yes," I said, although I wasn't quite sure what he meant. It was early in the day, not hours past the end of a shift spent dealing with angsty reporters and breaking news.

Then I got it. I was more than eight months pregnant, and would soon begin my four-month maternity leave. "Yes," I repeated. "I am still here."

But with that, the end of my newsroom career began.

A few years later – the day before my forty-first birthday – having abandoned the stress and long hours of management for a return to reporting, I took a buyout that the *Globe* was offering. My husband, a senior political reporter who started at the paper four months after I did, had accepted a position as the *Globe*'s first Victoria bureau chief. My bosses, however, would not agree to me working part-time during my husband's five-year deployment because, they explained, that would be precedent-setting. After fourteen years of rising through the ranks from copy editor to national beats editor, having two kids and dropping back to feature writing, I moved to Victoria with my family. While the *Globe* offices had overlooked the SkyDome (now the Rogers Centre) and Toronto's skyline, my new bedroom workplace at our suburban home had a view of the front walk. Once I had been paid well to write, edit, and assign stories; to help organize civic, provincial, and national election coverage; and to bring my beat reporters' work (health, education, law, police, Metro Hall, social trends, etc.) onto the front page. Now, I was a freelance writer, paid peanuts and irregularly, with no benefits or vacation pay. In Canada, freelance writers' incomes have stagnated for three decades at about $25,000 a year on average, about $5,000 lower than what is defined now as low income for a family of four (Cohen, 2012). (In the United States, only about one in ten freelance writers makes more than US$30,000 a year [Jones, 2014].) My income dropped by two-thirds, but I did have flexibility and more time for family. What I did not have was a challenging, exciting career inside a newsroom or a regular national platform for my stories, columns, and news decisions. Eventually, I took up teaching journalism, began media-training professionals such as lawyers, doctors, professors, and government workers, and established myself as a writing coach.

We never did return to Toronto. And because so many women like me were doing the same thing, I never stopped asking myself what daily print journalism, and by extension, the sociopolitical agenda in Canada, was losing by so many women's voices going unheard on the pages of daily newspapers. I wrote this book to get at the heart of that question. By asking women print journalists what their work means to them and to their communities, I hope to help energize a debate that will ultimately help Canadians redefine for themselves what news is and who is privileged to create it.

Over the past twenty or so years, many other women of my generation at the *Globe* and at other papers have privately told stories like mine of leaving daily journalism – mostly in frustration and sadness, some with fully stated regrets and others not looking back a moment – for public relations, teaching, homemaking, freelancing, and other kinds of paid and unpaid work. Recently, many women print journalists – and men, too – have been leaving newspapers in greater numbers, taking buyouts and being laid off, as the newspaper industry shrinks in the face of business and technological upheaval. My husband, who remained as a daily reporter, editorial writer, and columnist for nearly twenty years after I left the *Globe*, recently took a buyout package.

As I took up my new work, women journalists across the country recounted to me their stories of madly juggling long hours with increasing family demands inside a culture that offered no flexibility. Young, single women would wonder at conferences whether to stay at their newspapers or jump into public relations and gain footholds there rather than risk losing their nascent journalism careers after a few years' climb; newly married women fretted to me about whether to have kids now, later, or at all; more senior women saw men promoted around them, the door to the editor-in-chief's suite barred to outsiders in skirts. In university classes, young women, who consistently made up the majority of students, would graduate, not to take up daily journalism at all. Why go through all that stress, they reasoned, with little hope of advancement?

As an editorial consultant, I continued to work with journalists and saw first-hand how women who have stayed in the newspaper industry, along with those relative few who have joined it more recently, were still passionate about their work as they still encountered, submitted to, and fought against subtle and complex forms of discrimination.

This fight drags on today inside an industry that is either wheezing through its death throes or about to be reborn, depending on which evidence you prefer. The readership of print newspapers and ad revenues for dailies are declining in lock-step, and they have been for years. This is happening as media consolidation intensifies and the magic formula to bring sustainable ad revenue to newspaper websites remains undiscovered: print ad revenues still account for about two-thirds of daily revenues, while online advertising accounts for about 8 per cent.

Canadians still learn about their neighbourhoods, cities, provinces, country, and the world through dozens of daily newspapers – more than 111 in Canada, 92 of which customers pay for, while the rest are free. In this country, we still have an unusually high rate of newspaper readership compared to the rest of the world. Fifty per cent of Canadians read newspaper content every day, with print still the primary source, says Newspapers Canada, the industry's marketing arm. Eight out of 10 Canadians read a paper sometime during the week, whether in print or online. Older Canadians tend to pay to pick up the paper at the front door every morning; younger fingers click through news produced by multiplatform reporting. The Canadian Press, once a not-for-profit supplier of print and broadcast news to member papers and radio stations, is now a for-profit company co-owned by three media companies. Canadian Press Enterprises Inc. plays a big role in supplying news to Canadians, as it produces and relays stories, photos, videos, and more to Canadian papers, broadcasters, websites, and other clients in English and French. Currently, all eight members of CP's executive team are men.

Reporters, editors, photographers, and editorial managers make up about 15 per cent of a daily newspaper's workforce. As technology becomes more sophisticated and newspapers hunker down to fight financial losses, those journalists' jobs are changing. When I started in journalism in the late 1970s, editors worked on paper proofs to edit copy and handled metal line gauges to create page designs. Reporters took notes at an event or interview, came back to the office, grabbed a coffee and kibitzed, and then banged out the story on a clunky computer the size of a carry-on suitcase. (We still used typewriters at journalism school in the mid-1970s.) A pneumatic tube shot page proofs down to the composing room, where real humans took pieces of printed type and laid them out on the page. Any editorial employee who touched the pages could cause a downing of tools by the compositors, a fiercely protective band of male workers. They are, of course, gone, the work of creating pages by hand having long since been digitized.

Page design and printing are now done electronically, and more and more editing is done offsite by companies like Pagemasters North America, a wholly owned subsidiary of the Canadian Press and part of a global centralized editing service. In April of 2014, Canada's largest daily, the *Toronto Star*, laid off the last of its full-time page editors, leaving two part-timers and Pagemasters to fulfil the duties of eleven laid-off staffers. At the same time, the *Star* hired eight digital journalists at what it calls market-based salaries, less than other journalists already in the newsroom.

The days of the well-paid, union-rate, print-only journalism job are all but over. Increasingly, in its place, positions like digital journalist are offered, often as temporary contracts, with young reporters required to report across all media, using print-style forms, audio clips, photos, and videos to tell their stories. Journalism students used to be streamed into broadcast, print, or online programs. As news forms converge, they must learn to do it all and even tutor older colleagues. The most basic requirement of journalism – accuracy – is increasingly under pressure, as the demand for new material to fill multiple platforms speedily rises with each distressing quarterly report.

Inside this newspaper tornado – at its centre, the oddly quiet newsroom with noise whirling all around it – the traditional, hierarchical culture that has existed inside for nearly two centuries is preoccupied with surviving. The attention of senior administrators is trained squarely on fiscal issues, with apparently little interest paid to how gutted editorial staffing might play a role in circulation and advertising losses, and what news might go ignored or is underreported because of who does, or does not, remain to tell the stories. Those making these staff-level decisions are invariably men, shaping the careers of journalists who remain. For women in editorial departments, that means not only are business-related stresses increasing, but they must be handled in a culture with deeply ingrained gender-based attitudes and practices that already limit the trajectories of their careers.

A few years ago, I attended a Canadian Association of Journalists conference that brought me face to face with women journalists' dilemmas. During a session called, predictably, "Breaking the Glass Ceiling," women reporters in their late twenties and early thirties told how they were considering leaving journalism, largely because of a perceived family/career conflict. A reporter from the *Edmonton Journal* described how working while female was a problem, so she had started lowering the pitch of her voice and dressing in mannish suits to appear more serious. "I have changed the way that I am" in order to progress, she said. "I've cut out the 'girly talk.' I dress like a man at work so that I have more confidence." Kim Bolan, a long-time reporter for the *Vancouver Sun*, recalled how twenty-five years earlier, the all-male editing staff eyed new women reporters to see which ones wore bras. Female summer interns were sent to cover the Abbotsford air show to see who would throw up during the jet-fighter flights. They were routinely assigned to do features on Wreck Beach, which is a "clothing optional" beach, for the amusement of male editors. Many battles and a quarter-century later, Bolan said, things had improved, but women still faced obstacles in the newsroom, and were still rarely assigned to traditional male beats such as the legislature. Bolan herself covers terrorism and organized crime for the *Sun*, and said she received mail from angry people asking how she, as a mother, dared to do such dangerous work.

Hearing the women at the conference describe their daily work experiences in Canadian newspapers reminded me that, despite most of them never having met before, as women journalists they appeared to become an instant community, listening to each other empathetically as well as angrily, and vowing to push harder at the powerful, male-dominant forces in their newsrooms. Here were women (and a few supportive men, one of whom commented how many talented women had left his newsroom) exchanging nearly identical stories about working within a power structure that has been hostile to women for 150 years, across the country and across newsrooms, while claiming to interpret the world accurately and fairly to all who peruse the daily paper. As I would learn during my research, a newspaper's ownership, its maternity leave policies, or how long or whether it had been unionized seemed to make little difference in the women's concerns about their careers. When more women than men were at the top of the editorial ranks (rarely and briefly the case) and if there happened to be a company day-care centre onsite (and there was only one), then participants talked positively about their work culture. But that talk was tentative: the women at the top moved on and men replaced them, order restored. The day-care centre closed.

Meanwhile, newspapers that pride themselves on exposing social inequality on the page as part of their accountability discourse (roughly speaking, "we afflict the comfortable and comfort the afflicted") demonstrate myopia or are in denial about their own discriminatory practices. As I began my research for this book, a good example emerged in a *Globe* editorial on the importance of bringing more women into leadership positions in business and government. The *Globe* lamented that while women "have made great strides in four decades, they still remain a small minority in the narrower world of power and authority in society today" (*Globe and Mail*, 9 January 2010, p. A15). The editorial then described many powerful places where women were underrepresented, from Crown corporations to boards of directors to the House of Commons. But nowhere did the piece make the point that women are missing from the highest ranks of print journalism, including the *Globe* itself. The paper has not had a woman editor-in-chief or publisher to this day. A list of the paper's senior editors at the time (2010) showed just seven women among twenty-six top-ranked editors; the online version did slightly better with ten women among twenty-seven names. Two years later, the senior editors' list was about the same, with nine women among twenty-five senior editors, and the online senior staff consisting of four women to eight men. The sports section, as with most newspapers, was written and edited almost entirely by men, manifesting how sports reporting is "part of promotional culture, completely incorporated into the economy (and arguably) … exists in a parallel male universe" (Aldridge, 2001, p. 98). Another literally graphic example of this phenomenon appeared in the *London Free Press* on 1 March 2010, when the chain owner's Olympic Games reporters were congratulated for their Olympic reportage with a photograph that showed one (pretty) white woman, an employee of the broadcast arm of owner Quebecor Media Inc., among thirty white male reporters. As Hardin and Whiteside (2009) note, "Female sports journalists work as tokens in gendered organizations where masculinity is integral to hierarchical logic and newswork processes" (p. 627).

The voices of women I knew who left journalism, who were still in it but were feeling increasingly frustrated and excluded (Association for Education in Journalism and Mass Communication, 2010), or who never entered journalism to begin with, had gone from whispers to an invisible chorus; all of these intelligent, educated, and passionate people were looking ahead and seeing a career path leading nowhere. Understanding the pressures and stresses that caused so many women to leave, I found I kept returning to a question that was similar to the publisher's that day back in 1987 when he eyed my belly: given their continuing status outside of the top editorial positions, why were women still there?

I began to do more organized research, both on my own time and while at the University of Western Ontario (now Western University) as a Canwest Fellow in Media Studies. It struck me as I conducted research and spoke to colleagues across North America that a significant amount of literature examined how women have been portrayed in the media worldwide, and feminist theorists in particular had written thousands of scholarly papers analysing the impact of media representations of gender. Yet little in-depth research had been done on Canadian women print journalists, with the most obvious exceptions being work undertaken by Dr. Barbara Freeman at Carleton University, historian Dr. Marjory Lang of Langara College, and Dr. Gertrude Robinson at McGill University. Freeman has written extensively about Canadian women's experiences in journalism from a historical perspective, Lang has written a thorough social history of Canadian women in newsrooms, and Robinson spent much of her long career quantifying and questioning equity relations among journalists across the Western world. Their work, and that of a few others, such as historian Carole Gerson (2010), revealed to me the dimensions of women's historical struggles and achievements in Canadian print media (and elsewhere), and illuminated the path where I felt the next steps needed to be taken to understand their current status in print newsrooms and why it matters.

It is not as if the modern practice of journalism in Western-style democracies has been underreported. Since American journalist and social watchdog Walter Lippmann began critiquing newspapers in the early 1920s, researchers (Lippmann, 1922) have been exploring how news media influence the ways in which citizens in a democracy see their world and their place in it. Today, the daily press, while in great turmoil in terms of financial viability and technological challenge, continues as an essential site of public learning and debate and a powerful force both propelling and preventing societal change. Mass media's role in shaping and upholding public opinion is central: the media "amuse, entertain, and inform, and inculcate individuals with the values, beliefs and codes of behavior that will integrate them into the institutional structures of the larger society" (Chomsky & Herman, 1988, p. 1).

Despite the news media's fundamental role as public agenda-setters, little study has been done on the small group of historically influential workers within them: the subjects of this book, senior women print journalists in Canada. Some context here is useful. Worldwide, women occupy a small fraction of middle management in news media organizations, and they are even more seriously underrepresented in senior management. In its 2006 review, *Convention on the Elimination of All Forms of Discrimination against Women*, the United Nations drew attention to the lack of women newspaper executives globally, which it deemed problematic because of the great power and influence of daily newspapers.

In Canada, women have done comparatively better: their numbers in print newsrooms have risen to about one-third of editorial staff, including middle management, and in smaller-market French- and English-language papers, women have risen to about one-quarter of publishers and editors-in-chief. In 2014, *Convergence* magazine reported that at Canada's largest twenty-five newspapers, only four had female publishers and only four had female editors-in-chief (Shermack, 2014). According to a 2014 blog posting, about three-quarters of Canada's English-language national columnists are men (Mahtani, 2014). Stagnation reigns: back in 1994, researcher George Pollard found that young middle-class men dominated the Canadian daily news workforce, and women journalists' mean annual income lagged behind their male counterparts: the men earned about $36,000 a year, and the women, $30,000 (Desbarats, 1996). In that same year, only 2.6 per cent of Canadian newsroom staffers were minority journalists, "about five times less than the percentage of non-whites in the Canadian population" (Desbarats, 1996,

p. 107), a situation that has not changed much. Desbarats (1996) also noted that "93 per cent of the editors in these newsrooms felt that 'the climate in their newsroom does not discourage either the hiring or promotion of non-whites'" (p. 107).

Women's minority status has persisted even though women have been the majority gender in journalism schools for over thirty years in North America. At Carleton University in Ottawa, for example, since 2001, enrollment into the undergraduate journalism program has been 80 per cent female. (The program cuts the class size from 200 to 100 after the first year. Because of their higher grades, it is women who advance.) Women's rise through the ranks of journalism is slower than in the overall workforce: while nearly half the people in management or professional occupations in the United States are women, for example, only 24 per cent of women occupy supervisory roles in journalism. In Canada, the Conference Board of Canada reports that "contrary to popular belief, women have not made significant progress toward gender equality at the middle management level in either the private or public sector" (Wohlbold & Chenier, 2011, p. i), and puts part of the blame on media reports that headline the few female leaders who reach the top. An American study from the Nieman Foundation, called "Where Are the Women?," notes that gender disparity in leadership across industries is "especially pernicious in journalism" despite "overall historic gains and pockets of progress" (Griffin, 2014, paras. 10, 11).

The newsroom, like the majority of workplaces in Canada, is a gendered space. Women have experienced varying levels of hostility since they began working as print journalists in Canada (and other democracies) in the mid-1800s. Many women journalists in the Western world today find their minority position in the industry increasingly problematic, with more women than men (21 per cent compared to 16 per cent in a recent study of 715 American newspapers) saying they are burned out, frustrated, and thinking of leaving the field altogether. An already stressful environment is compounded for women by family issues, sexism, and the proverbial glass ceiling. In Australia, female journalists, especially those with children, say they find it more difficult to perform the journalistic tasks expected of them as the industry's financial instability continues. In New Zealand, Catherine Strong (2011) found that while women represent a majority of journalists in that country, the daily newspaper industry relegates women to lower career levels, and they are nearly invisible at the top editorial and executive level. The very few who do break through the gendered ceiling keenly feel the hardships of isolation from both management and journalism collegiality.

In Canada, scholar Catherine McKercher of Carleton University noted that right from the start of ongoing global economic difficulties, legions of women journalists in this country have been "laid off, bought out of, or denied entry to the full-time labour market in the news business: their only option if they want to work in journalism is to freelance" (McKercher, 2009, p. 370). Many women journalists who leave newspapers turn to freelancing, as I did; it pays poorly, with rates of between nothing to $1 a word, which has not changed in thirty years. Often, articles must be written "on spec," meaning "on speculation" that the editor will publish it. If rejected, the writer has done the work for nothing. Digital "content farms" pay a few cents for hundreds of clicks on a story. Freelancing is an unstable, powerless sort of intellectual piecework done mostly in Canada by women, while editorial work at the highest and best-paid levels of the daily newspaper business is still done mostly by men. Freelancers are emphatically outsiders, usually working from home.

Well, as newspaper editors ask every morning when deciding what stories will be covered that day, who cares? Is it a problem if senior women print journalists are underrepresented, under stress, and under the radar in terms of what might affect newspaper readership, and, by extension, what issues citizens think about and act on? Would listening to women print journalists discuss their working lives tell us anything new about them – and the newsroom and society – that would be worth knowing? At first glance, it would seem that while feminist scholars have produced masses of papers on the effects of mass media sexism on what is published and broadcast, few researchers appear intrigued by the idea of talking in-depth to women journalists who produce news. American scholar Linda Steiner (1998) concludes that most large-scale journalism studies ignore who specifically creates the news. Canadian communications theorist Gertrude Robinson also pointed out in 1998 that in a feminist framework, the role of lived experience, which once was snubbed as a possible source of knowledge, could be used to build theory. Yet, to date, studies examining women journalists have seldom looked at the role of lived experience. Historically, the precedent is there: Lang (1999) noted of women journalists in Canada in the early 1900s, for example, that "from their entry-level jobs to their career mobility to their retirement, the profiles of women's contributions to journalism and their experiences as journalists distinguished their career patterns from those of their male colleagues" (p. 9).

But rather than scholars' lack of interest, the problem may be one of limited approaches leading researchers repeatedly to get lost in the woods, unable to move forward. To date, "contradiction" and "ambivalence" are the terms most often reported in articles concerned with how senior men and women journalists influence news creation or think they do. Research on what factors motivate journalists is generally so inconclusive that we cannot say with confidence what *does* motivate them and so cannot yet draw precise, reliable conclusions about the nature of their personal impact on the sociopolitical agenda and their reasons for staying or going (Peiser, 2000).

Where media and communications scholars do take up the issue of women journalists' specific impact on the craft, their attention has focused on the effect of gender *in isolation* and whether it makes any observable difference to how journalists conduct their various tasks as media workers, therefore causing differences to show up in the final product. For example, the Global Media Monitoring Project, which is the biggest, longest longitudinal study on the representation of women in media globally, has been studying gender's influence on journalism since 1995. Non-profit MediaWatch Canada has been doing similar work in content analysis for years, primarily challenging sexism in the media.

Some scholars do content analyses and find gender differences in sourcing and story topic, for instance (Rodgers & Thorson, 2003). But in their landmark review, Craft and Wanta (2004) found studies "do not support drawing a straight line from reporter or editor to news content that somehow flows out of one's gender" (p. 136). Then we might ask if other intersecting lines of diversity – race, class, age or parenthood experiences, for example – could affect how and why women work in newsrooms and if their presence or absence can be made visible on the news pages and screens. If so, could any of these aspects, interacting with gender, be connected to what we currently label only as ambiguities in the search for how individuals affect news and how they experience their careers? Do these contextual variables perhaps combine *over time* to create for women enough reason to abandon the newsroom mid-career or to cling to it fiercely in the few numbers that they do? One recent U.S. study that did use a novel approach looked at short descriptions from more than 300 American reporters of what stories they felt constituted their best work and indicated that, unlike what many previous studies have suggested, "social and demographic characteristics of reporters can be linked systematically to news decisions" (Beam, 2008, p. 2).

Beam (2008) argued that not enough attention has been focused on how a journalist's gender, age, race, and even religious convictions can influence the nature and subject matter of stories, and so set about letting journalists describe their own best work, rather than trying to theorize from yet another content analysis. Beam found that about 30 per cent of journalists cited "serious, traditional" topics as their best work, with one in five naming articles on education and social services, then business and consumer affairs, as most important. More women than men cited education and social issues stories as part of their best work, while racialized journalists were more than twice as likely as white journalists to see education and social issues stories as part of their best work. Wrote Beam (2008):

> Research on the sociology of news clearly establishes that professional, organizational, economic and cultural factors have tremendous influence on news. The findings here suggest that in some situations, a connection can also be drawn between the demographic and social characteristics of reporters and the kinds of stories that they create and admire. (p. 10)

This was, to me, a promising finding born of an innovative approach and worth pursuing further, if we believe, as I do, that there is indeed a problem. Understanding the experiences, opinions and struggles of those few (generally white, middle-class) women who help define for Canadians what is newsworthy will help us to understand how social issues are prioritized as they are and whether these priorities are conducive to our progress as individuals and a nation. Could any connection exist between the paucity of women in senior newsroom positions, for example, and the fact that globally, women appear to know less about politics than men, no matter how democratic or advanced the country they live in, including Canada? A recent global study from the University of London suggests that worldwide, women were found to know less about public affairs, felt more disconnected from the political process and were more inclined than men to say that they found politics complicated and difficult to comprehend. Explanations abounded on why this might be so, but the researchers suspect that one reason is that news is heavily weighted towards men as sources, women are far less likely to be interviewed or cited, and women tend to appear as sources in so-called "soft" news stories about family, culture, and lifestyle. In Canadian newspapers, simultaneously, men journalists dominate political reporting, while women reporters and editors dominate lifestyle sections. A *Globe and Mail* article quotes James Curran, one of the (male) researchers conducting the study, as noting that the issue of women appearing to know less about politics than men matters to society because "in a democracy, governments need to be held to account and they can't be held to account effectively unless citizens are informed" (Daugherty, 2013).

I wrote this book because research in print newsrooms is needed to witness, document, and re-examine the impact of individual journalists' experiences and differences from both a public-policy/social-agenda perspective and in terms of the working lives of senior women journalists and those who might wish to follow them. At first blush, a story about Canada's shrinking pool of women print journalists might not seem of interest beyond the potluck dinner parties of those involved. But the story is the same across the United States, Britain, and Western-style democracies around the world, where corporately owned media dominate. The strength and progress of all these democracies *do* depend on all their citizens being well informed; editorial staffers *do* influence the news media for which they work in various, if contradictory, ways; and the media are among the main transmitters of information about what is allowable behaviour for both women and men. As communications scholar Augie Fleras (2003) writes, "male-controlled media have defined what was newsworthy because of their monopoly of power to make decisions regarding what to emphasize and what to ignore" (p. 312). With mostly male journalists providing much of this input into how citizens perceive themselves and the world around them, I saw a need to investigate in an original way how and why so few women stay at newspapers to become leaders and also to theorize on how their exclusion, as well as any of their own practices that exclude others, might affect the definition and production of news. As Barber and Rauhala (2008) observe, "it is surely valuable to discover who the [news managers] are, whether they reflect the society they live in and what they think about diversity both in employment and society at large" (p. 8).

I conducted individual interviews and focus groups with women print journalists across Canada to investigate and analyse how junior and senior women print journalists make sense of their career trajectory over time, focusing on the ways in which they say they have had to adapt to, reject, rationalize, and revolutionize the male-dominated newsroom culture which persists across Western democracies today (North, 2007). I have also analysed the ways in which the women say they have affected the sociopolitical agenda as a result of who they are as individuals and what they do as journalism decision-makers. By examining autobiographical data – most importantly, their narratives about their own working lives – I have studied power relationships as the women experience them, documented the ways their personal lives were affected by the work they do, investigated how their decision-making affects what is defined as news, and draw conclusions about women's exclusion from the highest ranks of print journalism in terms of its implications for them as individuals and for social justice. An important and connected sub-theme is whether and how the new industry focus – some might argue frantic obsession – on emerging media technologies might affect the entrenched newsroom cultural discourses that, historically, women find limiting. Media owners today appear to worry far more about delivery systems than content.

My starting point for this book was gender and it remained the primary lens of analysis. But by widening the focus to range over other qualities, I noted how they were bound up with gendered experience: participants' age, class, race, parenthood status, and physical ability also shaped women's newsroom careers. When I examined answers to the open-ended question "tell me about your career," I realized the women invariably told stories in which their gender, age, and parenthood status were central. If they had other qualities that put them in the minority in the newsroom – and very few did mention factors such as race or sexual orientation – those became part of the storytelling, too. Later, in focus groups, these qualities became part of their discussions about gendered experience, and what did, or did not, offer them positions of power in the newsroom. Readers with a background in feminist literature may wonder here if I decided to embrace intersectionality, a theory that studies how various forms of oppression or discrimination interact to influence how power works in peoples' lives. I thought about it long and hard, but no, I am not "doing" intersectionality in its most widely accepted meaning. Gender is my fixed line of reference to assess women's experiences in a male-dominated profession; but racialization and other forms of discrimination are critical to understanding those gendered experiences, as will be seen throughout.

Journalism Is Great for Men, at Least Historically

Members of the current generation of women journalists owe much to their predecessors, who faced – and endured and fought against – newsroom hostility. The facts of gender not only dominated what women journalists in Canada traditionally covered from the late 1880s into the 1940s, but how they did it: simply attending a political event made a woman reporter stand out. "The presence of a woman distorted the event just by her being there, and it made obvious the fact that what was defined as the public world of 'newsworthiness' was a world of men and that 'objectivity' was a privileged perspective, not a universal one" (Lang, 1999, p. 9). A brief look at the history of Canadian newspapers will help readers appreciate how entrenched powerful internal discourses still are in the industry, and how invisible – and denied – they are to this day. By and large, the North American print newsroom indignantly balks at change, is defensive about its own practices, clings to the myth of charismatic leadership, values long hours and competition among reporters, sees professional training as a costly frill, and prefers process-driven institutional coverage to more creative approaches. As David Ryfe (2009) found in a study of newsroom culture in a mid-sized, corporately owned American daily, reporters practically went through an identity crisis when a senior editor tried to change how they covered institutions, from daily visits to courthouses, police, and government offices to working on context, trends, and investigation. The reporters moved from feeling uneasy to questioning the legitimacy of the change: "In other words, they moved from feeling that (the) new direction was difficult to enact toward a sense that it was the wrong thing to do" (Ryfe, 2009, p. 198). This resistance is cultural (a "good" journalist is a watchdog, full stop, a view that can be seen as naive or even nostalgic [Deuze, 2005]) and institutional, based on a need to belong to a community of practice. That community is overwhelmingly white male dominated and always has been, since the days in the late 1800s when most newspapers needed only "an editor and two or three other men" (Sotiron, 1997, p. 5).

Over the past twenty-five years or so, scholars worldwide have been interested in the history of women journalists' status in newsrooms. But stories by and about women journalists themselves have not been integral to democratic journalism's historic male-dominated narratives, from everyday newsroom discussions to countless books and articles about the "great men" of journalism. (Even a simple Google search of "great men" and "journalism" brings up 142,000 sites, while "great women" and "journalism" brings up only 21,700.) In Canada, chronicles of women journalists' achievements and challenges are rarely mentioned in the Canadian historical canon, which focuses on historic relationships between governments and newspapers, business structure, and occasionally tales of colourful (mostly) male commentators and reporters (Kesterton, 1967). As historian Marjory Lang (1999) notes, "In Canada it has been relatively uncommon for women to reflect publically on their careers" (p. 13). These journalists are only occasionally written about in general-interest books (by women) with titles that indicate their status as interlopers or outsiders, such as *No Daughter of Mine* (Rex, 1995) and *No Life for a Lady* (Dempsey, 1976), autobiographies of roughly contemporaneous women journalists Kathleen "Kay" Rex and Lotta Dempsey, who worked at Toronto's *Globe and Mail* and *Star*, respectively. The theme of being in the orbit of male journalists is echoed in the scholarly text, *The Satellite Sex* (Freeman, 2001), which explores media and women's issues in English Canada in the late 1960s through a feminist analysis of coverage of the Royal Commission on the Status of Women. In *Women Who Made the News: Female Journalists in Canada 1880–1945* (1999), Lang borrows Arnold Bennett's 1898 term "second species," his definition of Fleet Street's women journalists, to describe the outsider status of early women journalists in Canada. Lang also notes that given the fleeting nature of news itself, those in the business tend to disregard their own past in it, just as readers toss out yesterday's paper or click to another website. Many of women's achievements in newspapering have thus been forgotten as the "path closed up after the path breakers," argues Lang (1999), whose work challenges the notion that women did not "'break out' of the women's sections until the 1960s and 1970s" (p. 11). However, most scholarly literature characterizes the antecedent of the modern newsroom as a smoky, noisy workplace, largely for men only, with the few women who worked for the society pages either writing from home (as so many freelancers do today) or in segregated offices until the 1960s, when women began to be admitted in small numbers to city rooms. Lang (1999) does note that while women may have been inside the city room in numbers greater than is noted in broad journalism histories, those women journalists were asked to provide the women's "angle" on current events. David Hayes, in his *Globe* obituary for journalist Heather Robertson, recalled an essay in which Robertson wrote of how the men with whom she worked in Winnipeg at the *Tribune* in the 1970s were dumbfounded by her generation of newswomen. "We had no tits," she explained. "It had been customary to measure the talent of female staff members at the *Tribune* by the size of their bra cups; the women's editor was a statuesque 38D, columnist Ann Henry a stunning 36 triple C. We were all As" (Hayes, 2014, para. 9).

While the earliest newspapers were essentially government flyers, political and economic developments in Canada, as well as technological innovations such as the telegraph, meant that by the 1850s the daily newspaper began to depend on advertisers (Fetherling, 1990). Thus began the defining relationship of newspapering that combined capitalism and democracy on one page, creating a dominant discourse of power and profit that both transmitted the intertwined business and political news of the day for moneyed elites, and displayed advertisements for the goods and services that the capitalist system produced and upon which fortunes were made. In *From Politics to Profit*, historian Minko Sotiron writes that this turn of newspapers away from partisan politics and towards business profitability came between 1890 and 1920, with growing cities, greater literacy, and good economic times (Sotiron, 1997). Writing about the first half of the twentieth century, Marjory Lang notes that while "bondage to the profit motive impinged on all journalists ... the fetters were plainly visible in the case of women writers, whose intended function on the paper was almost wholly commercial – to attract and instruct the female consumer" (Lang, 1999, p. 9). Men, meanwhile, had the playing field of the rest of the paper, with no low-status ghetto from which to try to escape. What male reporters traditionally wrote about was "hard" news: what happened in the public sphere of politics, laws, wars, business deals, and crime and punishment. The eventual inclusion of so-called soft news recognized that household products and fashion were being made and marketed to women. Over the early part of the 1900s, publishers created special sections that dealt with domestic concerns such as cooking, cleaning, and motherhood, reinforcing the private sphere as women's proper place. As newspapers moved from the political to the commercial, women journalists "were hired as a result of the major advertisers' recognition that homemakers were the primary consumers" (Lang, 1999, p. 8).

Beyond boosting consumerism, continues Lang (1999), "women journalists were employed to create a specifically feminine form of news that would popularize a gender identity for women readers within the existing newspaper or magazine" (p. 8). These women were part of a group that trickled into the craft as journalists, essayists, and short-story writers as female literacy and confidence grew in the late 1800s, when careers in other areas were barred to them. In 1891, just 35 of 756 journalists in Canada were women. Newspaper owners likely thought of the women's low-status work over the next decades as just filling columns around ads, if they thought about it at all. Of course, newspaper work generally was not seen as high status: one description of the field in Canada in 1878 was quoted by Paul Rutherford in *A Victorian Authority* (1982), and picked up by journalist and broadcaster Peter Desbarats in his *Guide to Canadian News Media*: newspapering then was "a means of providing men of ability, but lax in morals and irregular in habits, a means of obtaining a precarious livelihood" (Desbarats, 1996, p. **93**). That description might still fit today, were it not, at least in part, for the work of newspaper women throughout the 1900s who often saw themselves as public educators and even as agents of social change.

Three Generations, Three Women, Three Stories

One of the most famous of these women journalists was Kathleen "Kit" Coleman (1864–1915), who wrote advice on largely domestic matters in Women's Kingdom, which was first published in 1889 in the *Toronto Mail*, and continued from 1895 in the *Mail and Empire*. Coleman, an educated but destitute Irish immigrant and single mother of two, turned to journalism for a sensible reason: she needed the work.

Barbara Freeman, her biographer, writes in *Kit's Kingdom: The Journalism of Kathleen Blake Coleman* that her subject was a transitional figure in Canadian journalism who "sometimes defied, but always fulfilled, the expectations of editors and the public in what she wrote for women," walking "a creative tightrope between what was acceptable for a nineteenth-century woman and what was too daring" (Freeman, 1989, p. 5). In the first year her column appeared, a public debate erupted over whether Coleman was a woman or a man who was ghostwriting for her, such was the apparent need to hide her personal story.

Rather than reporting on events in politics, sports, and business, women journalists such as Coleman succeeded in their special sections by attracting readers' curiosity about their own lives, as living examples of slightly older, wiser, more worldly women than those for whom they wrote. And while she did not cover institutions, Coleman certainly expressed her opinion on social, economic, religious, and political topics of the day, including free trade. On these occasions, male readers often wrote in, indicating they were at least a small part of her constituency, writes Janice Fiamengo (2008) in *The Women's Page: Journalism and Rhetoric in Early Canada*.

Coleman appeared ambivalent regarding women's equality; she was for it, but not if it required agitation or campaigning. Since she worked for a paper that officially opposed women's suffrage, she could hardly be a noisy ally of feminism, even if she had supported it. While Coleman wrote that she would not champion suffrage unless ordered to do so by her editors, who opposed suffrage anyway, she did write about inequality: for example, as Freeman (1989) writes, castigating Toronto shopkeepers, who, she complained, paid starvation wages to working girls.

Despite reinforcing the domestic sphere as a woman's kingdom, Coleman encouraged women through her column to find paid work if they wanted it, whether in a factory or as a domestic, and supported women who wanted to be journalists as she was, although she cautioned that not much opportunity loomed beyond the women's pages (even though she herself would become the only accredited female correspondent to cover the Spanish-American war.) Freeman notes she "implicitly devalued her own work (by writing that) 'elections and single taxes and all kinds of men-fads are going on, and the Editor will crowd us out if we don't cut our chatter short'" (Freeman, 1989, p. 39).

Coleman was the first president of the Canadian Women's Press Club, which stood for expressing "Canadian national sentiments" (Freeman, 1989, p. 138) in members' work, indicating that the women journalists who joined the group felt that their published writing could influence the national sociopolitical agenda. Here we see the historical documentation of how, from their first forays into the hostile world of newspapering, women in print journalism simultaneously upheld and challenged the status quo. This strategy continued throughout the past century (and continues today), with women gradually moving, in small numbers, from reporting to signed columns, from women's sections into city rooms, and finally into the offices of senior editorial management.

Canadian print journalists Lotta Dempsey and Shirley Sharzer exemplified this development during long careers at their respective newspapers, both adapting to and pushing the constraints put upon them. Their individual stories bring to life how society's gendered restraints defined what opportunities they could expect in the newsroom.

Ten years before Kathleen Coleman died, Lotta Dempsey (1905–1989) was born in Edmonton, Alberta. In 1923 she gave up teaching after eight months to become a cub reporter at the *Edmonton Journal*.

In her 1976 autobiography title, *No Life for a Lady*, Dempsey played with the continuing common wisdom that journalism was not appropriate for decent women. (Years later, mining the same gender-defining vein, the 2008 anthology of articles by award-winning political writer

Christina McCall was titled *My Life as a Dame*. Her editors said she had chosen it before her death, to be used ironically for an autobiography she had been working on when she fell ill.) In *The Lady Was a Star* (1995), her daughter-in-law Carolyn Davis Fisher describes Dempsey's first job as writing about the social goings-on of Edmonton's elite; she was allowed to interview visitors of national interest only when men journalists were unavailable. Once she went to Toronto on a job-hunting trip, only to be told by the city editor of the *Mail and Empire* that he didn't have any woman reporters and he didn't want any.

Dempsey's motivation appears to be one of desire for the adventure her male peers experienced, gaining access to the lurid, the exciting, and the stories of celebrities and fallen heroes. She loved seeing her byline and knowing that people were reading her version of events. As stepmother to two and mother of one, Dempsey tried staying home for two years, but disliked domesticity. She was well off enough (having married an architect) to hire full-time help and return to work, finally settling in 1958 at the *Toronto Star*, where she remained until 1980.

Dempsey belonged to the feminist-oriented Canadian Women's Press Club (for which Coleman had served as first president) and won several of its writing awards. She appears not to have made an issue of gender discrimination in journalism in much of a public way, instead projecting the image of the glamorous gal reporter of the times, famous for her hats. However, later in her career, during the nuclear threat of 1960, Dempsey wrote about nuclear testing possibly endangering children and asked women readers to write to her if they wanted to do something about it. Out of those replies was born the Canadian Voice of Women for Peace (VOW), with Dempsey as a founder. VOW became a leading voice for Canadian women advocating peace, and is an accredited NGO to the United Nations.

She did her share of hard news reporting throughout her more than fifty-year career, but was never given a promotion to political correspondent or other prestigious beats. Dempsey's contributions as a columnist at the *Toronto Star*, first with a general interest column and then the Age of Reason column, which dealt with seniors' issues, gave her an opportunity to rally women to political causes.

While some "gal reporters" such as Dempsey were making indelible marks on the pages of newspapers throughout the last century, even fewer were on the inside as senior editors with responsibility for hiring and news decision-making. One was Shirley Sharzer, a Winnipegger who was born in 1928 and died in August 2014 in Ottawa. She was being considered for a job on the news desk of the *Toronto Telegram*, the first woman in line for such a position, the same year as the Royal Commission on the Status of Women was called into being. She had progressed steadily through the ranks, but in 1967 her career was stalling (Breckenridge, 1984). On this occasion, a senior editor was balking at the thought of a woman on the hard news side, where he figured Sharzer would cry under stress. But she got the job.

Sharzer, like many women journalists of her era, had long since figured out ways to repress her own outrage so as to continue working with the gentlemen of the press. She had begun reporting as a teenager in 1945, working for a paper put out by printers striking against the *Winnipeg Tribune*. She recalled that she felt the ways in which she was treated because of her gender and youth (for instance, being taken aside and having court or police proceedings carefully explained) were an advantage that increased her learning – perhaps an early example of the theory of power circulating, as experienced by a young woman reporter. At the *Free Press*, Sharzer became the first woman on a major city daily in Canada to cover city hall and then the legislature, while most women journalists were working on the society pages. She was moved to the desk when she became pregnant: the city editor did not feel it was appropriate for "a pregnant reporter to be running around in public" (Finlayson, 1999, p. 238).

Without maternity leave, Sharzer quit work and would not return to journalism for a full decade, after having another child. Later, at the *Telegram* in the late 1960s, Sharzer called in to work to say one of her children was ill and she needed to stay home. A benevolent male boss suggested she should lie and say that *she* was sick, so as not to be seen by other colleagues as having motherhood interfere with her job. Her husband's unexpected death in 1972 caused her to bury her grief in more work. She went to the new graduate journalism school at the University of Western Ontario, becoming assistant dean by 1977. She left daily journalism reluctantly, having realized that not even her progressive male mentors could move her past what would later be dubbed "the glass ceiling" – which held her at the level of features editor and ended her "youthful attitude of expecting to be able to do whatever I wanted" (Finlayson, 1999, p. 239). She returned to newspapering in 1979 as assistant managing editor of the *Globe and Mail*, working her way up to deputy managing editor. She was responsible for most of the hiring and development of staff, which put her in a position to hire and mentor dozens of reporters and columnists whose words and opinion would help shape the national discourse, including how the paper covered such issues as abortion, birth control, pay equity, sexual harassment, violence against women, and the growth in human rights organizations. Many of those hired were women, some of whom, like me, had been taught and mentored by her at the University of Western Ontario's Graduate School of Journalism.

From Coleman's lesser kingdom to Dempsey's globetrotting dispatches to Sharzer's influence as a career-maker, the work done by these three journalists, and other women journalists like them, helped to place what were deemed women's issues on the national agenda. They saw and experienced blatant and subtle sexism both in society and in their workplaces, denying or remaining silent about much of it in order to survive. But when it came to gross inequality, they fought back in their writing (or in Sharzer's case, hiring) on behalf of other women. Each journalist moved into more high-status real estate in the newsroom, from the women's page to the front page to the management office, chronicling and tacitly encouraging the expanding role of women in Canadian society. They learned the lessons of their male-dominated societies and workplaces well, but were not willing to repeat them unquestioningly to their elite and middle-class readers.

These three are exemplars of Canadian women print journalists, who, over decades of social, political, and technological change, succeeded in working their way, with difficulty, into exclusive newsrooms where they were often not wanted because of their gender. Their tenacity allowed women journalists of my generation and the current one to advance further inside. But equal numbers of men and women at all levels have not been achieved, nor do newsrooms represent the diversity of modern Canada (Fleras, 2011).

Stability and Neo-Liberalism Sell Papers, or at Least Used To

Profits, the primary concern of industry owners, are most reliably accrued in stable societies, so what is defined as news has traditionally tried to frame a messy, dynamic democratic reality through a conservative, status quo viewfinder. Part of maintaining that stability involves perpetuating conservative societal beliefs about woman's status, including maternity – beliefs that most women have been historically eager to support. Not surprisingly, then, the traditional discourse of neo-liberalism runs deep in newsrooms – the idea that one makes free choices in this world as a citizen and consumer, unaffected by the context of power structures. This conception of the news and public good being framed in terms of private ownership, free markets, and consumer choice runs from regulatory agencies right through to journalists at a personal level. Even when they are talking about whether to leave journalism or stay, or to have children or not, journalists tend to use a discourse of personal choice with researchers, rather than voicing the idea that they are often forced into making decisions by institutional inflexibility. A gendered effect is that women journalists, especially those with children, say they find it increasingly difficult to perform the journalistic tasks expected of them, and more women than men say they are burned out. On the page, the neo-liberal, status quo discourse plays out for everyone to see, especially in the lifestyle pages, where women are instructed on how to be "good" mothers and workers, have sleek figures while producing gourmet meals and model children, and to keep improving themselves to unattainable standards of perfection, as seen in the accompanying advertising. One study that looked at how the American press covers (indeed defines) the work/family conflict narrative noted that this neo-liberal discourse of choice, which is the typical frame for stories about work and family demands, does not apply to the vast majority of working women who might read those stories. Rather, the study indicates that press articles about women "choosing" to opt out of the workforce focuses on only the 8 per cent of working women who are in professional or managerial roles, which are the roles held by women journalists (Williams, Manvell, & Bornstein, 2006). Thus, those inside the newsrooms can be seen to be spreading the choice myth that they themselves have internalized and universalized to include (incorrectly) women in the working classes. What is exclusive to middle- and upper-class women becomes general truth.

That women journalists contribute to the culture's dominant beliefs and biases is hardly surprising inside an industry that fuels the media-saturated environment in which the middle classes live and work. So embedded are cultural discourses among journalists generally that professionalism can often be based on a sense of pride in resisting change in their own newsrooms, as discussed earlier. Journalists who demand transparency in others distrust any questioning of their news-gathering habits, cloaking themselves in a defence of public accountability. They guard an authoritative discourse with the power to convince and manipulate. Routinely visiting powerful public institutions such as the courts fulfils a function of that role and solidifies their sense of the importance of what they do and what makes a good journalist. And I note here that the watchdog function journalists cherish is deeply entrenched for good reason: a constitutionally protected free press can do the work of keeping institutions accountable, which is expensive and time-consuming for societies. What becomes problematic, though, is that this insistence on accountability does not seem to apply to the newspaper industry itself, at least in terms of self-reporting on journalism's influences on society that might perpetuate discrimination.

Journalists' access to sources in high places also feeds their sense of esteem, and a gender-specific effect emerges out of this discourse. One recent Australian study found that for men journalists, brushing up next to power can lead to an enhanced sense of personal power and confidence – power speaking to power – while the women journalists surveyed felt their access to individuals – both powerful figures and ordinary folks – helped them develop more compassionate feelings towards people in general (North, 2009a).

Politicians, business people, religious leaders and senior bureaucrats lead powerful groups and are in a position to order societal interests, so by primarily interviewing them, journalists effectively reinforce the dominance of male-dominated social and political institutions. If social stability is good for business, then the news media play a pivotal role in cheerleading for that stability.

The Discourses of the Majority

News discourse, as part of the workplace culture, is rife with subtle gender politics, such as the selective privileging of "masculine over feminine" discourse. Even when they act with what could be seen as a high degree of personal agency – because they are left alone to do much of their work – journalists act within the pressures and routines that are embedded in their organization (de Bruin, 2000). Those styles and values, especially around adversarial and competitive frames for "hard" news, are traditionally developed by and for white, male decision-makers and become professional standards. So strong is the institutional discourse that researchers have found that an individual reporter's voice can be muted on many levels in the hierarchy of a newspaper. For example, an English study found that any one reporter's ideas about who best reflects the local community is often trumped by a dominant newsroom culture that prefers elite and other white male voices as journalists' interview subjects (Ross, 2007).[1] A new scholarly book analyses links between an aggressive form of coverage by male-dominated media and the stubbornly low number of female candidates for political office at all levels of government in Canada: "research suggests the causal chain may begin with a hostile media climate that reduces the supply of will-ing [female] candidates" (Trimble, Arscott, and Trimble, 2013, p. xvi). Carole Stabile (2004), in an article analysing the widespread sexist cov-erage of celebrity decorator and publisher Martha Stewart's fall from grace, explains the pervasiveness of an androcentric culture manifested in the press this way:

> To suggest that sexist coverage of Stewart resulted from some rightwing conspiracy or masculinist cabal is to misunderstand how an androcen-tric culture reproduces itself. Rather than resulting from conscious inten-tions, this kind of coverage proceeded from the everyday practices of a journalistic culture that remains steeped in sexist modes of thought and behaviour. We forget at some risk that journalistic objectivity is every bit as androcentric as scientific objectivity. (p. 326)

To question that culture, I wrote this book from the perspective that knowledge is grounded in the lived experiences of individuals and is gained through subjective and inductive means, emphasizing the spe-cific stories of the participants. It is a feminist approach, and like any theoretical approach, will have inherent limits and flaws. But what better way to examine what shapes experience and how accumulated experiences become narrated and embedded in the public discourse, if not through analysing the stories of these members of the daily press? This book looks at the impact of power as these women journalists use it, and are used by it, in order to make sense of their own lives and to help make sense of the lives of those about and for whom they write.

How I Got the Story

Canadian women print journalists spend their working days telling other people's stories in the context of our society, with the idea that readers will make meaning of those stories for themselves and perhaps even act on them. But in what ways do these women journalists tell their own stories in order to live in that society and their workplaces? By analysing their narratives, I theorized as to what held them in their jobs, and what might cause them to leave, if they did. Narrative analysis invites participants not only to describe what has happened to them over a period of time but also to reflect on what those events mean, where they position themselves culturally, and whether they are agents, victims, witnesses, or critics inside those events. A review of the literature suggested to me that the long views of women in print newsrooms could reveal their evolving experiences of family and workplace and provide me with the tools to better understand why the underrepresentation of women at print journalism's senior levels continues and why those upper reaches remain almost exclusively white and male.

In *Analysing Narrative Reality*, Gubrium and Holstein (2009) define narrative, story, and account interchangeably and simply as "spates of talk that are taken to describe or explain matters of concern to participants" (p. xvii), and the research goal is to explore how "these accounts are socially organized and ... the process of storytelling is circumstantially shaped" (p. xix). Accepting that a storyteller "provides an account of experience or event of his or her own that is more or less credible" (p. xix) is the fundamental, respectful condition of this approach. This is not to say that narratives tell "the truth," but that they describe events in a person's life in a way that gives the events coherence and meaning. The narrator-participants are the experts on their own experiences.

Coffey and Atkinson (1996) say that "social actors produce, represent, and contextualize experience and personal knowledge through narratives and other genres" (p. 54) and ultimately, stories "are discursive structures that reflect cultural norms" (pp. 67–8). Of particular relevance to this book is the authors' understanding of how career stories express cultural norms in a workplace, giving us information about the perspectives of individuals in relation to the wider group to which they belong, as "careers are both individually constructed and structurally determined" (p. 68). Daiute and Lightfoot (2004) note that different types of narrative genres organize experiences and knowledge: feminist researchers, for instance, have used narrative analysis to show how dominant forces promote sexist values through grand or meta-narratives, as well as charting the counter-narratives that challenge those values (Snyder, 2008). Here we can begin to see the possibilities for narrative analysis to interpret journalists' stories, as they are at the hub of reproducing and challenging meta-narratives: the daily newspaper.

Narrative analysis also draws on a traditional view that explores how individuals position themselves, using stories within competing and contradictory discourses. With some power of agency, individuals essentially pick a cultural position and practise it, which then becomes the position to be drawn on when the question arises, *Who am I?* Another view posits that we perform identity, yes, but we are constantly self-revising, contradicting and flirting with ambiguities, not simply acting out established identities. Analysed from the former view, the stories that senior women journalists tell about themselves could be understood as anchor lines that help them remain securely connected to a practised identity; from the latter, stories are perhaps renegotiations of identity within a workplace that has been traditionally hostile to women and racialized minorities in Canada, the United States, and Europe (Robinson, 2005). The stories could, of course, combine both and might further speculate about the future, as the business is transformed by technologies assumed to be best wielded by the young, and perhaps not as competently by older women journalists.

Over time, stories about what we deem to be our pivotal life events reflect the impact of the passing years and the perspective they bring, so that we could, for example, start to tell stories about ourselves that are as much about the perceived impact of age as of gender. While researchers cannot essentialize by generation any more than by gender, ethnicity or ability, some elements associated with second- and third-wave feminism surface in narrative analysis, including mine. The wave metaphor has limits, however, including a false divisiveness as well as a focus on the activities of white American women and so should be invoked with these caveats in full view. No two women are the same, nor are men, nor are members of a generation or racial group. But using narrative theory, we can theorize how "merely idiosyncratic personal stories or confessions [can be seen as] examples of postmodern subjectivity that intend to destabilize dominant discourses" (Snyder, 2008, pp. 191–2). Life histories such as the ones told to me by the participants cannot reveal any "totality of social life" but offer for analysis "slices and glimpses of localized interactions to understand more fully both others and ourselves" (Roets and Goedgeluck, 2007, p. 91). This method of research takes the term "anecdotal evidence" and effectively removes the word "mere" from in front of it.

Narrative enquirers can begin either by engaging with participants through telling stories or "through coming alongside participants in the living out of stories" (Clandinin, 2006, p. 47). I chose the former for practical reasons: I could not abandon my paid work to come alongside my participants for any length of time. The average working print journalist would not be in a position to let someone shadow her for weeks on end, either. And globally, journalists have been found to ignore requests to fill out surveys. I needed to go to the participants for in-person interviews for as much time as we could all possibly manage, which turned out to be about a month for me. I interviewed twenty-seven individual women at different ages and career stages in person for about ninety minutes each at the five newspapers across the country, as well as one journalist-turned-academic, and conducted focus groups with the women, one at each paper, with most of the participants from each paper attending. I conducted two follow-up interviews on site nearly a year later with two participating women, and have had ongoing email exchanges with several of them.

I went back and forth a number of times on what criteria would determine the makeup of the participants. I concluded that the study needed to be national, so that I would be in a position to analyse their understanding of how they might or might not be influencing Canada's sociopolitical agenda from their positions at the newspapers, all of which have online components and share stories through the Canadian Press or other services. Unfortunately, I had to exclude French-speaking Canada, since I am not fluently bilingual and would not have been able to tease out important narrative aspects of the stories in French.

I also had to cast a wide net to avoid interviewing journalists who were employed by one chain of newspapers, in case a concern arose that the studied group was biased, with women participants potentially being seen to be operating inside a common corporate culture rather than inside a larger newsroom culture shared by the industry across Canada. A handful of owners dominate the daily press in Canada. Most recently, Postmedia Network Canada Corp. (publisher of the *National Post* and English-language dailies from Vancouver to Montreal) bought Sun Media Corporation's English-language papers (including the *Sun* chain of papers across the country and the *London Free Press*) from Quebecor Media Inc. Sun Media also includes papers in Ontario run by Osprey Media. Glacier Canadian Newspapers owns papers in British Columbia. Only a few dailies, such as the *Chronicle Herald* in Halifax, are the sole paper owned by a company. CTVglobemedia Inc. owns many broadcast outlets and is a part owner of the *Globe and Mail*.

The newspapers also needed to be roughly the same circulation size in similar markets, big enough to employ a number of journalists at various career stages who are women, and comparable in terms of how management responds to labour market factors (layoffs, buyouts, union agreements, etc.). I wanted to avoid interviewing people I already knew, so that I would have as few preconceived ideas about my subjects as possible, although it was not possible to avoid former colleagues completely: the print journalism world in Canada is small, and I have worked in it a long time. As a consultant for newspaper staffs, I have coached several of the women over a couple of months; one hired me to do some editorial training several years ago, and another was an acquaintance I had not seen in twenty years. I have socialized occasionally with a few of the women in Victoria, but none is a close friend.

The newspapers I eventually chose were the Victoria *Times Colonist*, the *Calgary Herald*, the *Winnipeg Free Press*, the *Hamilton Spectator*, and the *Chronicle Herald* in Halifax. The *Times Colonist* and *Calgary Herald* were owned at the time by Postmedia, but since October 2011, the *TC* has been owned by Glacier Media Group. The *Winnipeg Free Press* is owned by F.P. Canadian Newspapers Limited Partnership, along with the *Brandon Sun*. The *Chronicle Herald* is owned by Halifax Herald Ltd., and the *Spectator* is part of the Torstar chain in Ontario. All of the newspapers except the *Calgary Herald* have unionized editorial departments. Unifor represents the employees at the *Hamilton Spectator* and the *Winnipeg Free Press*. The Communications Workers of America represents employees at the Victoria *Times Colonist* (in editorial) and the Halifax *Chronicle Herald* (Law, 2014).

I recruited women by email and telephone follow-up, looking first at the papers' websites to see who would have begun her career in the late 1970s and early 1980s and who would have joined the paper more recently: who was a junior reporter, a middle manager, an editor-in-chief, a columnist. This offered the participants an opportunity to share their varied histories and experiences, as well as to reflect on possible generational differences and the industry's changing structure. If I could not tell from thumbnail photos on the paper's websites that the paper had any visible minority women journalists, I asked the first person recruited at each paper if they could recommend someone: only one newspaper of the five, the Halifax *Chronicle Herald*, employed a person of colour as a journalist at that time, and only the *Winnipeg Free Press* employed a woman with Indigenous status, a white woman who had married a First Nations man in the Maritimes and had long since been divorced. Only one person, also at the *Free Press*, self-identified as lesbian, and only one, at the *Chronicle Herald*, had any obvious physical ability issues she was willing to discuss. Most of the women were married or in long-term relationships but a minority of ten had children, and they included the only participant, Kelly Toughill, who no longer worked at newspapers at the time of the interviews. A former *Toronto Star* reporter and manager, she is the director of the journalism program at the University of King's College in Halifax, preparing the next generation of journalists.

Narrative analysis offers an opportunity to use a method of inquiry for a journalistic topic that aligns with the field itself: my book charts how the participants make sense of their lives as journalists using their own lingua franca of storytelling. Critical questions arose: Do women print journalists tell stories that help them accommodate contradictions in their work lives, or to be subversive, or both? Do the stories end with them remaining outside of power positions? Or are they creating new styles of leadership? What would I learn about my own story and whether it is about development, resistance or abdication, or all of those things? After all, as the narrative inquirer, I am equally complicit in the world under study.

Certainly, a prime reason to write this book was so that I could examine my own responses to the research. Unlike Kit Coleman, Lotta Dempsey, and Shirley Sharzer, I did not stay in daily newspapering. I am a former senior newspaper writer and manager who, like many other women of my era, left a leadership role at a daily newspaper in mid-life for many reasons, mainly the perceived demands of parenthood clashing with career. My experiences as a former daily newspaper reporter, columnist, copy editor, "women's editor," and manager inform my research, as do a decade as a consultant to newspapers in Western Canada and my recent position as a magazine editor who hired freelance writers, most of whom were women, for just 30 cents a word.

As a white, middle-class, university-educated, able-bodied, English-as-first-language, heterosexual person, I share many demographic similarities with the majority of employees in print newsrooms. Being a woman and parent at the mid-management (department head) level put me in a minority position, however. Taking up where Shirley Sharzer's generation left off, I have experienced journalism both in a segregated, low-status "women's section," writing up recipes and wedding accounts, and on the high-status national news desk, working on municipal, provincial, and federal political coverage. As a senior journalist at Canada's "newspaper of record," I felt the power of the dominant male culture of the newsroom both silence me in-house (as one of only two or possibly three women at a news meeting, for instance) and empower me as I interviewed national business and political leaders and as I helped direct coverage of issues from education to law and social policy to medicine and the environment.

In this book, readers will meet more than two dozen fascinating women who reinforce and resist the newsroom culture every day of their working lives, whether it has been for as little as two years or more than thirty. How their age interacts with their gender is a primary theme, with the women's stories revealing how, over time, they take the complexities of their multiple identities and the externalities and try to create a coherent whole. Assumptions about social characteristics such as race, class, parenthood, sexuality, and physical ability further complicate matters of their gender and age, offering other possible positions from which to hold on tight to their shrinking, turbulent newsrooms so they can continue their work or decide to jump ship. No matter what course they chose, the women saw themselves as different from their male peers in terms of their career paths. Wherever they were, they were outsiders still, for better or worse.

Structurally Speaking

In the following chapters, each of the participants' individual interviews and focus groups are described and analysed. The chapters are grouped into three stages of career trajectories by age: chapter 2 focuses on the longest-employed women, who recount their experiences over decades in the business, often with a sense of deep frustration but also with humour and satisfaction. Chapter 3 introduces the mid-career women who find themselves at a crossroads, where the demands of their careers and personal lives are most extreme and demanding. Chapter 4 analyses the stories of the latest recruits to daily print journalism, the young women who look warily ahead and worry that they will be sidelined by maternity if they are not ousted before their contract positions expire. In chapter 5, participants at each of the newspapers speak as a group and compare notes on their experiences and expectations across the generations. In chapter 6, those who left the business reflect on their achievements, regrets, and hopes. The final chapter draws conclusions about the study participants and their impact on the newspaper industry and the wider, more diverse society they seek to inform and even to represent.

Chapter Two

Senior Women Print Journalists:
So Stuck, Yet So Lucky

It was really only once, more than a decade ago, when Elissa Barnard, a nursing mother, felt that she could not do her newspaper job because of her baby. As a Halifax *Chronicle Herald* arts reporter, she headed out one night to review a performance by the Royal Winnipeg Ballet:

> EB: I went to the ballet and came home and I was going to write the review in about a half an hour and email it to the office for the next day's paper. And when I got home, the baby woke up, screaming to be fed. I called my editor, and I don't think he really understood, but he was a very good type. I said, "I'm sorry; I will have to write it tomorrow. I can't do this right now." I think that's the only time that I really couldn't get a story done because of being a parent.
>
> VS: Do you remember what he said? You said he was a good guy.
>
> EB: Yeah, he's her godfather [*laughs*].
>
> VS: [*laughs*] Lucky!
>
> EB: Yes! He said "okay." He was a wonderful editor. He delivered 110 per cent and he expected a lot. We usually always came through. He is the kind of person who always comes through. So I did feel very bad. There were no consequences, he said "fine," and I felt bad because I let the job down that night. In the end it didn't matter. We ran the review the next day. It didn't affect my job or our relationship at all.
>
> VS: Well, that's interesting, because we still beat ourselves up.
>
> EB: Yes, that's right.[1]

This section focuses on participants such as Barnard who, at the time of the interviews, had stayed in the industry the longest, twenty-five to thirty years or more, arriving at newspapers when historical, overt

sexism had only somewhat diminished, thanks to the feminist movement of the day, their own reporting on that movement, and their own
struggles.

The participants' positions ranged in rank from reporter to columnist
to section or department editor to editor-in-chief. They included Elissa
Barnard, Pat Lee, and Pam Sword of the *Chronicle Herald* in Halifax;
Michele Steeves of the *Hamilton Spectator*; Margo Goodhand and Alexandra Paul of the *Winnipeg Free Press*; Monica Zurowski of the *Calgary
Herald*; Lucinda Chodan, the *Times Colonist* editor-in-chief in Victoria;
and Janet, who asked not to be named.[2]

Each journalist explored with me the meaning of her own experiences
independently of the others, yet themes of frustration combined with a
sense of mission and the impact of parenthood connected the accounts.
Like the other two age cohorts (with one exception), this group of senior
journalists was comprised exclusively of white, middle-class, and well-
educated women. Five were mothers. Besides feeling lucky, they felt
"stuck" due to industry upheaval; they saw multitasking as a "natural" thing that women like them did and had to do; they had to choose
between work and family and constantly sought work/life balance; as
women journalists, they could change the world, but they could not see
changing the newsroom culture, and even suppressed their own ideas
about how to cover stories differently. Those who were in positions
of authority (such as editors-in-chief) spoke of how they enacted and
longed for a new model of leadership that had a clear gender component, based as it was on women's perceived communication and collaborative skills. These women, aged forty-nine to sixty-one, told stories
that relayed aspects of struggles taken on by second-wave feminists,
despite feminism being mocked inside newsrooms: they bristled at
overt, sustained sexism; expressed a lack of entitlement to interact with
men as equals; and felt, with some sense of a woman's duty to address,
the white, middle-class bias of their own privilege.

When Barnard told me her story in a Halifax *Chronicle Herald* meeting
room, I had yet to grasp the importance of luck in those stories told by
the participants who had been the longest at newspapers. It became significant as an indication of how, as noted above, they generally lacked a
sense of entitlement, with luck seen as equal to or more important than
their work ethic, skills, or talent in how they developed as journalists.
Simultaneously, they often acknowledged, but did not describe as matters of luck, the privileges of race, class, and education. That acknowledgment seemed to bear heavily on a sense of duty to tell the stories of

those they considered unable to tell their own. It seemed ingrained as part of their myriad responsibilities to stand up for the dispossessed in their communities, often while inhibiting the expression of their own gendered workplace problems.

Luck, Longevity, and a Passion for Story

In a small, corner meeting room at the half-empty suburban offices of the *Chronicle Herald*, Elissa Barnard, fifty-one, an arts writer, looked out at the darkening autumn sky. She asked me a rhetorical question about passion for story, which she declared to be undiminished in her after nearly thirty years at the paper, mostly in the same job, covering performances and writing about Nova Scotia's busy arts community. "I like a good story and I am interested in the mechanics of writing," she began, and then paused briefly. "How do you translate a good character, a good plot line into a readable story and convey the passion you have felt for the topic into the article?"

Barnard came by her passion for narrative by birth: both parents were print reporters, with her father eventually retiring from a communications job "to write a book he never completed," and her mother leaving journalism for a while to raise Barnard and her sister.

Trying to convey passion through story drove her working day. On a good one, Barnard said, she might interview an artist or entertainer who had a great tale to tell, and when she returned to the newsroom, she enjoyed joking with colleagues and loved to see that the photographer had taken a wonderful shot of the subject. That combination of passion and teamwork was magical.

But Barnard had bad days, too, in particular, the incoming rush of technology that management expected reporters to use made her fear she would be a "dinosaur," a word in common use around newsrooms to describe the oldest generation of workers who appear to resist new demands on their approach to work. Barnard wanted to "embrace" (a word she used several times) new technology but was not sure how: management had offered little training. She also described how one-quarter of the staff had been cut in recent layoffs and the once-separate arts and lifestyle sections had been folded together. What she wrote about seemed less important to senior managers, she said, requiring the head of her now-merged department to wage an almost daily fight for diminished space. Then she shrugged her shoulders and smiled, and talked about how journalists like to complain, effectively minimizing the importance of her own observations. She had been at the paper long enough to recall that the publisher gave out turkeys at Christmas, in the 1980s.

Barnard had an Arts BA and was married with one child, aged eleven at the time we spoke. After telling the story of how lucky she was that the editor on deck the night of the ballet performance was her child's godfather, Barnard said things were getting easier on the work/parent front. By rising at 6 a.m. and working until 7:30 a.m., she could take ninety minutes off later to get her daughter to piano lessons. "I can make it all work, usually," said Barnard, recalling an article she read once about how women are good at multitasking to explain why she was good at "juggling" family and work. It struck me how she appeared to have internalized the prevailing social belief that women are naturally good multitaskers when she said that "there is something to be said for trying to put all the pieces together." After years of being the family's main breadwinner, she described her husband's new job in terms of luck, too. He happened to have an understanding boss: a single mother, who was flexible about hours. But Barnard did not connect this situation with her own, at least not to me.

After all this time and experience, and with her daughter older, had Barnard considered a management job? No, she said, managers would make her work nights. She feared she might have to fire someone, maybe a friend. But women had not been encouraged to apply for management jobs at the *Herald*, although they had applied, she added. Four such jobs existed, all held by men. Once there was one female managing editor, and she became a politician.[3] Barnard regretted not having learned to edit, which made her feel stuck, unable to move up to the editing desk.

As for why so few women were senior managers, Barnard hesitated, then posited that it may have to do with a "bigger time commitment," the same reason so few women went into politics, she said, as well as management being boring, full of meetings with people who have a "corporate" style of thinking. Most of the men in the newsroom, especially in positions of authority, she said, didn't have to deal with the multitasking and schedule-juggling that she and other women did. "I don't think they understand it; I don't think they know about it, really."

Barnard's job, as she saw it, was to promote the arts in Nova Scotia, especially by women, Indigenous, and black artists. She, as a middle-class, educated white woman, didn't think much about her privileged position, but was aware of it, and complained about the lack of diversity in the newsroom, as other participants did. It annoyed her still that "women artists are not as validated or accepted by the establishment as male artists." But despite her personal commitment to promoting diversity in arts coverage, Barnard ultimately did not see herself as a newsroom decision-maker, rather as part of a small, struggling team whose work mattered most to the growth in the local arts community. Could the choices she made over three decades about what stories to cover have influenced the nature of that growth? No, she said, she didn't think so. When it came to the power of the exclusively white male management team to downsize arts coverage, Barnard felt that "breaking news ... has to be the priority in a daily newspaper."

Barnard's was a story of long-term adaptation and resignation and apologies, with a positive experience with managers depending on good fortune, not policy or even her own skills. In Winnipeg, meanwhile, Alexandra Paul, another long-time reporter, was feeling lucky, too, just to have a job. Like Barnard and others in this group, she positioned herself outside the dominant culture and cherished her opportunity to champion others from within the dominant news discourses. But for Paul, this meant recounting the stories of Indigenous peoples.

The Defining Business of Being an Outsider

When I asked why women print journalists were rare in senior management, general assignment reporter Alexandra Paul at the *Winnipeg Free Press* said journalism is so tough on family life that even talented women were not staying while men did. She also recounted a story about a young woman who recently left the business, even though it was her dream to be a journalist, because she could not get a permanent job in an unstable industry. Women like herself, said Paul, who still had reporting jobs – and "good days" of teamwork-driven journalism were fewer and fewer – were simply "fortunate," according to the luck theory of career longevity. In her own case, she positioned herself as "not really management material," because she was not part of the community elite:

> AP: [*pause*] I'm too independent. I remember a prof who said, "There are two kinds of journalists: the ones who maintain the status quo and the ones who rock the boat." I think a lot of the management people, men or women, are the people who maintain the status quo. They know how to work within parameters, they're part of the community's life, and

they're used to sitting on the boards, volunteering. Their parents have been part of a community.

vs: Do you mean the people who maintain the status quo tend to be part of those elites who are the power brokers in the community?

ap: Well, I'm the kind of reporter who's an outsider. I think you kind of have to be accepted as an insider to go into any kind of management position.[4]

After decades in newsrooms, Paul did not see herself as an insider who would fit as a manager, but as an outsider, a "rebel, contrarian, thorn, a real prick," going toe to toe with editors on certain stories, but ultimately having the support of her (female) bosses. As she got older, though, she was beginning "to mellow," while worrying that women were sliding back as the larger culture demanded entertainment over news, and entertainment involved women portrayed as they were in the 1950s. For her, feminism's gains were not necessarily sustainable. Women, she sighed, were "going to have to start all over again."

I interviewed Paul in a quiet meeting room at the *Winnipeg Free Press*. She was an only child, born twenty-one years after her parents married: her father used to joke that he was collecting the baby bonus and his old-age pension at the same time. He ran a brokerage firm in Montreal, while Paul's mother was at home, with six servants, including a Scottish nanny called Flossy Goodfellow. ("A name right out of a movie," laughed Paul.) When Paul was about six, her father lost his business, and the family decamped to St. Andrews, New Brunswick. Her mother died at fifty-three (the age Paul was when interviewed), when Paul was only thirteen.

Five years later, in 1975, Paul did something even more shocking to her family than being born. She eloped with a Maliseet man in New Brunswick. (She learned only after her father's death that he tried to have her committed to an insane asylum, but this was not legally possible.) Her new in-laws, militant about Indigenous rights, encouraged Paul to go to university, for which she was grateful. After earning two degrees (English honours, education), she took her interest in writing to Carleton University's journalism school, where she thought she might learn to write stories that would help white people understand the "parallel universe" of Indigenous peoples.

The marriage did not last long, but Paul's interest in Indigenous affairs did. She'd kept her husband's name and had not remarried: she paused when she said, "I wasn't able to have children, so I became a career woman." She went from the *Guelph Mercury* to the *Winnipeg Free Press*, with most of her career being spent at the *Free Press* as a health reporter. A series Paul did on regulatory bodies making decisions behind closed doors resulted in the College of Physicians and Surgeons requesting a change in medical legislation to open up disciplinary hearings:

> vs: Getting a law changed is not a bad day at the job!
> AP: Yeah, it was a very good day. Yeah, those were good days. When you feel like you're being useful and you're making a difference and you're helping and that you're valued, that's a good day for me.

For eighteen months before our interview, Paul had been on a leave to act as a director of communications for the Assembly of Manitoba Chiefs, which gave her a chance to see the difficulties of the Indian Act from the First Nations' perspective. She assumed that because she was "status by marriage and white by birth" that people in the Assembly would object to her ideas. However, she said, while that may have been a factor behind the scenes, she was considered neutral in her approach by at least one chief because she was not associated with any Indigenous nation. Sensing an insider/outsider moment, I ventured:

> vs: So [the chief] assumed that your neutrality came with being *outside* the group.
> AP: Yup, interesting, eh?
> vs: Yeah.
> AP: I haven't thought of it like that. But because I was neutral I was also independent, and I wasn't really answerable to anybody in the group.
> vs: Right. You didn't owe any particular group anything.
> AP: Yeah, which makes me pretty "not political." [*using finger quotes*]
> vs: And would your position as a white person also perhaps mean to them that you could craft their message in a way that was going to be understandable?
> AP: Yeah. I had people tell me they were glad I was there because I understood both worlds. "You understand us," I was told. "And you understand how to talk to those other people over there."

I was struck by how the chief who felt Paul was neutral in her dealings with all the groups in the Assembly thought so because she was non-Indigenous, or an outsider. Paul's comment that she had "never thought of it like that" alerted me to how our own partiality is invisible to us and how easily we allow others to define our own positions, often based on a balance of perceived power. It struck me as well that Paul's demeanour – friendly, listening, interested – could influence people as much as her Indigenous status by a long-ago marriage.

In terms of her own newsroom politics, however, Paul talked about that same position as a conflict of interest when it came to her reporting about Indigenous issues. She mentioned various Indigenous/non-Indigenous conflicts over the years, and how she had been afraid that her knowledge and relationship to Indigenous peoples would make her reporting biased, and so she held back on offering to cover their issues for years. That was changing:

> I didn't think I could keep an impartial focus. I could have talked about what had happened [in the Oka crisis] but back in those days there seemed to be more of a focus on an impartial, balanced, unbiased point of view. Today with journalism it seems more relaxed. They're all columnists and bloggers and everybody's talking about what they think. Well, back in the journalism world I grew up in, it didn't matter what you thought, or what you saw. What mattered were the facts, so the narrative, I just wasn't ready to do the narrative I guess. Not prepared. I would be now. Not that I wish for anything like that to happen again.

Paul had a conflicting insider/outsider position to negotiate, depending on whether she was perceived as Indigenous or not: her "independence" was an asset when working for the chiefs, but she had seen it as a newsroom liability, although that could change as more personal journalism was springing up around her. She was more ready to write "narrative" based on facts.

At the *Free Press*, the only Indigenous employees in editorial were a Metis man, who was a deputy editor and had no public profile, and Paul. Somehow, a white, educated woman born to great privilege had become the paper's only Indigenous reporter. Paul said nothing about that odd situation but mentioned the backlash against Indigenous peoples that cropped up in anonymous posts on the paper's website, echoing a concern Margo Goodhand, editor-in-chief at the *Free Press*, expressed to me about people hiding behind online anonymity to make sexist, racist comments. Paul found this racist backlash depressing, but lauded her paper for seeing the "human rights" issues it raised, citing gender balance as a key factor in that recognition. Racist comments seemed to be dealt with better because of women's presence in the newsroom:

> AP: They keep a very human rights attitude towards the whole thing and I'm thankful for that. I think that's as much due to having a newsroom balance between men and women as anything else.
> VS: How so?
> AP: [*pause*] I think in an all-male newsroom, because that's what it was when I first started, the mood's different. You bring women into it and it opens up somehow. There is something modulated about having a balance between the genders, you have additional viewpoints. And those additional viewpoints get more viewpoints. So, like, [if] you've got one, that's one; if you've got two, then you'll get more. That's the multiplying fact of nature.

By her account, gender balance made all the difference to how the paper responded to racist and sexist commentary online. Paul, like Barnard, did her work with difference and social justice in mind, even though both felt hampered somewhat by larger forces at work in the industry. Paul's and Barnard's career passion still burned, but back in Halifax, reporter Pat Lee, after twenty-one years at the *Chronicle Herald*, was finding it hard to get excited about her daily assignments.

"I'm happy where I am for now"

Pat Lee said that her years on the job had given her confidence; there weren't too many situations any more that she found intimidating. "With age comes experience," she told me with a smile.[5] Yet Lee expressed the least job satisfaction among the cohort of oldest participants: she had grown tired of routine assignments like Remembrance Day and cancer cure runs. She'd even told an editor she simply couldn't cover another such run. This would have been unusual, as most reporters whine about assignments, but rarely would they refuse one, or be allowed to.

After arriving at my hotel room a couple of hours before starting her afternoon shift, Lee told me how she was raised in a middle-class home, as were most other participants: her dad was a regional director for Colgate-Palmolive, and her mother was a homemaker. They moved a lot when she was growing up, ending up in Halifax. After high school, Lee, a "jockette," had a brief idea to teach gym but ended up moving to

Toronto. A few varied jobs later, she wandered into a community college and signed up for journalism, being something of a "news junkie."

Lee, a white fifty-year-old, also described herself as a late bloomer. She had been married only eight years, to a retired military man who had custody of two kids. She helped raised them for only a short time and they were now grown. She was hired at the *Herald* as a GA (general assignment) reporter and had returned to general assignment after a stint on the editing desk and ten years as a TV columnist. She also spent a year as the community reporter, which she liked. The job had been killed during recent layoffs, when about a quarter of the staff was let go.

She did not feel prejudice because of age or gender in the outside world, she said, and anyway, now people usually talked to her on the phone so they couldn't tell her age. (Invisibility, it seems, reduces the risk of possible ageism.) But a new regime of managers – all men – had caused a feeling among older staff that the new regime considered them lazy; managers' eyes "just kind of go over us," she said. She speculated that story assignments like Remembrance Day might be the kind of "not hot" stories older reporters like her were assigned:

> Well, unfortunately, this is the first time that I've ever felt this in my career. 'Cause I've had male bosses, I've had female bosses, but this is the first, and again this is just a newish crowd that has come in. It is somewhat anti-women to some extent and age-related as well, I believe. Just based on assignments, promotions.

Here Lee identified a meeting of age and gender that appeared to influence her new male bosses and might have an impact on story assignment. She then told a story about a man who was parachuted into the editing desk and then "the layoffs came." Lee stated flatly she would never want such a job. She continued:

> It was not any job that I ever would have been interested in, but it set the tone. You know? It set the tone because this guy goes around the newsroom, looking tough and cracking the whip. It's just one of those more of feeling kind of things. The guy who hired this guy used to quite severely bully a younger reporter, a woman. It was noted and she was one of the people laid off, and I don't think it was ever formally grieved. I know it was sort of taken up as an issue because he used to berate her in the middle of the newsroom, which was really unprofessional, at the very least.

Lee noted that a couple of plum jobs had come up – columns and the legislature beat – and men and women apparently applied, but men got the jobs. Lee said her history of being the president of the union local for four years may not have helped her: the paper has not always been a union shop.

Lee liked having some control over her work; in fact, the word "control" came up several times. She described a good day as having her own story idea turn out well, maybe going on the front page, and not having to take constant change in direction from editors. Those days didn't happen much anymore, however. Lee remembered the only woman managing editor they had, who gave her the TV column job. "The climate seemed more friendly under her," said Lee. Her main regret, she said, was leaving the column of her own accord, for reasons she did not explain. Lee had enjoyed the TV column because of the freedom and control it gave her, and how she would get good feedback from readers after drawing their attention to shows they would have missed. She saw the practice of writing just a few paragraphs for the website as a return to the old days of rattling off short pieces of hard news. It seemed difficult for her to find much fun in that, and she had pitched column ideas to no avail, while, she said, "they go and create columns for guys."

Women journalists tended to focus on different news stories, she felt, echoing others in her cohort and in the academic literature. The women took pride in covering welfare, children, education, social agenda stories, more than men generally did. It would also be hard for a man to write about a battered woman, she explained. But then, she asked herself, why make that assumption? It was like assuming women weren't interested in sports – no woman was in the *Herald* sports department – and she thought sports stories were fun.

Lee lamented the loss of energy at the paper when the young reporters were laid off. She had liked mentoring the young reporters, as their questions made her feel like she was not "out to pasture," echoing Barnard's concern about being seen as a dinosaur and the implications of being stereotyped by age. However, at that moment, with fewer young people and a more traditional male structure in power, Lee found the atmosphere irritating. "Maybe I am just sensitive to it because I am fifty, I'm not thirty-five," she said, observing the intransigence of newsroom culture from the perspective of her long experience in it. Lee said she hated to say it, but to a great extent reporting was a young person's game. It was hard at her age to be enthusiastic about covering a murder at eleven at night.

When I asked Lee why senior women print journalists were so few, she answered that "a lot of it is the sidetracking that happens with women." What was "natural" for women (making their first priority their kids) was seen as problematic by managers, and caused women to have to make a "choice" to step back from promotion unless managers helped them. But when I wondered aloud about the notion, she indicated that managers forced mothers into this so-called choice because the newspaper system demanded it. Male managers were "used to promoting men so why would they start promoting women?" This came as a rhetorical question, laced with resignation:

> PL: They [working mothers] can't put in the hours maybe that are required. Some managing editors we have work weird shifts. They come in at ten or eleven and don't go home till seven or eight at night. I don't know too many working mothers with young kids that can do that. You're not home for supper, you're not home for bathtime. And, well I shouldn't say, most women choose not to. Most women put their children, their young children over [their work] – I don't judge anybody for that. That's just [the] choices people are making, and it would be better if companies could accommodate working women, working mothers, better.
> vs: I often think of this idea that it's a "choice," and I think, "Huh? Is it?"
> PL: Well, it's the mother's choice 'cause you're given no choice.

Lee did give former managers credit for giving some mothers at the paper four-day (reduced hours) weeks when their kids were little, and that approach lasted even after the children were grown. Then she sounded resigned to her return to GA work, and spoke of being in "that weird age spot" where she could stay another ten years and protect her salary, or find something else. "I'm happy where I am for now. Let's just put it that way," Lee said. Only then, within a couple of minutes of the end of our talk, did Lee talk about her volunteer work in animal rights, and how she, too, now had a four-day week (and less pay). "I'm not 100 per cent happy in my work life so I've got to improve my out-of-work life to compensate for that," she said.[6]

Lee seemed to have ceded much of her coveted sense of power and control when she left the position (as TV writer) she loved, returning to the mercies of harried assignment editors and filing bits of news to the website, and reducing her hours. She talked about how workplace conflict was based on gender and age factors founded on status quo beliefs, but unlike most of the others, she still did not see herself as a crusader for change but rather as someone who endured her job and found satisfaction elsewhere. Still, she acknowledged women's preference for covering matters involving social justice for disadvantaged groups. Over on the editing desk, Pam Sword was even closer to the upholders of the dominant news culture, finding herself quietly at odds with them in meetings and suppressing her own views about the story line-up for the day.

"A story that connects with your heart is glued to you"

Like Barnard and Lee, Pam Sword was a veteran at the Halifax *Chronicle Herald* who described herself as being somewhat at odds with the news discourse. But her position was that of editor, not reporter, so she had the added possibility of affecting the paper more widely through her defence of certain stories over others. Sword began our talk in a meeting room by giving her age with a laugh, or rather not giving it: she "stopped counting after fifty," which turned out to be four years earlier.[7] Born in Belleville, Ontario, to "definitely middle-class" parents, Sword said she always liked writing, working for the high school newspaper (what she called the "cliché stuff" of budding journalists), doing a stint at community college for journalism, and then working in a string of jobs throughout the late 1970s and early 1980s in small-town Ontario newspapers. After she worked at the Owen Sound *Sun Times*, Sword said abruptly, "stupidly I got married."

She and her husband eventually broke up after they moved around the country for his job as a Snowbird pilot. Settling in Halifax, she had worked at the *Herald* for about twenty years, fifteen on the news desk, editing. She recalled a day early on in her career that underscored the notion of the journalist-as-superhero role she loved (but also gave an apologetic-sounding "hokey" label), which she hinted had been undermined by budget cuts:

> When I was a reporter, once I went to a career day for kids. There are so many cutbacks in modern journalism but I said to them, "a reporter was like being a modern-day superhero." Where you write a good story and you can change maybe not the whole world but [*pause*] you can change a little piece of it, you know? We've done stories about people that need help, or you shine the spotlight on the grievous wrongdoing. My dad was a bit of a social activist. So I thought, Ah, this is sort of a way to change the world for the ... Oh my god, I'm so idealistic, I sound so hokey ... A way to change the world for the better.

Sword, as the single mother of an eleven-year-old daughter, felt that parenthood cemented her interest in stories about ordinary people at the working end of policymaking, those struggling and overcoming problems. She covered the education beat before she had her child, and after becoming a mother became more interested in education as her daughter moved through the school system. At the time of the interview, Sword was a night news editor who was in charge "after the boys go," her reference to the male managers who worked during the day. She "carrie[d] out the wishes" of the earlier news meetings and supervised the night desk, the editors who produced the pages, wrote headlines, and so on. After talking about why she found certain sports and business stories less interesting (it was not the subject, but rather the repetition of the Team A versus Team B paradigm), Sword said:

> I try and be cognizant of people, when we're talking about stories ... maybe this is a girl thing, but you get in meetings and people are like, "Oh, this is a great story," and I don't know. Maybe it's an older thing, too, but there are certain things I'm very interested in, and I might know that 80 per cent aren't interested. I'm a vegetarian, so if there's a story about vegetarianism, I'd be super interested, but probably most people wouldn't.

Here Sword positioned herself, as Paul and others did, at odds with the majority of the senior people in news meetings, who were middle-class white men. Rather than seeing herself, for instance, as being well-positioned to assign stories to reporters that appealed to vegetarians because she was one, or seeing vegetarianism as a national phenomenon that was worth a story, she saw herself as excluded from the news meeting or as a small undercurrent in the mainstream news. She equivocated over whether this thinking was a gender or age issue, as her colleague Pat Lee had, adding that she "wouldn't push a story because it was something I embraced." But as a parent and environmentalist, she tried to ensure "important" stories were at least "briefed," meaning an editor made a paragraph out of a potential news story as part of a digest of items (that is, a column of briefs or one-paragraph news items). She gave the example of taking a wire story about cadmium in children's jewellery and making it into a "brief" so that it at least got into the paper, and running stories about BPAs in baby bottles, as part of her interest in environmentalism and child safety.

Sword said on the night desk, she couldn't assign stories on anything but breaking local news, like a break-in. But still she tentatively expressed (apparently for the first time) how in those meetings, she stands in (or not) for all womanhood:

> I guess 'cause I'm usually the only woman there too. So, I've never really vocalized this before – not having thought about this before, right out loud, but I probably feel like I'm somewhat there representing and not representing women in terms of an activism sense but the interests of readers. 'Cause they (the male managers) all have wives, most of them have children ... but I don't know how a man thinks. Maybe I do. [*laughs*]

Being the only woman – and she was in a union job, not management – at most news meetings had become so routine for Sword that she thought of it rarely and in non-gender terms, along the lines of "I am the only one in here wearing a T-shirt and everyone else is wearing a blazer." If that was a metaphor about internalizing structural differences, Sword had put on the uniform of the casual weekend worker, not the power suit.

Like Lee and Barnard, Sword felt the layoffs that took out the youngest reporters caused the *Herald* to lose valuable energy and new ways of thinking. Class-related matters seemed off-topic: she felt strongly that representatives of an age group were valuable for insights they brought to what is news and how it is reported. Sword felt senior staffers felt the "hot breath on the back of the neck" from young people's ambition, which kept the older group sharper at their meetings:

> Just as we were talking about, things that women might be concerned about, or whether you're middle class, or whatever. We sit around trying to figure out what this allegedly desirable demographic of young people who are turning away from traditional media, what are they interested in? I can bring what ten- and eleven-year-olds are interested in to the table. But, I don't know, what are teenagers interested in? What are people in their twenties interested in? And how do we know that? I guess if you have kids, but it's not the same as having the people in here in their twenties who can say, "That story's boring" or "Why are we doing it like this?"

When asked why so many women leave print journalism, Sword said she didn't know, but maybe job pressure increased the higher up the career ladder women went. Then she started to tell me about her own situation:

> I work terrible hours. It's harder on your family life. If work's stressful, I try not to bring it home. Sometimes I do, and I'm cranky. And child care

is probably an issue, too, if you have a family, the old work/life balance. I got to my position before I had Emma. Now if I had had Emma first ... I've been really lucky, I've had the same childcare provider the whole time. But if I didn't have a super-flexible – because I work nights, right? So if I didn't have that, I couldn't do my job. And being a single parent, too, and having to pay for a full-time childcare provider? I still do it because I love it, not because it makes my life easier.

So while not being sure why women's voices dwindled at the senior level, she talked about handling the night shift by being "lucky" with consistent child care, and commented that throughout her career, nobody with the power to change things ever saw women as a valuable resource who might be held back, or questioned why that was so, as I was doing with her:

> I don't see any place I've ever worked where, anyone has said, "Gosh we need more women in the higher ranks" and "So how can we facilitate that?" Or "Let's talk to women who we think would be good managers or supervisors, and what stops them from applying for these jobs?"

She also speculated that women's reluctance to go into management had to do with not wanting to go outside of the bargaining unit. Because it was easier to lay off managers rather than people with seniority within the union, she explained that women at the paper with "years and the experience and are talented" are "far enough off the seniority chain so that the paper would have to close before they'd be laid off."[8]

I noticed Sword articulated the ambivalence I felt in meetings where I was the only white woman among white men. Using rhetorical questions, she outlined the central false binary and gendered thinking about "hard" versus "soft" news, what supposedly interested women and what didn't. In meetings, she negotiated this tension by telling herself (using finger quotes in the air) to "shut up," suppressing her own defined – and gendered – views of what constituted news, and giving way to a fear she could not name. In the place where the culture was easy to reinforce – the news meeting – she felt silenced, but passionate about what seemed invisible to the men:

> We have this four o'clock story meeting. I know the managers are fairly interested in politics, and maybe sports, and a bit of crime. I appreciate those stories, too, but if there's something else, I don't want to say just

human interest, but something that women would be interested in. And not just women, I mean, we all, it's almost like, "Shut up, Pam." Why are we so afraid? We all eat food. But is food a women's issue? Well, it's not. What's happening to your kids' school, is that a women's issue? No, it's not. Is pay equity a women's issue? Well sadly, maybe yes, but it's not. Is the fact that a woman could get stoned to death for adultery a women's issue? No, it's not. Are animal stories women's stories? I hate animal stories. But I call it emotional resonance. That makes a connection. You can read a story out of Ottawa that's important, and maybe it makes you mad, but it'll make my brain mad but it won't connect with my heart unless it's about something like the [teen girl suicide in jail] story. That connects with my heart and that's a systemic problem, too, with Corrections Canada. But a story that connects with your heart is glued to you. And you might even read it twice.

Once again, we see flashes of passion for the craft, followed by hesitation on contact with the male-dominated, traditional news model; cultural myths about motherhood repeated; and being able to continue in the business (working terrible hours) seen as a matter of luck, in her case because of the good fortune of having reliable child care for a daughter born at just the right time. As she told her story, what she described vividly – systemic inequality – was not actually named as such. While Sword carried these complexities up from the reporter's cubicle to the assigning desk, the *Spectator*'s Michele Steeves took them further, to the department head level, where her luck was to have an editing job that aligned with her domestic interests.

"Journalism is easy if you have a wife at home"

Michele Steeves, the oldest study participant at sixty-one, warmed gradually to being interviewed: she started with one-word answers, then slowly increased the length of her responses. Her enthusiasm grew when she described how lucky she felt because her own personal interests intersected with those of the pages she filled. As style editor at the *Hamilton Spectator*, Steeves was responsible for fashion, gardening, décor, and lifestyle coverage, as well as for a Saturday section, similar to the *Globe*'s Focus section in its emphasis on issues and feature news. She had also been life editor from 1979 to 1999. When I commented that she had a lot of responsibility in her current post, she said "yeah." When I asked how many reporters worked for her, she replied "none."[9] Like

Kathleen Coleman, who ruled Kit's Kingdom in the late 1800s, Steeves commanded a broad field every day with few troops.

Without her own reporters, Steeves hired freelancers and used whatever staff-written material the city editors gave her. This scenario was typical for lifestyle editors, the whirling dervishes of the newsroom, who cobble together freelance stories, event calendars, syndicated material (such as health columns), so-called soft features and items about the arts, health, social issues, parenting, hobbies, and so on from wire services. These sections pay close attention to design matters, as much of the content deals with aesthetics, and this is especially true for section fronts. Lifestyle and weekend pages must be completed earlier in the workday (and earlier in the week for weekend sections) to leave more press time available to breaking-news pages, so the lifestyle editor and her/his (usually her) assistant, if there is one, are continually run off their feet.

Steeves was the youngest of three children whose father was an airline records employee and whose mother worked as a sales clerk. A Maritimer, she earned an English degree from Memorial University in Newfoundland, and says she "fell" into journalism when she took a job as a copy editor upon graduation. After moving to southern Ontario and working at several editing jobs, she landed at the *Spec* thirty-three years ago and has remained there, always in the lifestyle area. She was married, with one grown daughter, age twenty-six. Her personal characteristics, she told me, certainly informed her work, as a woman, wife, mother, gardener, and someone interested in decorating, cooking, reading, and "caring for a home and that sort of thing." These characteristics seemed to define what choices she made at work, and she expanded that approach to all editors:

vs: Do your personal characteristics bring something to the way you do your work?

ms: Certainly they do. As a content editor you are always looking for stories that other people want to read and you have yourself as sort of an example of, well, I'm a woman reader, "this story is fascinating.'" You know?

vs: You're putting yourself in the place of the reader.

ms: Yeah. I think every editor does that. It's pretty hard to take yourself out of who you are in this job. For instance, I couldn't be a sports editor because I don't know anything about sports and have no interest in sports. I'm fortunate that the content that I edit includes a lot of things that I personally enjoy and do and are part of my life.

After more than three decades in more or less the same position, it is not difficult to see how and why Steeves would interweave her job with her personal life, where she found pleasure in the same activities that her sections described, and that was "fortunate." In terms of her impact, she made a point when deciding how to cover consumer stories to spotlight local, independent retailers, and to give readers a feeling that she covered "personal consumer shopping" to make their lives easier and their money go farther. Reader response was huge, she said.

Steeves's big challenge was to source and edit enough content to fill her sections well and in a timely way, because the inexpensive material that came from wire services had declined as U.S. newspapers shut down or cut back. She noted that when cuts came, "it's usually the life section and style departments that go first." Concurrently, her freelance budget had been reduced with "all resources really in news these days." Like the *Chronicle Herald*, where the arts and life sections were folded together, the *Spec* sought to squeeze the pages that happened to be most read by women and most likely to be edited by women journalists. If she had any plans to start aiming copy at male readers, she did not mention them; her section was by, and about, women.

As Steeves talked about how the *Globe* had begun to emphasize lifestyle stories, even on the front page on Saturdays, she began to use more emphatic language ("for me, it's thrilling to see") as she contrasted the *Globe* with the *Spec*, from the perspective of someone who had seen – and overseen – much change. "We're almost 99 per cent wire-dependent," she said of her page content. "It's tragic in a way, to see that erosion." (The *Globe* has since combined its life and arts section into one, effectively reducing those pages, just as the Halifax paper had done.)

Still, like the other senior participants, she saw herself as lucky. She had been a working mother who rarely left work on time, with a husband at home. It was a dream situation:

vs: To what do you attribute women's low numbers at senior positions in Canadian newspapers?

ms: I would have to point to working conditions.

vs: What would you mean by working conditions?

ms: Well, my main experience is the *Spectator* and I would say it's the lack of flex time, flex schedules and certainly no onsite day care. There has been reluctance, from the company, to even entertain different ideas that women have brought with regard to flex time, working at home or different schedules. So you're either in a traditional working environment or you leave. Take a break and hope you can get back in after a few years. I think too, it's just the same way it is in our culture in general, the old boys' network has been around for a long time and is taking a long time to go away.

vs: Yeah.

ms: Journalism, like many other professions, is easy if you have a wife at home.

vs: And for those who have a husband at home, it is not the same thing.

ms: No, it's not the same thing. Although I was lucky when I had the years as life editor when it was just me, and five or six reporters and doing the assigning, editing, layout everything myself. During those years when I was never home on time I did have my husband who's also a journalist and had much more flexible hours than me and could work from home because he was a columnist. That was when my daughter was a baby and that was just a dream.

The *Spec*, said Steeves, did not have a level playing field for women. She hesitated to answer the question at first, since she said she was "so marginalized now from the newsroom." Things looked better "on the surface" because two senior editors were women, but she also noted the newsroom "whispers" about gender issues, a fear among women of speaking out (biting their tongues as the Halifax *Herald*'s Pam Sword described), and the reality of the "high-pressure, twelve-hour-day senior jobs" being unappealing to women who preferred family and job balance. Her experience a decade earlier, of having expressed interest in a senior editor's job only to be ignored, made her feel disappointed with management generally.

We discussed how difficult it still was to get to a day-care centre on time (a problem I had twenty years earlier at the *Globe*), and Steeves remarked, "You know, I can't think of a time when I've heard of a man in the same position." I also noticed that Steeves was articulating the notion that journalism operates in lockstep with society (e.g., in her comment about the old boys' network) rather than considering how journalism might actually reinforce societal norms, including assumptions about women being primarily interested in stories about the home. In Calgary, Monica Zurowski was taking "toddler steps" to address gendered aspects of that idea.

"If I had kids, I don't think I'd be where I am"

Lots of luck and a lack of kids figured in Monica Zurowski's story, as did themes widely shared among participants regarding beliefs about multitasking, choice, and women's communication skills. But Zurowski, whose position as managing editor at the *Calgary Herald* was higher

than that of Barnard, Lee, Paul, Sword, and Steeves, felt she was positioned to do things differently to create a better workplace for both men
and women, and somehow to begin righting the wrong of gendered
career barriers.[10]

If Zurowski had had kids, they might have attended the day-care
centre downstairs from her sun-filled office beside the newsroom hub.
Earlier that day, as I waited for my appointments at the *Herald* in the
large cafeteria, a day-care worker went by pulling a trolley full of tod-
dlers around the building. I recalled how a few years earlier, when I led
coaching sessions at the *Herald* in a seminar room, we emerged once for
a break to see a gaggle of preschoolers in tutus trundle by with caregivers. What an uplifting sight in a workplace basement.

Like most in the cohort, Regina-born Zurowski, forty-nine, had
middle-class roots and a university degree. After a disastrous insur-
ance job, she tried an education degree, since many of her relatives
were teachers, but got "lucky" and found a journalism program in the
same university.

"I loved it from the start," said Zurowski, citing journalism's lack of
routine, the privilege and fun of talking to interesting people, of developing a global view. She had an internship at the *Edmonton Journal*
("very lucky") and ended up at the *Calgary Herald*. She described herself
in her twenties as naive but competitive, turning down the out-of-town
bureau the *Herald* offered at first and starting as provincial court reporter.
By twenty-nine, she was assistant city editor, with people much older
than she reporting to her, including "curmudgeonly, grumpy, fifty-five-
year-old men." She told me about one male staffer who had refused to
walk over to her at the assigning desk, even though she was his immediate boss. So she would go to his desk and "pay homage to the great
journalist that he was." After management training (which is largely a
thing of the past, as consultants are the first casualties in hard times)
and gaining experience, Zurowski persuaded the older reporter to meet
her half way: sometimes he went to her desk, and sometimes she went
to his. Her story was a stark example of the lengths, literally, to which
many women managers will go to accommodate the dominant cultural
norms in a newsroom, as expressed in everyday contact.

Zurowski was appointed features editor, encompassing eleven sections, and stayed there for years. Moving to features had been her choice;
looking around for experience in other departments, she applied for the
editor's post after spending more than a decade in the city department.
Plus, the features department oversaw the weekly news review section

called "Observer." It was her first department head position. When reorganization occurred, the next job up, that of deputy editor, came open and Zurowski said she thought that, while there might be other good candidates, she was best suited for it. She also thought about all the times she and women colleagues talked about not being risk-takers, while men were more likely to see a chance for promotion and apply. Zurowski did not continue suppressing her own competitive streak. She got the job. Eight years and another restructuring later, Zurowski was the managing editor, reporting to the (white male) editor-in-chief. She was "lucky" this man recognized the extra things she did and supported her. She was responsible for the day-to-day running of the newsroom, and "arm-wrestled" each night with other newsroom leaders to decide what went on page A1. She was the only woman to hold one of the half-dozen powerful positions in the newsroom.

Invited to consider how or if any of her personal characteristics intersected or acted in concert to affect how she did her job, Zurowski responded that she had been thinking about this, since she had had time to read the questions ahead of our talk. Her answer was multifaceted and focused on commonly held views about gender differences. She saw being a woman as having a positive effect: women had a "fabulous ability" to multitask, while men were more likely to focus on one thing, and that mix brought strength to the team; interview subjects tended to find women more open, approachable and better listeners, so they opened up more; women had a greater connection to community, so they would likely adapt better to the new demands for community-based online reporting and blogging; and women were better networkers.

Regarding what might hold women back, Zurowski talked first about society's "expectation of women doing the bulk of the childraising" and that taking long leaves was "a choice" women were making. But as she talked more, she began to question this notion:

> There's still that society expectation of women doing the bulk of the childraising. We've had lots of couples in the newsroom. And 99.9 per cent of the time it's the female journalist who stays home for a year. I've had a few cases where they've split it, actually not even evenly, like maybe ten months for the woman and two months for the guy or something. So it's a choice that women are making. And it can be a great choice. And it's great, women raising their kids is a fabulous thing, and I obviously have no problem with that, and I support that. I don't have kids. So I don't

know if it's a societal expectation. Is it their own wishes that lead them to that point?

Whatever caused the inequity, Zurowski saw herself as part of the solution, a manager who helped women if they wanted to work part-time, for example. But how could they then keep a senior writing job three days a week? She had been part of "endless" discussions about this, so it was clearly on the *Herald* agenda. Zurowski speculated about why so few women were at the top, touching on parenthood, age and work/ life balance. Later, she cited a lack of confidence women held regarding their own experience, echoing uncertainty expressed by others, like Elissa Barnard in Halifax:

> I could go out in the newsroom and pick the next ten or twelve people who might want this job and I don't know if any are women. Some of it is because they have kids. Some of it is the hours. Maybe women are smarter [*laughs*]. I mean they have a better sense of the work/life balance. They see how, as you climb the ladder, it becomes increasingly difficult to keep any kind of balance outside of work. So maybe that's what discourages them. It might be because they know they can't have that same drive at work and at home and where is their priority. But in the last five years, I can think of one young female journalist who has come to me and said, "I want your job some day." I can think of nine or ten young male journalists who have expressed, "I want to be a managing editor and editor-in-chief some day." So, I don't know. Maybe women don't apply for as many jobs. They don't promote themselves. They don't apply for promotions.

Zurowski saw herself as having the power to negotiate personal time and to do so for her staff, and she accomplished that in part by breaking down some "myths" about management life. She described telling a young mother with leadership potential that senior positions had some flexibility, despite journalism not being a nine-to-five job and that it was not "the most conducive thing for women, especially women who have a lot of family pressures." In a follow-up email, Zurowski explained she was urging the woman to consider applying for a senior job, and wanted her to know that while management could be difficult, it was not impossible.[11]

"Toddler steps" were being made at the *Herald* in work/life balance, said Zurowski. She made sure that the sports editor had a regular date night with his wife and another editor left in time to coach his son's basketball team once a week; she did not make these arrangements as "favours" the way male managers tended to do. This was all part of her responsibility – and power – to set the tone, to keep things as positive as possible, keeping up creativity and productivity, and, using gendered decision-making, not to put a Calgary Flames photo on the front page as often as the male editors would like. Her competitive juices still flowed: she loved knowing that the *Herald* had an exclusive story or a great photo that the Calgary *Sun* or CTV didn't have. That was a great day at work.

Had not having kids (Zurowski had a male partner) changed how she was experiencing her career?

> Yeah. And I do think that's one of the difficulties for women who have children is that they can't always do the – if there is a big news story breaking or special initiative or special report or whatever needs to be done. If I need to stay tonight, if all of a sudden [someone] needs me to stay and do something until ten at night, I can do it. If you're a mother and you've got a kid who you have to take to soccer or cook for, you can't do it. So, you know, not having children probably makes it easier to get ahead or to do that kind of job. I don't know what the answer is. I don't think it's right. I do think that's the way it is, yeah. I've probably said before, "If I had kids, I don't think I'd be where I am." Yeah.

Even with an onsite day-care centre, it seemed that the mother-or-journalist conflict was unsolvable. Still, after more than twenty years of climbing the ranks, Zurowski tried to change the culture of her newsroom for men and women in small, but she hoped meaningful, ways. If tackling other diversity issues was on the *Herald*'s agenda, she did not say so. She did not discuss age as a factor that might sideline her or how age might intersect negatively with gender. She was the managing editor, after all.[12]

When a woman print journalist leaves the business, it is often out of frustration with newspaper culture and/or a sense that her personal life suffers, or will. One participant, in an off-the-record comment, said that this was so common that it was "normal for women to disappear" from the newspaper business. And even if they do not disappear, they can still feel invisible.

This was the case for Lucinda Chodan, one of the two editors-in-chief I interviewed, who recalled long-ago experiences of sexism that led her to understand she did not exist in the minds of her male bosses. Did this invisibility fuel her wryly self-described megalomania? Chodan thought she was the right person to fix the industry and to champion social justice, despite not having much confidence herself, and being hamstrung by tight budgets.

"I still think this business needs me to change it"

Lucinda Chodan's entry into the world of print journalism was unusual. She began as a typesetter (at the *Edmonton Sun* in 1978), after stints as a teacher (Chodan has an education degree and grew up in small-town Westlock, Alberta) and a test-designer for the Alberta Ministry of Education. She quit journalism twice, each time going back to the education field, but then finally returned to journalism for good. She drily framed her own kind of luck as a "gift from God." The second time she decided to return to print was after the assistant deputy minister of education walked by her office one day:

> I was resigned to a life developing tests. I was having a meeting with my boss at Alberta Education. I didn't like it there very much, but my boss was a woman, and I liked her a lot. She and I were sitting in her cubicle, talking about some aspect of the Grade 3 test and where it needed to go, when the ADM walked by and he said "I hate to interrupt your hen party" and I just thought "Fuck this, man." Later that day, [a *Sun* editor] called and he said "I won't bother you again, but [the editor's wife] says to just ask you, 'Are you happy there?'" And I go, "Wah! I'm not! Get me out of here!" Since then, it's been a pretty unbroken trail.[13]

In an editorial department meeting room at the *Times Colonist*, she told detailed stories about her early days as a typesetter, a proofreader, and a features writer, and how she moved to editing jobs that took her to the *Montreal Gazette* and then the *Times Colonist*. Chodan, who was fifty-three, described "awful, humiliating" hazing rituals at the hands of male editors and pressroom men, sometimes together. She talked about several such highly charged incidents at length, borne at the time with suppressed fury and still keenly felt.

Chodan framed her career as a series of big breaks she was able to exploit because of what a friend called, she said, her "quietly aggressive manoeuvres" and what she characterized as a dogged work ethic, honed by her small-town upbringing. Unlike her male peers at the *Gazette*, she had no sponsor, so Chodan battled the inevitable presence of whichever "fair-haired boy of the managing editor" was in vogue in the office at the time by metaphorically "doing windows," the grunt work of editing copy instead of something high profile like flying "to Cuba to cover the FLQ." It would never have occurred to her to put herself forward for such a marquee assignment. Nor did she speak out when senior male editors engaged in everything from leering to making audible sexist remarks about young summer interns to even "hitting on" them. As for how it felt to see these events happen but feel powerless to stop them, Chodan explained that these men held the fate of editors like her in their hands and it was "part of the landscape," as inevitable as the fact that not having kids helped assure Zurowski's career, as she told it. "I don't think I really existed for them," Chodan said of her male managers in the 1980s. "I wasn't one of the curvaceous, brown-haired, brown-eyed young interns."

By the end of the 1980s, from her position as assistant entertainment editor, Chodan began what she called a "fairly serious assault on management ranks in a fairly weirdly passive way." I was not surprised by how she described herself as accommodating her quiet nature to a war-strategy metaphor, since military conflict dominates newspapers as a narrative construct.

But Chodan's motive was to make her paper "a better place, a better newspaper." Having come up on the arts side – as was typical for the senior women in the study – she felt her lack of news experience held her back, describing a feeling shared by other participants that she needed more experience before taking on a new assignment, instead of learning on the job. Rather than taking on a more senior position immediately, one that her (male) boss thought she could quickly grow into, Chodan asked to work on the foreign desk:

> I didn't have a lot of confidence, about my familiarity with news, so I said to [my boss], "You know, I don't feel that comfortable doing this. Can I work on the news desk for a while?" And he said, "Oh, you don't need that," but I think I have felt all along, I don't really want to do a job that's built around my own bluster. I think men that I have worked with have felt a lot more confidence in that the office itself has authority attached to it, whereas I have never been comfortable with having authority without having expertise attached to it.
>
> [*Few seconds pause*] I think that's probably held me back, held women back, because I want to know when I say something that it's true, or that if I think something can be done. This probably is a limitation as a manager, I have to know that something could be done if people stretched, rather

than just saying that something needs to be done and making people do it, however they have to do it.

Chodan echoed the self-doubt expressed by Elissa Barnard and others, which she generalized to include all women: her long experience did not give her enough faith in her ability to do the next higher-level post, even though her male manager felt she was ready. She took a dim view of the traditional model that allowed the holder of a job title to take authority from it (what she later called the "magic wand" approach), preferring to inspire rather than ordering a task to be done.

As Chodan continued to describe how her career evolved to her position as editor-in-chief of the *Times Colonist*, a pattern emerged: self-doubt or insecurity appeared before each next step up the ladder, while simultaneously she described (sometimes with a wry laugh) her own sense of "grandiosity." A sense of mission, of passion for social change, for giving readers what they wanted and needed: these ideas dominated her reasons to stay in an industry she feared was in peril. She was the only one, Chodan said with a smile, who could "save" the *Gazette*, and would serve in that job, if asked.[14] And like her counterpart Margo Goodhand in Winnipeg, she saw her abilities to make change thwarted by forces beyond her control. Why then, did she stay?

LC: I still think this business needs me to change it. I have always loved newspapers. I think we play such a huge role in a democratic society. And we're only going to continue if people like me stay in and help them change. Number two, I still have a lot left to do in journalism that needs to be done. Number three, it's a great job. On the days that I'm not profoundly depressed about my inability to change even the smallest thing, I am buoyed by a sense that I have made changes and I continue to make changes, and eventually the rest of the world will catch up and see what the rest of those changes are. I think absolutely you have to have a degree of megalomania to do this job, and for some reason, in spite of not having a lot of personal confidence about many things, I do have an absolute conviction that I have a sense of how to save newspapers.

VS: You have this sense from where?

LC: I don't know. A gift from God. Same as my proofreading. Excellent. No idea why.

VS: Is any of it to do with the fact that – as you said, and I say to people, too – it's not rocket science? Is it simply by being that part of a society that newspapers historically have simply appealed to?

LC: Maybe. [*pause*] … Well, first it comes from the success that I've had doing it. Measurable success, repeated in different places in different times, that makes me comfortable that I should have faith in my own decisions because they work. Also, I don't think of newspapers … the kind of approach that I see … what has … Oh, gosh. [*pause*] I think that one of the things that has been in many people's eyes a weakness of my own career and my approach is that I'm not a particularly hard-news person. I don't come from that traditional hard-news background. I'm not a ballsy Christie Blatchford or Rosie Di Manno. Or any of the great newspaper leaders that existed before, or the models of them anyway.

Chodan politely countered my devil's advocate suggestion that her "gift" of saving newspapers was perhaps more a matter of journalism being the kind of business that could be fairly easily saved. Obviously, it is not. She pointed out that she had measurable successes, repeatedly, throughout her career. But when she reached the part of her story where she could have cast herself completely as the wise leader/heroine – the one who killed a "women's" section that she created herself just because it had run its course; the one who took a deep breath and fired people (I nod here) because she had to; the one who had fended off a publisher who only thought about the sports department – she stumbled, equivocated, then described herself as a victim of the old, male image of a successful woman in journalism, somebody she was not, which was "ballsy" with a "hard-news background." Still, elsewhere in our talk, she described male managers as "gutless cowards," and said women had more stomach for dealing with the hard, complex people issues that men tended to avoid. She saw women as far more adept at change, because the vested interest men had in keeping power made them reluctant to give it up. "I think that great leaders welcome change," said Chodan. Male managers, in refusing to be open to change, she continued, were weakening an industry already in a panic, where the standard answer to fighting the unknown was to stop hiring. She predicted that the Canwest head office, which had not noticed that the *Times Colonist* readership had increased on her watch, would do so eventually and offer her a promotion. She was right: it took them three years.

Chodan did not mention that she had no children until near the end of our discussion. This was partly because I knew, partly because it appeared she hadn't worked out the reasons why "for the record" herself. She had the usual reasons: the work was hard, the hours long and crazy, the business unforgiving, the news culture sexist, she "forgot" to have children (which she said with a laugh). As well, she named her musician husband's peripatetic life as an important factor. Echoing Monica Zurowski at the *Calgary Herald*, Chodan said that she told women entering the business that "for me it would not have been possible to have children and have this job. So maybe things will be changed when you're in this kind of role, but that certainly was the case for me." Change for women journalists in the future was left to a "maybe," while she could imagine herself as Superwoman, saving print journalism single-handedly.

Conclusions

The higher the rank of women journalists I interviewed, the less they attributed random external serendipity to their own success, but the vast majority did attribute their decades of successful journalism to being plain lucky. Lucinda Chodan did so with humour, talking about her "gift from God" success. While those good-luck stories perhaps allowed them to feel they had improved their community or society as a result – an important factor for these women's job satisfaction – they also saw their own careers as circumscribed over the years by what they took to be immutable truths. Women, they mostly agreed, were multitaskers, so they were asked to do more and they obliged; women had babies, so they naturally made more sacrifices for family than men (and when they did not have babies, many reasons were given, but never that they just didn't want them); journalism was a 24/7 job, even more as media technology was imposed on them, and there was no getting around the hours for work/life balance, so women naturally could not keep up the gruelling pace. Here we see the most senior participants tending to support the idea through their stories that narratives reflect dominant cultural norms, in this case industry norms of how journalism production "works" and how larger society "naturally" operates. As social actors, the participants describe their working and private-life arrangements as largely outside of their control and position themselves as aware but passive accomplices, their agency undercut by powerful forces. Their stories appear to indicate that the oldest participants, in order to remain on the job, have internalized – or grudgingly accepted – the gendered oppositions they experience daily. They felt powerful and simultaneously powerless, unsure yet confident, often feeling stuck in whatever career position they found themselves.

They were aware of their own racial and class privilege (not described in terms of luck, however), which seemed to motivate them to focus on social justice issues. A contradiction arose here: they felt they could change things in society, but seemed to see structural inequalities in their own workplaces as inevitable. Three of the participants named age stereotypes (the "dinosaur" worry) as part of what might increase their sense of powerlessness, along with gender. They could clench their teeth and bear it, suppressing their own views about the situation, or leave. As time went on after these interviews, more and more of them did leave; the majority of those who have left are from this oldest cohort.

Ideas about power were contradictory, too, often expressed as an absolute where men were concerned (they have it, want to keep it and if they lose it, it's gone) but as women, they saw their power as an energy supply to be tapped to fuel social-justice projects, if only they could get – and keep – their hands on it. Social characteristics, here primarily age and gender, may cause them to accentuate the social-justice aspects of their journalism.

Much of what the participants in this cohort said was offered with a mix of pride and resignation, after a lifetime of working inside a male-dominated workplace, striving to chronicle the experiences of those outside mainstream power sources (lifestyle and arts news), while the newspapers placed more value on the exploits of the powerful (political and economic news).

While individual stories of senior women print journalists related wide-ranging experiences, observations and opinions, and an under-standing that we cannot force individuals to stand in for a genera-tion, the participants' stories had common touchstones regarding the forces that order the women's relations between themselves and their workplaces. The women were all white, spoke English as a first lan-guage, were well educated, able-bodied and mostly raised in middle-class households. Most were married and several had a child or two, mostly teens or older.[15] Several described their stay-at-home husbands as making their careers possible. Where participants had stories about immigrant experiences or difficult or unusual circumstances early in life, those were described as formative, disrupting privilege in a good way. They seldom had women mentors and only a few remembered male mentors fondly. These most experienced participants saw them-selves possibly at the height of their abilities, maybe already as stale as yesterday's news, worried about the industry itself, as well as the women coming after them. Embedded in the newsroom culture and responding to the increasing list of daily tasks, they often felt immobilized, exasperated but unable or unwilling to do little more than recognize their gendered accommodations and lament the lack of diversity in the newsroom. Instead, they saw themselves as standard-bearers for "the voiceless," whoever they might be.

These oldest participants told stories that helped combine their multiple identities as women, newsroom veterans, wives and mothers, into a coherent whole. Looking back on their own histories, I found less ongoing revision and fewer contradictions than emerged from the stories of mid-career and younger women, still in the thick of negotiating complex identities. With narrative available both to give their lives clear meaning and purpose, and to expose life's ongoing discrepancies and inconsistencies, the oldest cohort tended towards the former.

From their perspective as women developing their careers during second-wave feminism, they told stories about their own luck, more than skill or effort, reflecting what feminist researchers have identified as a lack of a sense of entitlement, and sometimes confidence, in that generation. At the same time, they used their version of the war story to describe their own resilience – especially as women and mothers – to show strength and resistance. Lacking further characteristics of diversity themselves, they let gender bestow on them the right to speak for others with less power, taking up the cause of those whose own characteristics (such as race) effectively banned them from the newsroom.

The next generation of women print journalists describes struggling at the epicentre of young motherhood and mid-career challenges. Their negotiations with the dominant newsroom culture are less resigned than the oldest group, and their stories of life and career interactions more frenzied.

Chapter Three

Mid-Career Participants: Hard Work, Sacrifice, and Missing Family Pizza Night

Having spent years grinding through the water for over four hours a day as a competitive swimmer, editorial page editor Licia Corbella knew something about the interplay of privilege and sheer determination: she was once the fastest female swimmer in North America in the eleven-to-twelve and thirteen-to-fourteen age categories. But by the time she finished high school in Point Grey, one of Vancouver's most exclusive neighbourhoods, Corbella had abandoned the pool. Her dream to swim at the 1980 Moscow Olympics ended with the boycott of the Games because of the Soviet invasion of Afghanistan; her swim coach moved away; her top grades dropped; she felt, she said, "shattered."[1]

But remembering this when we talked in her *Calgary Herald* office, Corbella said the life lesson for her was not to stop trying when adversity hit, but to reset her goals. Yes, the Olympic dream had been ripped from her, but she could have tried out for a competition in Japan. Olympic trials were still on, so she could have at least found out if she would have qualified for the Moscow Olympics. "I should have stuck with it," she said.

Corbella has more than stuck with her chosen career: she was the oldest of the mid-career cohort of participants, who ranged in age from thirty-two to forty-seven. Most had been in the business between ten and twenty years: she had been in it for twenty-five. Her story about regretting the abandoning of her sport reflected a theme common to these participants, which was to attribute hard work more than luck to their career rise. Also, rather than singling out gender as central to any outsider status they felt, many white women in this group named their parents' immigrant status as an important factor in their professional lives. The only black participant in the study was detailed and emphatic in her description of the impact of racism on her life and newsroom career, naming it as both motivational and painful.

Parenthood, whether they were mothers or not, was a key element to their understanding of how careers developed, and those who had children felt keenly how they were in the thick of a work/family tug of war, often naming self-sacrifice and a sense of duty to family on the one hand, and society on the other, as a necessary component of survival. Five of nine had at least one child, and those children were in the toddler to preteen stage. This helped to explain why workplace flexibility (or lack of it) was a crucial issue for this group, even for the three who did not have children but hoped to or who observed their colleagues in the midst of childrearing. Their stories reflected the change that has occurred in many newspapers, due in part to women journalists' increasing presence: they showed how they reinforced the continuity of the hierarchy, too. The managers might not be flexible, but these mid-career women were the Gumbys of the newsroom.

Unlike the most senior group, all but one mid-career participant – the above-mentioned Corbella – did not rise through the arts and entertainment side, reflecting women's increasing arrivals directly into hard news from the start of their careers (Freeman, 2011). They did not mention the path-clearing done by the women who went before them, but it appeared they benefited from the hard work of those "lucky" journalists. Being sandwiched between baby boomers who wouldn't retire and ambitious twenty-somethings also made a few feel stuck in the middle of the newsroom hierarchy, while the oldest cohort more often cited industrial upheaval and cutbacks for their sense of being stuck. These mid-career women were significant for having inherited the media-hyped "have-it-all" meta-narrative, only to find they were *doing* it all. They embodied continuity in the workplace and in the society on which they reported or commented, and they simultaneously manifested its change as they named, and often challenged, the same oppressive social norms they described so richly in their stories.

The mid-career cohort included Corbella, who ran the editorial pages of the *Calgary Herald*; Carla Ammerata, city editor of the *Hamilton Spectator*; Paula Arab, then columnist at the *Calgary Herald*; Sherri Borden Colley and Patricia Brooks Arenburg, reporters for Halifax's *Chronicle Herald*; Denise Helm, online editor at the *Times Colonist* in Victoria; Nicole MacIntyre, reporter for the *Hamilton Spectator*; Sarah Petrescu, reporter, columnist, and online editor for the Victoria *Times Colonist*;

and Stephanie Coombs, then city editor of the *Times Colonist*. Only one participant in this cohort, Mary Agnes Welch, worked for the *Winnipeg Free Press*. At first I thought it was coincidence, but this was likely due to a "lost generation" of women this group told me about, who had left years earlier and were lamented by the *Free Press* women journalists who came before and after.[2]

"I've found what I love to do and I just want to get better and better doing it"

Despite her sharp early lesson in broken dreams, Licia Corbella expressed satisfaction with her life. At forty-seven, she had been married for twenty-five years, her sons were thriving, and her position was a pivotal one as editor in charge of representing the editorial board's opinions at the *Calgary Herald*. She worked her way up from city and beat reporting through lifestyle and travel editorships, sections where women who rise up the ranks were routinely installed, and she had been an assistant city editor. Her "ed board" was comprised of five members, three of whom were women, including herself and Paula Arab. The third edited letters to the editor and wrote columns and editorials.

As she told stories about her childhood, young adulthood, and career as a journalist, Corbella often referred to determination, tenacity, and sheer hard work to account for her position. However, the luck theme did appear a couple of times, in her being "very lucky" to have been chosen for an internship at *The Province* in Vancouver as she was starting out, and also lucky in being freed up to write more upfront news columns in addition to her editorial page columns, which was going to be announced the day after we talked. "It's fantastic!" she said. Corbella loved the process of reportage: her joy was in digging, making calls, observing, and getting the big, hard-news story.

Like many participants, Corbella was singled out early as a good writer. After a year in Europe post–high school, she worked on a newspaper in Mallorca (her mother is Spanish, and Corbella speaks Spanish), and despite being rejected twice by Langara College's journalism school in Vancouver, she was finally accepted. Also, like other participants across cohorts, her goal, she said, was to "have a career that had meaning, where I could make a difference." Her parents' divorce made her realize, too, that as a woman, she needed to be financially independent. Her husband had a good job, but "staying employed for all these years" had been important to her.

Corbella told a story about her first few days working weekends at the *Toronto Sun* in the late 1980s, which illustrated how her well-honed work ethic influenced her career trajectory. She figured at the time that if she could hustle on those weekends, "they'd never let me go":

> There was a plane crash, a hobby pilot was taking his inaugural flight in a plane he built and it crashed and he died. This was in Oshawa. So I drove down to Oshawa and, this was before cell phones, and I left *Sun* business cards. I wrote my phone number and my name on them and I left messages on people's answering machines who were involved in the flying club in Oshawa and got some calls back and got together a pretty good story of this man, and the irony of this being his inaugural flight and blah blah. But no photo. So it's 6:30 at night, and I file the story and the phone rings and [the caller said], "I do have a photo of him with his plane!"

She drove back to Oshawa, got the photo, brought it back, and the next day, Corbella said, she knew she was "in" at the *Toronto Sun* for having gone – driven – more than the extra mile.

Gender did add to her efficacy as a journalist, she said, listing commonly expressed beliefs about women's qualities. Women were more empathetic than men as reporters: an example she gave was in "bawling my eyes out" when talking to the mother of a child who had been raped and murdered. A male colleague told her she wasn't being "objective," to which Corbella replied, "Well, you want me to take the side of the friggin' rapist?" Because Corbella felt for the mother, and let it show, the mother was able to tell that important story, she said. Women were also better at "smoothing out the rough edges" in heated newsroom situations, Corbella said, and could mediate arguments between men staffers, allowing them to "kiss and make up" without losing their dignity. Making a positive difference in the world was more important to women journalists (and women generally), she felt, and being able to share personal stories has helped women journalists reach out online as bloggers and excel on that increasingly important media platform.

As to why newsrooms continued to lack diversity beyond gender, Corbella cited the tendency of immigrant parents to want their children to pursue science degrees rather than arts degrees, but she added that this was changing. To address why women were scarce at the highest levels, Corbella offered that the business concerns of publishers and editors-in-chief didn't make women "happier and more fulfilled" because those roles were more about budgets and "firing" people, echoing Halifax participant Elissa Barnard's distaste for such responsibilities. The issue was much on her mind, as Corbella assessed the current hierarchy, especially as corporations were exerting more control over editors-in-chief and publishers' offices. She increasingly felt that real power lay in reporting and commenting on important stories rather than in being in increasingly hamstrung top positions. Like Lucinda Chodan in Victoria, Corbella had a bit of the messiah in her:

LC: When I was at the Calgary *Sun*, my publisher wanted to groom me to be editor-in-chief and then to try to work towards being a publisher. I eventually said to him, "There's parts of those jobs that I would love to do and there's parts that I would absolutely hate doing," and I said "I'm really not interested in heading down that road." I've found what I love to do and I just want to get better and better doing it. What is attributable for the top echelons of many corporations, not just journalism, is that women are more in tune with who they are and what makes them tick. They recognize that moving up in itself will not make them happier and more fulfilled. I'm where I want to be and I really don't want to be editor-in-chief and I really don't want to be publisher.

VS: Why not?

LC: I dislike doing budgets, for instance; I find that to be drudgery. I don't like firing people and that seems to be a growing part of the job. The whole business side doesn't interest me. Don't get me wrong, I want newspapers to be successful businesses, I want them to make lots of money because I love newspapers. I understand that, but what I want to do is help shape where society goes. And help prevent bad things from happening. Expose wrongs. Speak truth to power. All of that stuff is what makes me tick. So why put a square peg in a round hole?

Corbella talked about how she had already had to deal with cutting her freelance budget by 40 per cent the previous year, and watched as what she called a lack of workplace flexibility (the onsite day-care centre notwithstanding) sidelined many women who were general assignment reporters because "let's face it, if you're on the roll doing shift work as a general assignment reporter, you cannot stay in the business and have small kids. You can't." In a later email, Corbella explained that by the time she had children, she was already working regular editor's hours. If she had had her children earlier, she would have likely left the news business.[3]

Corbella told an intensely personal story about parenthood that she said she had not told her colleagues at the time. She had kept it to herself that she was trying to become pregnant through in vitro fertilization, even though a few men in the office described how their wives were doing so, because, she said, "I thought that would be career-limiting." So she suppressed sharing that experience, but now wondered if the delay in pregnancy that seemed problematic for so long was actually "planned divinely," harkening back to the luck theme. If her kids had come earlier, she thought she might have been in public relations work by now, rather than overseeing the *Calgary Herald*'s editorial stance and, as of the next day, having the added platform of a news column.

Like Corbella, Carla Ammerata found that being the daughter of immigrants drove her work ethic. But it was not the only way to feel like an outsider in Canadian newspapers. Being a rare female manager also gave her the feeling that sometimes she pulled the wool over male eyes.

"They're going to find out that I am a total fraud"

Carla Ammerata, city editor at the *Hamilton Spectator*, worked about ten to twelve hours a day, but longer on Fridays, because she was responsible for organizing city news for the Saturday and Monday editions and for the *Spec*'s website. She carried an office-issue BlackBerry with her twenty-four hours a day. With newsroom staff having shrunk from about 120 to roughly 80, she said her most difficult task was organizing the people to do the work for even the next day's paper, let alone for two issues.

The trouble was, Friday night was movie and pizza night at her house, where her stay-at-home husband and two sons carried on the tradition whether she made it home in time or not. Usually, she did not. On Fridays she rarely got home before 10 p.m. At least she had been spared the guilt of her long work hours because her husband had always been the at-home parent, doing the meal preparation and picking up the kids. That "non-traditional" arrangement allowed her to succeed in her career. "I have been lucky in that way," she said.[4] That way was slightly different from the luck described by most in the oldest cohort, whose sense of a lack of entitlement permeated their stories. Only one senior participant described the luck of having a husband at home during the day: in her case, it was because his employer let him work at home, so he could help mind their own child. Ammerata's husband is a full-time, at-home parent of two.

At forty-three, Ammerata saw success as having achieved her goal to become city editor. That would not have happened at the North Bay *Nugget*, where she had started her career twenty years earlier, she said during our interview in a *Spec* meeting room. Ammerata was born in North Bay to parents who emigrated from Italy: "Dad was the immigrant story," she said, meaning that he came to Canada for ten years, and then returned to Italy to marry and bring back his homemaker bride. He started with nothing but a Grade 5 education – reading newspapers in English was a struggle, but important to him – and built a successful auto dealership. Ammerata learned about hard work and the importance of an education, with her parents making sure all their offspring graduated from university debt-free. After obtaining a degree in political science, Ammerata decided to pursue an early love of reporting. But the idea was not well received by her father:

> He wasn't happy. He always thought I should either go into teaching or into law, some other type of profession just because he felt I didn't have a chance to succeed, just because I had a vowel on the end of my name. Let's put it that way.

Ammerata laughed, because, when her father said he did not see how she could succeed in journalism as an Italian immigrant's daughter, she became determined to do so. After nine years at the *Spec* and reaching her city editor job goal, she had begun to consider what might be possible next. But more than being an immigrant's daughter or a woman, she felt sandwiched between a generation that seemingly had all the opportunities that the journalism profession had to offer – and who were stretching out their careers because of such factors as the economic downturn – and the younger, ambitious generation coming up behind her.

Still, when gender came into play, she was aware of how she simultaneously reproduced and challenged the newsroom power structure. Ammerata described, for example, how by working such long hours, she was patterning herself after the male power model in the newsroom. This was due to how tough it was to break through as a female "outsider." And she had begun to notice others (including women without kids) rolling their eyes whenever a woman staffer wanted to leave the office to pick up her child from day care. It also surprised her that a corporate committee, brought in to implement an overhaul of how content would be processed, consisted of only men. Sexist language bothered her, too. Yet Ammerata also valued her experience and position as a woman, because it did afford her a different perspective, she said. In a big series the paper did on bullying at school, for example, while male editors questioned the sanity of a bullied boy's mother, Ammerata made sure that relevant school-board documents were produced as evidence that this woman was not "crazy."

While the top tier of management at the *Spec* was still male, plenty of women were thriving in mid-management, Ammerata noted; the paper had just hired four young, female reporters on contract, so she hoped things would improve. What might hold women back, she thought, was feeling like frauds. Ammerata said she shared this fear in conversations with women colleagues, who experienced what the popular press calls "imposter syndrome" and what the academy has defined as the imposter phenomenon, first described by social psychologists in the late 1970s as feelings of inadequacy or deception despite having achieved success through one's own efforts. Often those experiencing the phenomenon (including men and women) attribute their success to perceived outside sources such as luck, as many of the older participants in this study did. Ammerata described the feeling of constant insecurity:

> [The impostor phenomenon is a] conversation that we have quite often, and I wonder if this is a female thing. It wasn't until one of my colleagues voiced it [that] I thought, "Oh my god, it's not just me." She had just been made a manager and she said, "What are they thinking? They're going to find out that I'm a total fraud." And I thought, "Oh my god, you're in my head!" 'Cause it just struck me that, we bring that on ourselves, where we think "I'm not smart enough to be in this position. I don't have enough experience. What are they doing promoting me?" We're our own worst enemies in some ways.

Her story highlighted how, by suppressing their own insecurities as well as achievements, she and the women around her helped keep a "secret" that perpetuated their outsider status while they busily emulated the male leadership model that would eventually reject them. The power of luck is not named as much as hard work, but in this sense, it seems to be at play underground. Ultimately, said Ammerata, the choice for women was to look at the situation of feeling "disconnected" from the newsroom power structure and "either change it or leave."

Despite replicating the long hours and worrying about being an imposter, Ammerata tried to level the playing field: she'd been a part of a committee that hired four of the best candidates for contract work, all women. She had the authority "to bring human faces to stories" and to give those stories prominence. She felt the *Spec* needed more staff diversity, and served on a civic diversity committee that existed outside of the paper.

Back in Halifax, Sherri Borden Colley was experiencing the realities that a lack of newsroom diversity brought to her newsroom, to the community it purported to serve, and to her own experiences as a black print journalist who was not, as most other participants were, raised in a middle-class household.

"If you've never experienced racism, you will never know the pain of it"

On the day in the mid-1990s when Sherri Borden Colley picked up her journalism degree at the University of King's College in Halifax after years of hard work, she was so happy she felt like kissing it. But when it came to making a small bow before the university president as she accepted her degree, she refused. Earlier in her journalism studies, when she was interviewing this high-status white man for a story, he told her about an art exhibit mocking black stereotypes that had made him "embarrassed for every nigger joke" he had ever told.[5] He said this after she had turned off her tape recorder, she remembered. Even in the context of his own learning, his use of the "N-word" offended Borden Colley deeply. She would not bow to him:

vs: Did he remember you from that incident do you think?
sbc: I'm sure he did. And it was a silent statement but it was very powerful for me to say, "You know, I'm not going to allow you to have that power over me." And that I consciously made that decision. I'm not going to bow to him. No. And you know, it's all based on my experience. It really is just as a black Nova Scotian. I won't bow. I quietly fight racism. I've done it all my life. But, sometimes that's as effective as anything. I'm not a shouter, like out there "black power" kinda thing, but I fight it through education; I fight it in a more quiet way.

Borden Colley had been at the Halifax *Chronicle Herald* for fifteen years when we met in the same small corner meeting room where I interviewed Elissa Barnard and several others. She started at the paper when "things were really good, when summer students got to stay on." She was one of those summer students, working weekends until she finished her degree, and then hired full-time. She was a general assignment reporter at forty, in her "dream career," like others.

Borden Colley drew more attention to the interplay of identity markers than the other participants: she was the sole black person interviewed and did not have a middle-class upbringing as most others did. These aspects were both motivational and oppressive. They also reflect the notion that black women's multiple struggles in relation to gender, social class, and race give them a unique standpoint.

The youngest of five siblings, Borden Colley was born in New Glasgow, Nova Scotia, to a homemaker mother and a father who was a self-employed garbage man. She barely passed classes in an education system that "was not friendly towards the black community." But in Grade 11, her English teacher did something that changed her life: it was a turning point of the kind that helps social actors situate themselves or find ways to operate within the structures that try to define them. Journalists, as well as fiction writers, also seek out these turning points in their narrative work:

> We were asked to write about a favourite Christmas gift, and I had written about this little black doll that my aunt had given me, and I talked about how it was so important because the doll reflected me. She was dark complexioned like me. I compared it to the dolls you see with the blue eyes and fair skin, and what defines beauty kind of thing. I remember he read it out in class and that was a turning point for me because the Nova Scotia education system was, when I was going to school, hostile towards black students. To have a Caucasian teacher think that much of a project that I did, it was life-changing and he didn't say "You should go into journalism," but I felt so proud.

Spurred on, after high school and a few jobs, Borden Colley took a transition program at Dalhousie University for black and Indigenous Nova Scotians, and then attended journalism school at King's. As one of two "visually black" students in the program, both women, she found the environment tough. One student told her she only got into King's to fulfil a quota for black students. Her story about that episode showed her vulnerability to racist expressions, as well as her resilience in the face of it. She kept getting on the bus:

> It was rough. Honest to goodness, when I used to take the bus to university, I would physically get sick when I walked on that campus, because,

if you've never experienced racism, you will never know the pain of it. If you've never experienced what it's like not to have privilege. King's is a very elite school, you know what I mean?

Her comment regarding my not knowing what this pain might feel like cast me as an outsider, which I certainly was: those who have not shared such an experience may not fully understand it. However, narrative analysis and a feminist approach allow researchers to highlight such "secrets of repression and resistance" (Sosulski, Buchanan, and Donnell, 2010, p. 3) with the participants' permission. We carried on.

Borden Colley made it through on sheer hard work and student loans, as her parents had little money, and she was grateful to be taken on full-time at the *Herald*. At the time of the interview, she was the only black reporter there, the other having been let go in a recent round of layoffs, since he had been one of the most recently hired. After spending six years covering the Supreme Court of Nova Scotia, she said her general assignment job suited her, except for being assigned an increasing amount of what she called "fluff" stories.

Borden Colley had a five-year-old son with medical problems, and her husband, who was in the navy, was often away at sea. So the nine-to-five day worked well: she often ran out at lunch to grocery shop. She most enjoyed the voice her work provided – she said "when I leave this Earth I want my work to have spoken for me" – and was glad of her benefits, pay, an understanding supervisor, and great colleagues. She felt she had good workplace flexibility, offering the example of asking to work a night shift for eight months for personal reasons in 2006 after maternity leave, with management agreeing. This seemed to me not so much a sign of flexibility, but that she asked for something the paper always needed but few reporters (or any workers, for that matter) usually would choose to do.

Her racial background had shaped her experiences in multiple ways, Borden Colley said. She took it upon herself to educate other reporters and editors about racism, whether it was language used in copy, or what stories they covered and how. She encouraged her contacts in black communities to contact the paper when they saw racist terms or coverage. The paper tended to cover drug busts and violence in black communities such as North Preston, rather than writing about the community itself. So Borden Colley tried to counteract that by writing stories, for example, about black veterans and businesses. She suggested that rather than focusing on attracting youth readers, why not appeal more to the growing black middle class? But tokenism crept in, too, with editors once expecting her to go to North Preston to accompany white staffers who feared going alone. She laughed: she was so tiny, she said, it was hard to imagine herself as a bodyguard. (As if white reporters needed one.) Here, her physical size interacted with her race and gender, complicating and enriching her experiences.

With four white males ahead of them in management, Borden Colley said she and her women colleagues felt "kind of stuck" in their careers, but she also felt that she was most effective getting out into the community as much as she could under new budget constraints, talking to people, and "making a difference." A striking example she gave were her 2010 stories about Viola Desmond, an African Nova Scotian who refused to leave a New Glasgow theatre's white section in 1946, and was arrested and fined. Borden Colley's stories ultimately resulted in the province issuing a posthumous pardon and apology to Desmond, who died in 1965.

It did bother her that not one of the *Herald*'s columnists was a person of colour, but when I asked her why she wouldn't apply to be a columnist, she answered with a little hesitation:

> SBC: I can – I don't know. I don't know how to write a column. I really
>   don't. I don't know what I would write about.
> VS: Ah, come on!
> SBC: Honest to goodness. But you know what I mean, for my community,
>   I'm not the "black reporter," but I'm most effective doing news. I really
>   am. I think. I think – right now at this time, those are the stories that
>   need to be told.

Despite her sense that her gender and racial identities guided her social-activist approach to journalism, and despite a unique position at the paper as its sole black editorial employee, Borden Colley could not see herself having more power as a commentator there than as a reporter. (As we will read in the final chapter, she may be changing her mind.) In any case, she had a new posting coming up at King's College to teach a short course. That university president to whom she would not bow was gone.

Her colleague, Patricia Brooks Arenburg, had similar views on scheduling flexibility and she came to acknowledge that any move to offer it was as much about the employer's needs as hers.

"Will my son be proud of me and what I do, or will he think I just wasn't there?"

Patricia Brooks Arenburg, who was thirty-six when we spoke, graduated from King's the same year as her friend and colleague Borden Colley. She, too, talked about the benefits of what she described as workplace flexibility. As a parent with one child and a husband who worked part-time, she was the main breadwinner in her family: as such, she was grateful that the *Chronicle Herald* needed a general assignment reporter to work a weekly rotation of early day shifts (filing to the paper's website) alternating with a week of nights. Even though it was tough to cope with the constantly flipping schedule, she said she was glad she could see her then five-year-old after work on the seven-to-three day shift, and to be home before midnight on the four-to-eleven night shift. The opportunity for these shifts arose after she returned from maternity leave, and found the regular twelve-hour shifts on the Supreme Court beat were too much: she had been at the *Herald* for thirteen years, and had covered police and the courts. In fact, on her first day back at work after six months of maternity leave, Brooks Arenburg's son said his first words, which made her feel bad. Early in 2010, she asked to go onto general assignment, and was pleased with the results:

> I needed some more time with him. And that's the one really good thing about here is that they're flexible with – as much as they can be. As long as you can fill a need for them, and they needed somebody to work a week of nights, on rotation because they already had someone doing it, and they needed an early morning shift and here I am.[6]

She later added that this "flexibility" was brought on by the company having laid off a quarter of the newsroom. With so many gone, most of whom were young people, many holes needed to be filled. Brooks Arenburg noted that men were assigned to the main beats (health, crime, the legislature), and that mostly women were general assignment reporters. She also thought that it was interesting that most of the women in the newsroom who had kids had only one or two, while the male editorial staffers each had more children – one had six.

Born in Cape Breton to a homemaker mother and a salesman father, Brooks Arenburg, who had two older brothers, always loved writing. She took up the family habit of watching TV news and reading newspapers early. She studied journalism and French at university and in the midst of her degree took a year to study in France: several other participants had made similar treks in their early years. She described herself as nosy and curious, always wanting to talk to people about their lives, but said she also had "terrible cases of nerves," and was happy to cloak herself in the anonymity of print, rather than face the limelight of broadcast journalism. After several summers interning at other papers, Brooks Arenburg, who had a "whopping student loan," got a job at the *Herald*. Because she had previously been turned down for internships there, she felt that "it was just luck, luck, absolutely" that she was hired in 1997. Here was an echo of the luck theme of senior participants. Today, she said, "if I lose my job, we're toast," the "we" being her family.

Brooks Arenburg said she worried that she might be seen as having "gone soft," by which she meant that her experiences as a mother might "get in the way of getting a story and getting the facts of a story." She struggled with this, citing a decision not to volunteer to cover biker gang stories.[7] Brooks Arenburg had trouble composing herself when she talked about not wanting to cover "kids" in court and her responsibility to raise a child who would not end up in front of a judge, as well as to provide for her family:

> I've been to court. I know what could happen if you don't focus on your children. I don't want that to happen to him. I love him dearly, but I have a responsibility to society to make sure that he, you know, does not go down that path. And uh, I also have a responsibility here. I've been the main breadwinner for a number of years.

Brooks Arenburg went on to describe how her age and experience changed her perception of other parents at work and told a story about how that shift in thinking came about. Her story can be read as an example of how social actors use narrative to help describe the constant self-revision they undergo as various characteristics come into play:

> I remember, before I had my child, going, "everyone's leaving at five o'clock: they all have to get home to their kids and I'm stuck filling holes." I resented that. Later on I started looking around, and went, "You know, these are busy people, it's not that they are not committed." Now that I have a child I know that every minute I spend beyond the end of my shift is one more minute I'm not spending with my child. And working a seven-to-three shift is great, 'cause I get home early enough that we can

have a day. When you work nine to five you don't get home 'til 6:30 or seven. By the time you get settled, have supper, it's time for bed, so when I was younger I resented it because I didn't understand. And now I do. I hope everybody else understands when I do that.

Not only did Brooks Arenburg feel the weight of her family respon-sibilities, she also felt that as a new mother, she owed it to society to keep her offspring out of legal trouble. As a GA reporter, she wanted the kind of understanding from her colleagues that she had had to learn herself.

Related to her concern about providing for her family was a recol-lection from when the paper became unionized. She found out she was paid less than men hired after her:

> vs: What did that make you feel like?
> pba: Garbage. Garbage. I came here in the same year that I graduated, but I did have experience. I spoke two languages. Some people didn't. So to look at that and to go "Okay: so I have a unionized job now, the pay is so much better than I thought it would ever be, here at least." And you know I have benefits, I have all sorts of protection in place. It's not perfect, it's not utopia but, what happens if I leave that?

There was a hint of internal conflict, with Brooks Arenburg asking rhe-torical questions that seemed to indicate she might like to leave, but understanding that without that job her family would suffer. And while expressing this worry, Brooks Arenburg said she also thought that women across the professions may have become "complacent" about the lack of women leaders, from CEOs to politicians to union leaders to the newsroom. Speaking of her own career trajectory, she said that she did not feel at this mid-way point in her work life that she was succeed-ing, but rather "surviving." This led her to speak movingly about what was most important to her. This exchange returned us to the choice nar-rative that women tell each other, that we are told, and that is repeated back to us through many media:

> pba: I'm surviving. When I think about, sometimes, when my son is older, will he be proud? I don't know. [silence]
> vs: That's a very deep and personal thing to say. Thank you. I think that's something a lot of women feel. And if I could ask, why wouldn't he be proud of you?

PBA: Hmm. [*silence*] Hmm. I don't always do the most flattering stories. Like I do a lot of "doom and gloom" stories still.

VS: So, "doom and gloom," by that you mean what?

PBA: You know, so-and-so is a murderer and let's look into his background and let's call his family. I do those stories. [*laughs*] ... Will he be proud of what I did? Will he be proud of me and what I do, or will he just think that I wasn't there?

VS: Ah. I'm here to tell you that he will not feel that way at all. I have been through exactly this and lived to tell the story. And believe me, he will be proud of you. What is striking to me is how this feeling that you have is not just you. Most women I think feel that way because we are the ones who think we have to choose.

PBA: And do we? And do we really?

With that rhetorical question, Brooks Arenburg looks over the cliff edge of social norms and wonders if it could possibly be narrower and more bridgeable than it seems. Her question also hints at how participants tell stories about their lives to fit larger society's value system, but counter-narratives lurk that challenge the status quo.

Of course, Brooks Arenburg said, her success was not defined by her job and whether her byline was on the front page. With the layoffs, she continued, came the realization that she could control nothing: it didn't matter that those who lost their jobs had skills and talents, they were gone all the same. Now she saw job success as perhaps broadening her writing skills, into reviewing and more multimedia techniques. She had already begun to add videos to her reporting repertoire. If her employer was not totally flexible, certainly she could adapt and keep up with change.

When I suggested to her that instead of using the pejorative "soft" to describe her new attitude towards journalism and try the term "richer," she laughed. "Maybe," she said, "but that is a hard sell internally, for me." Still, despite having internalized the higher status of hard news, Brooks Arenburg agreed that political reporting needed to be more "humanizing" and that more "people" stories were needed. With the staff depleted and a demand for more short stories for the web, she also said getting out into communities in Halifax was more difficult than before: she spent more time on the phone than in the field. That made "people" stories harder to report.

Just as her colleague Sherri Borden Colley could not picture herself as a columnist because she said she did not know how to write a column, Brooks Arenburg said of seeing herself as a senior manager that she didn't know "what people in those jobs do" and therefore she couldn't see how to be interested. Those senior positions looked like accounting or human resources jobs, not journalism. (Research by U.S. business professor K. Anders Ericsson and others shows how important a coach or mentor is in demythologizing the kind of expertise required to achieve at senior levels in business. For the Halifax participants, those kind of mentors didn't seem to exist.) However, Brooks Arenburg also saw managers as shaping news, whereas she did not see herself in that role. I pressed her on that point:

> vs: Let's say you decide your boss or your assigning editor has given you an option to cover A story or B story and your gut tells you that A is more interesting. Or it's not usually covered by the paper. Or maybe it's about some aspect about human life that the paper hasn't covered and you decide to cover that: isn't that helping shape news?
>
> pba: I guess. [*laughs*] Again, hadn't thought of it that way. It's one of those jobs that you do what you do and you don't know why or how. Sometimes it's your instinct.

At the end of our meeting, she returned to the notion of flexibility, but her comments about what constituted a flexible newsroom were revised and expanded, and new ways of working, she reasoned, were restrained only by outdated issues of trust. Would managers trust reporters who work hard even if they did less "face time" in the office? They could do the job better, Brooks Arenburg intimated, by getting out into the community and talking to real people:

> vs: So face time –
>
> pba: It seems like an outdated way of running a business. You can telecommute, you can video conference, here's the camera on my computer. You want to make sure that I'm here? I'm here writing. Or, log in or whatever, but face time? Yeah, seems like an issue of trust. But it's not very efficient. But this place is more flexible than others, so –
>
> vs: If you could change what the newsroom does or how it does it, [what would you change] then?
>
> pba: I can't speak for everybody but I can speak for myself. I wish I could go out more and have that coffee with that person and ask them, "Hey, what's happening?"

When the women at the *Herald* received my questions by email, the topic generated discussion that prompted them all to look around at the newsroom, Brooks Arenburg told me. Two themes emerged: the first was to question how far they had really come, since no women were managers and the younger women, except for one reporter in her late twenties, were gone. The second was that the women tended to forget their successes as they worked "through the grind." Brooks Arenburg and Borden Colley were part of a team that won an Atlantic journalism award, for instance, and other women had gone to Bosnia and Rwanda to report. After the interview, Brooks Arenburg was nominated for a prestigious National Newspaper Award for her part in a series called Nova Scotia Burning, which looked at a cross-burning incident in Hants County. It was nominated in the Multimedia Feature category and included stories, videos, a historical timeline, court documents, and an online panel discussion. It seemed her decision to work on the new media aspects of reporting paid off, but raising her head to see her success was rare.

Brooks Arenburg grappled daily with how to serve her child, husband, job, and even society itself through her work, and referred to leaving her job as an impossibility, although she still spoke of it. In Hamilton, reporter Nicole MacIntyre had more recently begun to experience these whipped-up career/family waters, and she was ready to abandon ship the same day we spoke.

"How can I be a journalist and a good mother at the same time?"

On a bright winter morning in Hamilton, Ontario, in the cafeteria of the *Spectator*, I met Nicole MacIntyre, thirty-one at the time, who had been employed at the daily since 2004. Born in New Minas, Nova Scotia, MacIntyre was an only child, raised by her mother, a banker. MacIntyre arrived at the *Spec* after working on short-term contracts at three other papers in Ontario.

Having failed calculus in her first year at university in New Brunswick, MacIntyre abandoned the idea of being a doctor and took arts courses, which she loved. She told me a story about how in high school, she had written a letter to the local paper, and became so excited seeing her name in print that much later, in her fourth year of university, she started to write for the student newspaper. "It was my calling," she said.[8] When she arrived at the University of Western Ontario's graduate journalism school, she felt she had come into her own. "I loved it beyond anything," she recalled. Her career took off quickly, despite a time of feeling intimidated:

> NM: I was a night reporter, a police reporter, as most young journalists start their career are, and then did some GA and then they offered me city hall, and I was scared shitless but took it. And that has become my defining thing in this community, is that for five years I was the city hall reporter.
>
> VS: Why were you so scared after covering cops and everything else?
>
> NM: I was intimidated by the bureaucracy of it. I felt out of my [depth], like cops I was good at. I knew it was essentially about people. City hall was more about the bureaucracy, the budgets, the numbers, things like that. I also thought that it was dreadfully boring, which is why they sent me there because they wanted it not to be boring. And so, I was just intimidated by that. I remember my first budget, I would have been at city hall maybe a month. And they were talking all these figures, and I'm a crier. I came back to the newsroom and I went to the city editor's office and I started crying. "I don't know what they are talking about and it's my job to tell the city about this." I was intimidated but I came to love it. I mean it has defined my career being the city hall reporter.
>
> VS: And why did you come to love it, do you think?
>
> NM: I loved the game of it. I loved the challenge of having sources and busting things open. And that's what I became known as. As someone who knew the inside; the things that they didn't want you to know. I thrived in that. I hated the planning meetings and stuff like that, but I absolutely loved the politics. I also would say that I loved the importance of the job. I loved being on the front page three times a week. You know what I mean? Like it was a status job and I loved that.
>
> VS: And then what happened?
>
> NM: Then I got pregnant.

Meanwhile, representatives of a larger newspaper had contacted her and asked if she would like a job as city hall reporter. She had been trying for years to work at this other paper, and wrote to say that absolutely she wanted to work there, but felt bound to tell them she was pregnant:

> NM: I never got a response and, to this day, I have never got[ten] a response.
>
> VS: Not even a, "Gee, wish we could have figured something out" or "Come see us in a year" or anything?

NM: No. So that experience with having, finally, my dream job come up, what I took away from that, was suddenly now I was less valuable to them. The fact that I was becoming a mother, in my dreams, I had thought that maybe they would say, "You know what? We don't care, we think you are a good reporter, come to us for the next five months, and it's more important for us to have you in our future." But the fact that I was becoming a mother meant that they no longer even wanted me. And that had a real profound effect on me and continues to.

This continuing effect showed itself dramatically at the appointed hour of our interview. I was unaware when I arranged to talk to *Spec* journalists that this would be the final day of a company buyout offer, and that MacIntyre, who is married to a journalist, had about four hours to decide if she would apply for that buyout. She was torn over whether she should abandon daily journalism, having had her baby and returned to work part-time as a GA reporter. Unfortunately, the baby was having problems in child care. With her husband doing well at his bigger paper, she and he debated constantly whether she should quit and stay home. This sounded familiar to me.

A few hours after I left the *Spectator* office, its lobby full of sport trophies and the hulk of an old press, MacIntyre made her decision: she applied for the buyout. She told me later that it was better to put her journalism career aside than to continue to suffer from what she saw as an inevitable, wrenching conflict between doing good work and the needs of her growing family.[9]

But as it turned out, the *Spec* was not done with her. Rather than see their part-time GA reporter leave, managers said no to her request. "But they have handled it well and have made me feel valued," MacIntyre told me in an email months later. She and her husband hired a nanny and she returned to the *Spec* full-time, moving into the Go (lifestyle) section, which was difficult for her as a "hard-news gal." However, she said, she was proud of having written a series on infant deaths, stillbirths, and miscarriages, and well, just had to laugh at having to conduct a Halloween candy taste test for the next day's paper.

MacIntyre was still worried about how to balance her job and family and what the future held for her careerwise. In a follow-up interview at the *Spec* office less than a year later,[10] MacIntyre summarized the events that saw her return to the paper to a position that, after six months of difficult adjustment, made her feel that managers saw value in her as a future leader. In fact, they had picked her to be part of a new initiative called Leadership University, which involved identifying about a dozen employees throughout the paper as having potential to advance, and offering mentorship, classes on leadership techniques, and one-on-one meetings with the publisher. This was encouraging to MacIntyre, who felt her career had "just *tanked*" after having her child. But reassurances aside, her worries continued:

> I am still struggling with that idea of career aspirations and being a mother. Several jobs have come up in the past year that I would have been *very* interested in before, that I feel like I can't apply for now because, how am I going to do that and be a mom at the same time? So I feel sad that for the next few years I am not going to be able to chase opportunities. I always wanted to be city editor by the time I was thirty-five. I don't think that's going to happen anymore. Simply because the nature of our newsrooms is that those jobs are twelve hours plus, because you have to be on call all the time, and again, I still feel like I could do that but I would really be sacrificing a lot of my homelife. I don't know that I want to do that to my kids. I'm now pregnant again.[11]

This last comment brought together what MacIntyre and everyone else in the newspaper business – and beyond, into most other workplaces – accept as inevitable: that senior, mid-career positions require long hours at work, and that children put women out of the running.[12] At a time when career possibilities glittered ahead; having been given management's seal of approval as a future leader; and having seen how her husband took on more childcare duties when she was ill early in her second pregnancy, MacIntyre still observed that "it really is difficult to see how much my career has changed in order to make it work for my family." In the here and now of her busy life, she focused on the fact that the next day was the provincial election, and it was the first time she was not covering it, but instead was pregnant again and doing candy taste tests:

> vs: What interests me about your perspective is the word "confidence." You've been pegged as a leader, even though you've had what could have been career-stopping things, and yet they're saying, "We see you for the long term; we want to invest in you." So you don't feel that says "we really believe in you"?
>
> NM: I do. I guess I worry when I see the women above me, who have gone for those roles. I see that they make severe sacrifices in their homelife.

I guess part of it is that I think those opportunities will be there. I'm wondering if I am going to be willing to make the sacrifices to do them. How long is it going to be before I am willing to work twelve-to-fourteen-hour days every day and be away from my children that long? And it's a shame to me that we've structured some of those critical jobs to be jobs that I think a lot of women are nervous about entering.

MacIntyre saw the structure as immutable, as a shame, and her job as choosing between sacrificing family or career, echoing the *Spec*'s Carla Ammerata, who said she had done the same, missing all those pizza nights with her family. The women who could be MacIntyre's role models were, to her, models of untenable sacrifice. I talked to her about my sense from participants that women were powerless to change newspaper culture, while in their own journalistic work they felt they were changing the world:

vs: When I asked them, "What do you think of your own power and influence?" people said, "I change how people vote by what I write, I can affect how people think about civic issues. I can bring voice to people who don't have voice, and I am quite powerful, in that sense." So what I see – and this is not a judgment – is a disconnect between women in journalism who understand they have this kind of power through their writing and editing decisions, but when it comes to their careers, they see themselves as having to fit into the structure, as opposed to having power to change it.

NM: I think it's always a double standard that exists in the whole "lion in the world, lamb in the newsroom" type of thing, and I often think there is that double standard where we're asked to go out in the world and challenge the powers that be, but sometimes in the newsroom that's seen as disrespectful, or not respecting authority.

So, as she understood it, the male-dominant newsroom discourse was to challenge power in her role as a reporter, but her role as an employee was to suppress criticism. She went on to note how senior managers paid lip service to supporting work/life balance, while mid-management positions still imposed onerous demands. The long-hours imperative emerged: MacIntyre, like city editor Carla Ammerata, said rising journalists "mirror the person that came before them and they think that if they don't put in those hours, then maybe they are not doing a good enough job." She told me how she would do a city editor's job, a dream she had abandoned, at least for five years. This involved realism (this is a fantasy, after all), communication, and trust:

> I've fantasized about how I would do that job differently, and one of the things I think newsrooms don't do well is that we tend to act like silos, especially with managers, where if they had more respect for one another's skills, and more co-operation, understanding ... So I am a city editor but I can trust that when the night editor comes, I can hand over this file and it's going to be fine. I don't need to stay until nine o'clock to see the story through. I would like to see that people could work realistic work days and still have families and things like that.

But in thinking about the chances of that job changing, MacIntyre sighed. She allowed that perhaps she could start to change the culture, as she had the luck (good old luck again) of feeling heard by her bosses:

> NM: [*sigh, pause*] I feel like I've been fortunate that I feel like I have the ear, the respect of my leaders. I feel comfortable going into their offices and talking to them and I feel that they come to me for opinions. So in some ways I feel that I can. [*pause*] Although, I'd have to say I feel like I'm fighting against a lot of history and tradition.
>
> VS: What kind of history and tradition?
>
> NM: Well, traditionally in newsrooms we don't have a lot of time for work/life balance; we're not really into "touchy-feely" workplace values. I also feel like it would be difficult for me, like many of the women. When I look at our newsroom, at the women who have had families, many have gone part-time, many have gone from major reporting roles to lighter, feature-type roles, many are in roles that don't demand them to be in for long hours.
>
> VS: Go, lifestyle, entertainment.
>
> NM: Yeah, that type of thing. Our city editor is a woman and she has teenaged children. But I look at her hours and they are just exhausting.

For a mid-career woman like MacIntyre, someone targeted as leadership material, the view ahead revealed side-lined or exhausted women, stuck enforcing the culture, all too aware of its punishments. MacIntyre mused on how newsrooms could redefine what dedication looks like to the next generation, what might define success differently. "I don't know what the right way to do it is," she concluded.

Meanwhile, she had her new pregnancy, the mix of pride and envy for her journalist husband's successful career at another paper, and feeling a little like a "cliché." She felt like just one of many women who had the hot-shot career but was now writing lifestyle articles and leaving to get to the day care on time.[13] She talked about other things that had happened since we first talked: a nice power shift in the home towards her husband's expanded role there; reporting important stories about miscarriage; and talking to others about the issues her participation in this project had raised. She worried that newsrooms did not handle younger women's careers well, and wondered how the company was "going to manage their transitions," noting that almost all the women with whom she started journalism had left.

Thousands of kilometres away, in Victoria, British Columbia, Sarah Petrescu was having mid-career survival issues, too. She could see all the factors pressing down on her that others in this cohort described, and had decided that work boundaries would have to be explored and established. It had even become a health issue.

"I've always been a storyteller; I think that's it"

In a busy Victoria coffee shop, Sarah Petrescu laughed and said maybe she did "too much work."[14] She had seen an online post of Arianna Huffington giving a TedTalk, and liked Huffington's message "to get enough sleep and stop trying to kill yourself by being everything."[15] That, said Petrescu, was an important message for women right now, herself particularly. At thirty-two, she did a fashion column for the *Times Colonist*, covered breaking news on weekends, and spent the rest of her shifts handling the *TC*'s web page and doing multimedia work. As a rare "destination" paper, meaning that once reporters are hired at the *TC* they seldom leave, turnover was such that only two reporters were younger than Petrescu. Having so many responsibilities, Petrescu said with a wry smile, was causing her to "find some of her strengths," but her expertise with new media (all learned by trial and error, she said) was also causing serious health problems:

SP: That's my struggle right now, finding a balance because it has affected me healthwise and careerwise to try to do everything. Because you realize that as much as you try your hardest and do the best work you can, that doesn't mean that in the end you're going to be rewarded with the same schedule. Or you may get lots of pats on the back but with the pat on the back also comes the next assignment.

vs: Like, "What have you done for me lately?"

sp: Yeah, it's sort of "Oh, that's great that you can do that. Fantastic. Can you do twenty more tomorrow?" And so I'm in looking at boundaries and recording how long it takes to do things and recording the process and making sure the process is acknowledged.

It seemed to me a smart, practical move, figuring out exactly what resources she needed for her new multimedia work, so her editors could see what support was required. But it also seemed a familiar pattern of self-sacrifice. Petrescu was educating her bosses at the expense of her well-being. "The problem with being able to do everything is you end up doing everything," she said.

Born in Prince George, British Columbia, and raised in Sechelt, Petrescu had feminism and social justice issues bred into her early by activist parents. Her mother, an Italian immigrant who worked with victims of violence, and her father, a carpenter, shop teacher, and ardent unionist, instilled in her a sense of community and a championing of the underdog. (Petrescu's father died of cancer when she was in her twenties; she has one brother.) Petrescu showed her narrative bent early, as she revealed to me in this story. While many participants told tales of their early writing being recognized at school, this had more of a twist:

My first introduction to writing that I can remember was in Grade 4. My teacher, I still see him around, loves to tell this story. I had been writing these mystery stories and I wrote one about a kid who had been abused and had to go to jail, and it was a little dark for a nine-year-old and so he called my mother in, my parents, to ask them about this, and [asked] "Where's she getting this?" My mom hadn't [realized] that I had been listening to her debriefing my dad at night about working with victims and crime and that I had been kind of taking it in and had come up with these narratives.

Her early adulthood was peripatetic, which makes good yeast for journalism. She had hoped to be a poet, dropped out of musical theatre study in New York, worked at a women's centre, lived for a while in a van when she moved to Victoria to attend Camosun College, studied at the University of Victoria, and then went to Ryerson University in Toronto, where she had a *Globe* internship. "I've always been a storyteller; I think that's it," she said of her life. Her best days happen, she said, when stories come together and "I don't care if I haven't eaten or I've been up all night."

Petrescu was hired at the *TC* to write about classical music two days a week, then started to fill in on the copy desk and did TV reporting for CHEK news (then corporately connected to the newspaper), and then came on full-time at the *TC* in 2008. At that time, she worked Wednesdays through Sundays, starting at 5:30 a.m., a schedule she found "exhausting." Throughout her career to date, Petrescu has always been drawn to the creative side, absorbed in ideas about how better to tell stories that are "human, newsy, timely" and that deal with social issues; she also enjoys writing about fashion, which is her second passion. On one of her recent great days (which she said were few), she had told the story of an extremely obese man, describing his struggles and telling part of his story with a video:

> I think my last great day was putting together that video because I worked so hard on it. I was teaching myself the medium. I was doing it and using a tiny $150 camera. It's just hard to do that kind of storytelling with that kind of equipment. I overcame a few technical hurdles and put together what I thought was a heart-warming story, dealing with the challenge of how you present somebody who is in that situation of being obese without making a mockery or a spectacle of them. When I met this person I just truly loved him right away because I saw that vulnerability and respected his openness with me and sharing with me. A day when you can honour someone who has shared with you in what you create is a good day. And that is getting everything right and telling their story well, and putting it into a meaningful context.

In her description of that day, she brought together her ideas of what journalism was for and how it expressed her characteristics – someone who championed the underdog and who was, in her own words, a "humanitarian." Being a feminist was important, too, an aspect of herself in which she took increasing pride. She didn't "care if it makes people cringe" when she used the word in the newsroom. All of these little bits of herself were important, said Petrescu, to how she did her work: being "a BC girl" and being interested in BC politics, being a feminist, feeling she had a responsibility or an awareness to look out for story ideas that reflected her generation, as well as standing on guard in the newsroom for language or story approaches that she felt were sexist.

Was the gender playing field level at the *TC*? Petrescu first said she didn't know, but talked about both editorial writers being male, how there had never been a female publisher, and that mostly men worked on the editing desk. The women she worked for had gone, too.[16]

Partly because of her early and odd hours, and because she worked alone so much, Petrescu said that she often felt "unsupported" in her career. (Working alone gave her less opportunity for mentorship in general, she said in a later email.)[17] There were those she called "creative mentors," older women journalists and instructors with whom she could talk shop, but who were not in a position to offer her promotions. One woman mentor at the *TC* did help her get a permanent job, however. Her journalism mentors outside the workplace had usually been men.

Having three female bosses during five of her seven years at the paper up to this time provided opportunities for a mid-career reporter/columnist/editor/multimedia journalist to observe women leaders in action, especially as Petrescu considered the possibility of having children. (Only one of the three bosses was a parent, with one child.) Of course, she joked, her crazy hours meant that she had "no optional time to go on dates." Single at the time, Petrescu noted that like her, most women reporters waited until their late thirties or early forties to have families. They seemed to "manage fairly well," but the idea of "working so hard and so much and then coming home to a kid" was scary:

> I don't think I'd like to be in the position where I was working full-time and trying to raise a child. Twenty years of hard work into a career and finally starting a family, I'd want to not be putting as much work into the career, I'd want to be putting more into the family. I hope that at the time I would have no hang-ups about that. No financial hang-ups and no personal hang-ups about having to sacrifice one for the other.

While others like Patricia Brooks Arenburg and Nicole MacIntyre, at roughly the same age, had young children and felt that sense of sacrifice and struggle between family and career, Petrescu felt that with experience and enough income, she would not find that stepping back from her career would be a sacrifice. (Later in this chapter, Paula Arab at the *Calgary Herald* speculates that she would not have made sacrifices if she had chosen to have kids.) Petrescu also commented, as Elissa Barnard in Halifax did, on how young fathers in the newsroom didn't "seem to recognize anxiety and tiredness in the same way that the women do. It's a personality type or something." Gender was not the issue here, as Petrescu saw it.

At this stage in her career, Petrescu had come through the "ruthless, competitive" years of establishing herself, only to be surrounded by co-workers twenty years older than she was, who talked of little but retiring. She couldn't fathom her own retirement yet (officially 2033), but every day she heard older staffers (mostly men) talk about onerous financial responsibilities for offspring (college, etc.), which kept them on the job. Meanwhile, the idea lingered in newsrooms, she said, that if you put family first you were not serious about your career. And, if you were someone of Petrescu's generation, managers expected you to bring new media technologies to bear on reporting, and she was complying on that score, teaching herself. So her next career moves would have to be made carefully, taking into account these contradictions and uncertainties. But she had an idea that encouraged her, which came out of the experience of competing for jobs and the new approach to online journalism that leaned towards "branding" reporters by identifying them publicly as individuals. I foundered a bit, then realized this could have some impact on a more individualistic – and possibly more diverse – kind of journalism:

SP: What's interesting about the new media element is that newspapers aren't breaking stories anymore. It's *people* who are breaking stories. So I think when you look at what is going to become valued in journalists, that competitive edge, [it] will be a different kind of journalist. Maybe more of a holistic thinker, maybe someone who has a different skill set who isn't that "go-get-'em, I'm available any time, at any moment." It may be a new kind of talent or a different set of talents.

VS: I'm sorry I'm not following you. You think that with the new media aspect, the competition will be less?

SP: I think the competition will be less focused on breaking news and being what they call journalism school "news-bots."

VS: So less focus on breaking news but more focus on what the person produces as an individual, is that what you're saying?

SP: I think so, on maybe a more varied skill set.

VS: What do you think that skill set might encompass?

SP: For me, it's multimedia tools, which is also male-dominated at this point. [And] creating writing with personality. I think is going to be something that we're going to see or seeing it already. Good thinkers.

A few months after we spoke, Petrescu went on sabbatical, which the *TC* allowed for staffers who take every seventh year off by taking less pay on the previous six years. When I checked her Facebook status some months later, she was anticipating seeing acres of hand-loomed silks at a fabric expo in Mumbai. She has since returned to the *TC* full-time.

Stephanie Coombs, with whom Petrescu had worked, also spoke of possible future motherhood and of hard work, and went on to expand the definition of workplace flexibility. For her, age was a major career factor.

"This is a whole new world and we have to look at stuff differently"

City editor Stephanie Coombs of the *Times Colonist* – one of Petrescu's bosses and, at thirty-two, the same age – was recounting how she clashed with the (white, male, sixty-plus) publisher over readership strategies: he said they needed more people reading the printed paper, and Coombs replied, "Nobody under the age of thirty-five or under is ever going to buy the paper, full stop. You can't do anything to make them buy it," so "a lot more crazy ideas" were needed for the *TC* to survive:

> If it were me, we could buy an iPad for everybody in this region and send them a paper every day on their iPad. And that would be cheaper than printing it and delivering it every day to people. In all honesty, it would be. We can't do that because we can't close down our press and we'd have to lay off people, and that's a problem, but I think we need to look at things differently and radically.[18]

Handling change was a big part of Coombs's career story, as was continuity, in the form of long-standing industry issues. The problem-solving she did every day, like her counterpart Carla Ammerata at the *Spectator*, largely resulted from the fact that there was not enough staff to get the work done. Many long-time reporters got lots of holiday time, called in sick, and took leaves, and only occasionally was someone hired to replace the few who retired. Advertising was (and is) precarious: in fact, the *TC* stopped publishing on Mondays in June 2009 to save money.

To be city editor of a major daily in Canada at thirty is unusual: Ammerata felt that having that position at forty-two meant she had achieved a major career goal. Coombs's path from Edmonton to Victoria, and then to Ottawa for two degrees (a bachelor's and a master's in journalism) led almost directly to the *Ottawa Citizen*, where she went from being an intern copy editor at twenty-two to running the night copy-editing desk at twenty-six, before reaching management.

Luck did not emerge in her narrative: during our interview in a *TC* meeting room, Coombs described how she worked hard, was keen, curious, and loved to learn, and throughout our talk she exuded a confident, relaxed demeanour. She acknowledged off the top another possible reason for her quick rise, along with print journalism's haphazard approach to leadership development, and the night shift (3 p.m. to midnight) being a job few wanted:

> I made good contacts in the sense that I knew the senior editors socially and I think that does make a difference. I, of course, say that's part of it, I'm not sure how much of it was. I was keen and interested and hardworking and anyone who works at the night desk knows that the quality sometimes is lacking. I think often night desks are full of people who don't really want to lead and often are kind of put on a desk because the paper doesn't really know how to manage them. I was excited and I wanted to do it. Night news editor is a thankless task in a lot ways and very few people actually want to do it. At the *Citizen* it was a burn-out job in the sense that people didn't last more than two or three years before they'd had it.

Coombs said she loved the pressure of "turning a mess into something really good" on deadline, of knowing that she would be the last pair of eyes on the paper before it went to the presses, writing the lead headlines, deciding what stories went on the front page and being "the one making the decision alone if there [was] a breaking story" that would have to be switched on to the front page and something else removed. She described herself as a "Type A person" and "slightly a control freak" and felt that in her position she helped set "the city agenda every day" with her decisions about what late-breaking city stories to cover and how they should be displayed on the page, conveying the story's relevance or level of importance to readers.

For Coombs, age, rather than gender, was the characteristic that would most likely affect her career trajectory, noting that "the age gap is a bigger issue than the gender gap" at the *TC*. She described several times the difficulties she has encountered – and had overcome with persistence, respect, and "baking cookies" – as a young person in a job usually held by an older, more experienced person. At the *Citizen*, she asked to go to a management seminar because "I was conscious that, at twenty-six, I was the youngest person on the night desk and I was going to be the boss." Older men might have had gender issues regarding her, she said, since they seemed to begrudge her the post, while older women on the night desk did not.

Coombs said it felt odd to say that, at thirty-two, she had already turned down the offer of becoming assistant national editor at the *Globe*. (I rose to an equivalent post, national beats editor, in my late thirties.) It was indeed striking to see a woman of her age already having developed a senior-management-level sense of confidence, in that she realized she did not have to jump at any offer, even one from the *Globe*: her destiny was not a job that would require her to follow the same stories that other outlets did. "Five years ago I would have leapt at that opportunity; I would have been, 'Oh my god, yes! Let me slave away for twelve hours a day, let me do it,'" she said of the *Globe* offer. But on that day, Coombs said her preference was to stay connected to readers where she had more of an effect on her community's "collective consciousness" on a daily basis than she felt she would have at the *Globe*.

When asked how (and if) her characteristics such as gender, age, class, and race affected her practice of journalism, she said she knew how to manipulate those factors to her advantage:

> I think that you are who you are, and if you don't use what you've got in a positive way then you are going to be stuck thinking there's something that's negative about it. When I worked in Ottawa and I was a manager, we had about a dozen managers and only two of us were women. Did that work to my advantage? Definitely. Did I exploit that? Yes.

Coombs identified how an individual's social characteristics, such as being perceived as too young to be in a senior role, work in positive ways, in her case through humour and respect:

> I always flip it into "I'm really good at what I do." Because I think that you can take things in one way, we all have that inner dialogue in our head. Or you can turn it into something totally positive for you. I joke about how young I am. I joke with my reporters, I say, "I don't know what you're talking about, you're all so much older than me." If you are a good journalist, if you're good at what you do, people forget how old you are or if you're a woman or not.

And the other thing for me is the mutual respect. I always showed the older deskers the respect that I felt that they were due and, in many ways I would say things candidly: "You've been here longer than I have, can you explain this to me or what do you think because I know you know this issue more than I do." And I find that the strategy that always works extremely well with people is to not pretend that you know everything.

Identity also played outside the newsroom. Coombs said it wouldn't matter to her whether a potential source talked to a reporter because he/she was "cute" or smart or tall or whatever. Coombs was pleased to say, for instance, that Victoria's chief of police was unlikely to forget her, because he noticed her tongue piercing. "He takes my calls and discusses things with me: is it because I have a tongue ring? No, but that is how he remembers who I am."

Of six management positions at the *TC* at the time, three were held by women (none is at this writing), which Coombs found odd, since there was rarely gender parity at that level. Coombs, who was single and had no children, described, as others had, the exclusionary effect of motherhood and of the need for adaptation to the prevailing culture:

sc: People become columnists or editorial page editors usually after they've done senior management jobs in the paper. And you don't get to be a columnist if you haven't been around for a while and have that sort of track record, and women tend not to take those positions. This newspaper is extremely odd to me in that in our six management positions, three are women. But if you look at that, of the three, only one of them has children. Women tend not to take the positions to rise up to the top levels.

vs: So why don't they?

sc: I look at what it takes to do these jobs. I wouldn't tend to try to do my job and have children. I think that would be extremely difficult. I don't work seven and a half hours in a day. And if you want to have it all – to me having it all is to have a career and children – you can't necessarily do the jobs that get you to those positions. It can be done, and I have former colleagues whose husbands are much more flexible in their schedules so they become more of the primary caregiver. I couldn't be responsible in this job for picking up kids after school because on really good days I'm done at five-thirty or six, on bad days I'm here until eight. Because I can't predict the news.

vs: So a large part of the unpredictability that's embedded in news is, if not the defining problem or issue for women, then a big part of it. Is there anything else?

sc: I think at some other papers, it was a boys' club. And some women don't operate well in that atmosphere. I was fine with it. I can sit down and tell dirty jokes, you know I don't mind doing that and I think that I consider myself the kind of person that can adapt to the sort of people they're with. This newsroom, in all honesty, there's usually three women and two men in our afternoon news meetings. And [our male colleagues] have to sit there and hear us talk about how hot Colin Firth is.

Since all three women in management have left the paper, presumably Colin Firth's hotness is no longer a topic for debate. More importantly (perhaps), Coombs shed light on how gender and motherhood combined to remove women from competing for influential positions as senior editors and columnists. Other people, whose workplace was "flexible," would have to be relied on to take care of the children. She elaborated on the intractability problem with a personal story:

sc: The fact of the matter is that women actually have children. I thought about it the other day. I was talking with a friend about where I see myself going, and I said, "If I do want to have kids, it [will be] weird if I'm a managing editor because [usually] you want to go away for a year and then come back." And do you come back to that same job, which is a very high-level, specific job? How do they fill in for you for a year? Does that person who replaced you now jump back down the totem pole? It doesn't happen a lot and I know logistically it can happen, but we as women, whether we have partners who do a lot of the work, we actually physically have to be out of the newsroom for a year.

vs: But if it did happen more often, then it wouldn't be weird, right? If a sixty-year-old man has a heart attack and goes off for a year on stress leave, he comes back. Or you could also give a woman, who's not quite ready to be managing editor, an opportunity to try out the managing editor's job temporarily by putting her in that position as a caretaker while the managing editor is on stress leave.

sc: I know you do stuff like that, and you're right, it doesn't happen very often and maybe we'd think it was more normal if it did. But again I think, "Could I do what's expected of a managing editor while wanting to get home and be with a baby?" Because even if you leave it to your husband to do more of the caregiving, you still want to spend time with your kids; and most women do subscribe to that sort of thing.

While she saw the biological aspect of motherhood in nearly inevitable conflict with expected journalistic practice, Coombs named another kind of workplace flexibility as being absolutely necessary for papers to survive and which required a new kind of introspection:

sc: I think flexibility hasn't been in this business. I say that for so many reasons; we need to be able to look at ourselves differently in what we do. One of the reporters was waxing poetic about the great days of Randolph Hearst and I was saying to myself, "Those guys were paid cents a day, weren't unionized, had no benefits, and people paid to read the paper because it was the only way they could get any news." I think often we look back at that and think, "Aaahh." Well, this is a whole new world and I think we need to look at stuff differently. We need to be flexible and say, "I'm not going to run the same story that everyone else has." We don't have very much money. And we don't have very many people, so we're saying, "This is how we've done it so we're just going to keep doing it so we can just survive." And yet that's not the way to revitalize or make a good product. We need to say, "Well, this isn't working." Maybe make radical decisions about how we're going to present stuff.

Coombs's description of her skills and confidence, gained with years of news experience at an early age, and honed with an adaptive approach, led her to question historical narratives about the "good old days" of newspapering. She was willing to challenge meta-narratives, in this case, one that threatened the industry financially, but at the same time did not talk about defying the notion that women must choose between careers and children. Rather, she felt that the career versus motherhood issue did not apply to her. Coombs's personal life, not the newspaper industry, shaped her stated attitude on motherhood.[19]

Like Coombs, Mary Agnes Welch regarded biology as heavily affecting a woman's journalism career. But with two women leading her Winnipeg paper, anything seemed possible.

"There's room to be ambitious at the *Free Press*"

In a busy Winnipeg café, Mary Agnes Welch, public policy reporter for the *Winnipeg Free Press* and a two-time National Newspaper Award nominee (among other accolades), was telling me about how she got the second-year blahs while studying history at the University of Alberta. She went on to finish her honours history degree in 1996, but that blah-time resulted in her journalism epiphany, that real-life turning point for which journalists always hunt and which narrative analysts identify as a storytelling tool to self-revise (Bamberg, 2003). Just as Sherri Borden Colley did in Halifax when she received that black doll, Welch experienced her own self-revision:

> I started volunteering at the student newspaper. At the *Gateway,* my first assignment – I think this was the story that got me into Columbia because I used this on my application to get in – was covering Sheila Copps, who was on the campus for the 1993 election. It was winter, [and] she was there at 7 a.m., not a student in sight, so I trailed behind her and her entourage. I had my clipboard with my heavy metal and alternative band stickers on it and [was wearing] my Doc Martens – I was so nervous that I couldn't read my own writing. I tried to write the story, not having any idea how. It was exciting and fun and I was interested in politics, so I realized I wanted to be a journalist. It was a good story and I wrote it all fancy and it is one of those rare times where you have an actual epiphany, something happens that changes the whole course of what you were thinking you were going to do.[20]

When we spoke, Welch, thirty-six, had been at the *Free Press* for about eight years, and had covered city hall and the provincial legislature before starting her public policy beat, which she described as "open-ended, feature-y, document-y." She grew up in Edmonton with one sister, her father, who went to law school at age forty, and mother, who worked for the Alberta government in health policy. She described her upbringing as solidly middle class. Being a relatively young Canadian at Columbia in New York made her an outsider there, "with kids who came from very wealthy families who did the year in France." Rather than be part of that competitive group, she went her own way after graduation in 1997 to a newspaper called the Odessa *American* in west Texas, and then returned to Canada for three years at the *Windsor Star.*

In the "mixed-up ball" of factors that affects how she does journalism, Welch said age and gender did have an impact, and she recalled being the only woman present at meetings she was covering and how she would have to spend "a bit more time listening even harder, asking smarter questions, putting your game face on in a way you might not normally have to do." Ultimately, though, she felt that "personality trumps those immutable things like 'I was born in Kamloops' or 'I'm a girl.'" Curiosity, scepticism, ideology, interests, and personal experiences had a kind of immutability for her, too, but these qualities were different than, for instance, having a disability or being a new Canadian. She described a great day as "getting a document that tells me something I didn't know and using that to do a story that nobody else has thought of." A bad day involved spending a lot of time on a story she thought was important, and it not having any impact: "no comments on the website and no angry emails."

Welch saw her success as stemming from the independence she had over her own assignments, "the big think pieces that challenge people to think more critically about their city, about poverty, about the environment and Aboriginal people," as well as the feeling of "sync" she had with her supervisors. "I feel like there's room to be ambitious at the *Free Press*," she said, expressing a sentiment rare among participants.

While Welch did not describe her father's return to school to study labour law or her mother's involvement in health policy as central to her world view, I began to wonder if that might be the case. I found her focus on matters of social justice, for instance, were reflected in her articles and Tweets, everything from Indigenous maternal health to civic parking problems, and even in her blog "Gripe Juice." One example she gave of story choice that came out of her personal interests involved fetal alcohol spectrum disorder, "a huge issue that affects moms and kids and crime and poverty in Aboriginal" communities, while simultaneously, a big story in Winnipeg about a football stadium was "interesting to the guys, it's just not interesting to me":

vs: What about those things – homeless kids, crime, Aboriginal people, social issues – what about that interests you, and why do you care?
MAW: They're complex, they really, really matter to people who are not often reflected in our newspaper – they are reflected more and more, because I think we're getting better at that kind of thing. The football stadium still takes up a hell of a lot of space: poverty and single moms and why the housing allocation is too low and simple things like that don't take up as much space, and they're harder to tell because they're soft. That's why I like data, because data puts hardness to soft things, I think, they're kind of nebulous and there are real stories involved, real people.
vs: The idea that stories about real people are what we call "soft news" and what I'm hearing you say is that by getting the data – getting the statistics – gives it a newsier, more persuasive kind of feel?
MAW: Yes, yes.

Welch commented on the lack of babies being born to *Free Press* women as "weird" and a "funny thing" after describing the particular nature of female leadership at the paper at the time:

MAW: I think that the *Free Press* is kind of an anomaly because either the most powerful jobs or the people in the newsroom who are most respected are women. I think of Helen Fallding, she's the smartest, the moral centre of the newsroom in a way, and Margo Goodhand, [one of] the most powerful [people] at the paper, in the newsroom ... I think they are held in more respect.

VS: So not just because of the position they hold but because of who they are as well?

MAW: Who they are, yes.

VS: What qualities do they exhibit that make them so –

MAW: They're calm, they're rational. They are creative, they have lots of integrity. They don't put up with too much crap. They're political – Helen especially is political. She reads a situation – she knows who wants what, and how to manage them. Not political, like stirring up trouble, but really smart about people and how to figure out what somebody else wants and what you want.

VS: So to use that horrible cliché, it's kind of "win-win" or strategic –

MAW: – that's the word, strategic. But I think there would be way more women in those kinds of jobs if there wasn't this – I know for Margo, she has two kids, she's there until six-thirty, seven o'clock and it's a stressful thing. You take it home, and your BlackBerry's always on and it's like that for reporters, too. That's hard on a family. The funny thing is there haven't been any new babies born since I've been there, practically.

VS: Why is that, do you think?

MAW: I think there's an age gap, or there's a whole bunch of women who are just about to have kids and they're going to, or are younger. There's a new generation of twentysomething reporters, so they haven't thought about it yet. It's a tricky job.

VS: The women you describe – Margo you said has two young kids ...

MAW: ... Helen doesn't have any kids.

VS: There might be a correlation between the fact that these women have few children and they're doing well, they're able to do the hours and all that kind of stuff.

MAW: I think that's partly it, yeah.

vs: Any other thoughts why women might not do as well, aside from your newspaper?

maw: I don't know. I don't think it's true anymore that women aren't seen as tough or good managers or that they can't make hard decisions – all the things that you want of managers or expect them to be. I don't think that that's the case anymore, so this inherent gender bias in the newsroom – I don't know if that still exists.

Having talked about family/work stress for women, though, she said she did not know why there were few women in senior jobs in Canadian newspapers. Her own situation, with a male partner (also in the media) but no kids, meant that she was more flexible in being able to stay late. Again, we see a member of this cohort accept that flexibility is something the participant can cultivate and adjust, not something that the company is offering. Her partner's job was more "stable," said Welch, and it was "just sort of a fact" that women did most of the childrearing for the first few years of a child's life. People didn't quit journalism because of becoming parents, they did it "because they have lost their mojo or they feel the practice of journalism has been converted by demands of technology or daily shallowness." Women who have kids make it work, she said.

Having children herself might actually be a benefit, Welch said, because she might think less about her job and the downside of blogging and Twitter, which had made journalists "much more public targets," echoing what her boss, Margo Goodhand, will say in a later chapter. Welch waved away most of the personal attacks as coming from "cranky, pajama-wearing basement dwellers," but still, their irritating, even enraging responses became another way in which journalism followed her home at night:

Every time you open your BlackBerry there's something else out there that you have to deal with. I think that having a kid in some ways allows you to realize that crap's not important. It probably reorients your perspective and your priorities in a good way. In a way, a kid would be – it's not really the only reason why I would have a kid but it would help me take my job way less seriously, which would be a good thing, I think.

Welch spoke at length about projects she had spearheaded or been involved with: a whole section of stories about downtown issues, which prompted a city summit, and a story about maternal health in northern

Manitoba that showed how "pathetic" maternal care was for Indigenous women. But even a big political story that fizzled was useful: Welch learned she could write the first story then do more work on the follow-up stories herself until they did have an impact, because nobody else would.

Conclusions: Twisting and Turning on a Middle Rung

The spotlight has moved from the oldest participants to those who were mid-way through their careers, in their thirties and forties. They were all well-educated heterosexual women who felt squeezed by traditional newsroom demands at a time in their lives when they felt that reproductive organs and cultural imperatives were issuing their own deadlines. No wonder many of these participants felt their lives seemed barely in control: as one participant said, using a movie title that has become a newspaper cliché, she was caught in a "perfect storm." Older workers clung to good jobs above them and younger ones circled impatiently below. Age, gender, and parenthood did not so much intersect for these participants as collide at top speed.

For Sherri Borden Colley, add in the complicating factors of race and class. While the other participants referred to their white, middle-class privilege mostly in the context of feeling a duty to be the "voices of the voiceless," Borden Colley was unique as a black journalist from a working-class family who experienced racism at university and on the job. Yet she, too, saw herself as speaking for others who could not. While rejecting tokenism, she took on the role of in-house monitor of racism in the paper, as well as focusing her own work on fighting racial stereotypes, being a mentor to young people in the black community and "making a difference." Borden Colley used her experience as a victim of racism to motivate herself, not to perpetuate a "victim" narrative in her work. And she was still in her dream job.

Borden Colley was not alone, as most others felt they were in their dream jobs, too. At the same time they felt forced to work harder as resources dwindled and they were made responsible for creating stories across multiple platforms. The mothers were grateful for what they described as flexibility, but recognized that flexibility was also a handy cost-saving measure for the paper.

The invoking of luck as a source of professional success diminished as the age of the participants dropped, until only sheer hard work was their main career-building factor. Luck did linger for Carla Ammerata, though, who experienced the imposter syndrome, in which externalities such as luck are seen as guiding someone's success. Some professed ignorance, or a lack of awareness about senior editorial positions to which they could aspire; a couple, like Ammerata and Stephanie Coombs, were working hard and long at those very jobs; others had seen the pressure on the lives of the few women in senior roles and said an emphatic "no" to those jobs. They still believed in the power of their own distinctive storytelling skills to fight for social justice. But unlike their older counterparts, these participants began their careers inside the city room, not arriving by way of the lifestyle and arts pages. The idea of being sent back to "soft" news after becoming mothers was troubling to them, even if they did exactly that.

The mid-career women positioned themselves as survivors, as did many in the senior cohort, while glorying in their best stories. They did not see themselves as victims of sexism (and occasionally ageism) as they sensed older female colleagues did, but described subtle cultural (and obvious) racial exclusions, as well as gender-based sacrifices. One described her fight against sexist tradition and history; another accepted the "fact" that women are the ones who spend years looking after children; and a third, fast-rising editor defended her "exploitation" of her youth and gender to help her rise in the hierarchy that would eventually hold her to account for her reproductive choices.

The industry upheaval that is clashing with its own male-dominant cultural imperatives resulted in the women feeling torn, scared, excited, exhausted, fraudulent, confident, intimidated, and adapting creatively. Ammerata saw herself repeating patterns of behaviour learned from senior male managers – such as doing more "face time" to show commitment – but was aware that these patterns were unhealthy and unproductive. Another accepted that her job required putting in consistently gruelling hours. It was as natural to her as the fact of women giving birth, requiring them to make decisions that pitted career against family. Another described the pain of racism as well as its motivational power, and being the daughters of immigrants similarly added complexity to identity for several participants, in mostly positive, empowering ways. Off the record, one even said that it was *normal* for women in newsrooms to go, to disappear.

The key theme of using narrative to create a coherent whole out of one's intersecting characteristics and experiences (the most senior group) or to accommodate contradictions and ambiguities (mid-career participants), takes another turn in the next chapter, which describes the youngest cohort. This group went farther in its storytelling, often spinning identity stereotypes to perceived advantage, as Stephanie Coombs foreshadowed in the mid-career group. And while most participants across age groups expressed concern about a lack of diversity in the newsroom, the characteristic of race as they might experience it personally was as invisible to the youngest group as it was to all but Borden Colley in the mid-career cohort and to the most senior women. The youngest participants felt they could handle all the challenges of gender, age, ability, technology, and parenthood that were thrown at them, if only the industry survived. Like their senior and mid-level sisters, the least-experienced women had internalized the notion that work and family were in natural and inevitable conflict, and it was their duty to suck it up.

Chapter Four

For the Youngest Journalists,
It's "a Game of Chicken"

Jen Gerson, a *Calgary Herald* general assignment reporter, was twenty-six at the time of our interview, which took place in her Calgary apartment. She described her career trajectory as "a bit of a convoluted one."[1] This seemed to understate the case, as she described at length and in compelling, colourful detail how she came to be where she was and how her big worry was not that gender or age or motherhood would affect her, but that she had chosen a career in a dying industry. The problem for young journalists, she said, was bigger than any debate about male or female newsroom experiences; it was about the very existence of newspapers:

> The challenges are so different for people at the bottom of this pyramid and they're so distinct that I don't think gender is an issue anymore. I'm not worried that I'm going to be kept out of the top echelons of the newspaper hierarchy because of a glass ceiling; I'm worried that there's not going to be a newspaper there. I think those concerns are shared by everyone who's getting into journalism now and there aren't very many of us anymore. You could go across this country and count on maybe four hands how many journalists under thirty are in newsrooms. I can tell you this because I know most of them.

I actually had gone across the country; and while researching this book did not require doing a head count of under-thirty print journalists nationally, and I did not seek a set number to represent age groups, the youngest participants – six – did turn out to be the scarcest. Since I conducted this study, one, Melissa Martin at the *Winnipeg Free Press*, was laid off and then later rehired.

They ranged in age from twenty-five to twenty-nine, were, predict-ably, white and middle class, and only one did not have post-secondary education. Two were married and none had children. Unlike most par-ticipants in the older cohorts, all but one started her career in "hard news" rather than the arts or lifestyle pages, reflecting women's increas-ing presence in that higher-status area of print journalism.[2] They were all in their "dream" jobs. None had a mother who worked exclusively in the home.

The cohort's priorities were meaningful for how, unlike the more – but equally privileged – senior groups, they rested on notions of individual power and independence as being key to their survival at work, along with a contradictory, residual bit of luck. This reflected how feminist researchers often characterize the "third wavers," young women who embrace a more individual approach to gender matters than previ-ous generations. The threat and promise of the personal identity or "brand" journalism being promoted by publishers was associated with this individualistic power. So was playing with gender and age stereotypes while on the job outside the newsroom, where they found themselves more often than the older cohorts, whose members were more likely to work inside the office. While not articulating a need to make sacrifices to further their journalism careers, members of this cohort still felt that work/family conflicts lay ahead and were inevi-table. Other themes included the daily impacts of media technology; competitiveness; being mentored and mentoring others; and a con-cern for honing their craft, which, for most in this group, involved public agenda-setting.

In thematic terms – that is, how narratives reveal meaning-making over time – this cohort appeared to court contradictions, actively prob-ing for ways as complex individuals to exploit expected norms, while simultaneously decrying how structures beyond their control held them back. If we accept the theory that social actors position them-selves through their narratives somewhere along a continuum (and sometimes all at once) marked by victimhood, witnessing and effec-tive personal agency, then the participants who were oldest tended to see themselves more often resignedly in the first category; mid-career women exhaustedly in the second, and youngest participants found themselves fighting like hell in the third.

This group included Gerson, general assignment reporter for the *Cal-gary Herald*; Katie DeRosa, crime reporter for the *Times Colonist*; Laura Fraser, general assignment reporter for the Halifax *Chronicle Herald* and the only participant to describe herself as not being able-bodied and how that affected her relationships with managers and her reporting; Melissa Martin, then a general assignment reporter at the *Winnipeg Free Press*; Nicole O'Reilly, crime reporter for the *Hamilton Spectator*; and Emma Reilly, city hall reporter for the *Spec*.

"We're going to be well-positioned – if we can hang in"

Having decided in Grade 10 that she loved writing stories for her Coquitlam, BC, school newspaper, Jen Gerson went on to a high school newspaper internship, then to Ryerson University in Toronto in 2002 for journalism (while writing for the student newspaper and working part-time at the *Toronto Star*), and received a National Newspaper Award while at the *Star* full-time. The story of how that job in the *Star*'s youth section ended was, she said, even more "fraught and complicated" than how she told it to me, but the result was she moved to work at a paper in Abu Dhabi, which she described as a poisonous, disrespectful workplace. To escape the rigid hierarchy, she decided to move to Yemen, but an offer from the *Calgary Herald* arrived and she accepted, returning to Canada in May of 2010 as a GA reporter. So far, she had found the *Herald* to be "lovely," with consultative processes and opportunities for her to have input into story ideas. Managing editor Monica Zurowski, whom we met in chapter 2, was her boss.

Gerson was raised by a single mother who had no university degree and was smart. Her mother worked her way up through Shell Canada from various jobs in Burnaby to a senior-level position in Calgary. When Gerson was little, her mother took her from wherever they lived to a school and day care near her office so her daughter would be close by:

> We lived for a time in Pitt Meadows and Maple Ridge, but we were going to school in Burnaby. I would do that commute at six in the morning with my mom and she would make these godawful bran muffins, they were vile, which is an ongoing joke between us. And it would be an hour to get me to day care every day. I would quietly throw these muffins out the window because they were so awful. Every once in a while she would treat me and we would go to Robin's Donuts. That was a good day. We would get into day care at seven, I would curl up in a corner and sleep and the day care would take me into school, and she would pick me up at six. That was hard for her for a long time.

This childhood experience, which she deemed as something more difficult for her mother than for herself, seems to have had a lasting effect. Gerson opposed the traditional construct of motherhood as personal sacrifice and denial of selfhood, as described by the middle cohort. "That's a major issue we have to overcome," said Gerson, who was single (with a boyfriend) and had no children. She felt this attitude came from her age as well as gender and experience:

> JG: I see women who are so wrapped up in being a mother that they've forgotten all sense of self. Their identities are just gone. I can't relate to that, I have tried talking to those women, it's not pleasant; this is all they talk about. I can't picture that for myself. But that's got a lot to do with the age that I am as well. I would love to be able to have a kid and have a kid grow up and see me be a strong, full-time working mom who is Jen Gerson, just as I am Jen Gerson today. And raise that kid to have a strong sense of self.
>
> VS: As your mother did.
>
> JG: As my mother did, exactly, my perspective is probably different because of that. My mom didn't have that choice. I think that if my mom had that choice she probably would have stayed home and been a typical mom, but she didn't have that option.

When I asked her whether those personal factors that are immutable affected how she practised journalism, Gerson said "kind of yes and no." She also said her own approach of putting others at ease was a "powerful" tool she used to get past the externalities and to the core of what is human:

> JG: As you and I both know, when you're sitting down to have an interview with someone, that's always going to be affected by who you're having the interview with and how they perceive you. So yeah, when I'm approaching a 200-pound cop at a murder scene, I'm going to play it a little differently than I would if I were a 200-pound white guy. You always have to tailor how you approach things to how people perceive you and I think there's an element of intuitiveness to that.
>
> VS: So how might you approach a 200-pound cop at a murder scene?
>
> JG: Well, everybody knows if you're female and you approach a 200-pound cop at a murder scene, you kind of play it simple. Simple and sweet a little bit. But I also think there's some value of playing against that stereotype in different situations.

vs: How so?

jg: If I'm talking to someone who is high up in the corporate world or a scientist, not playing it down and just being dead-on smart. I'm playing against that expectation of how people might expect me to be, judging by my job and my looks and my age and my gender, it is a powerful thing to do, because the second they can see past how I look and to the fact that I'm actually engaging with them as a person, I get a better interview and I get somebody who is far more willing to take time to explain things. I think the best interviewers can connect with people on a human level and can get past the external stuff. I don't know if I'm one of the best interviewers. I can't really be a judge of that.

vs: It sounds like you're sensitive to stereotypes or expectations that others might have because of these combinations of things.

jg: Probably not consciously, probably intuitively. I'm okay with that. I'm okay with playing with those stereotypes a little bit either by dealing with them or by challenging them, depending on the scenario.

vs: So it's adaptive behaviour.

jg: Yeah, it's totally adaptive. I don't think that's unique to young female journalists. I think every journalist has to be somewhat conscious about what they put off, when they walk into to an environment. They have to be conscious about putting people at ease.

Gerson observes here that externalities such as age, gender, and looks do have to be gotten past by people in her business. As well as this adaptive behaviour, or playing with stereotypes, being helpful in interviews, Gerson added that she felt women were probably better at mirroring their interviewees, which might be a learned behaviour, but "if you're a successful journalist, period, you know how to do this." She noted a different approach for broadcast journalists, who needed the "sound bite" and would have to get more "in your face" with sources to get quotes. She also suggested that broadcast journalism was more focused on "young, attractive females" than print journalism. Gerson also thought that because of the long hours, stress, and relatively low pay of newspaper work, women would self-select to leave as long as they were expected to be primary caregivers for children, and that this held true for politics, finance, and other demanding male-dominated lines of work. Her story reflected how from her position and experiences, cultural norms seem immutable, as Daiute and Lightfoot (2004) posit such stories do.

Gerson said she could understand how someone starting in the business in 1977 (meaning me) could find gender an important aspect of newspapering. But it was no longer a boys' club, she said, and she could see herself "choosing" to be an editor-in-chief of a daily in twenty years. She introduced the social variable of class without using the word, rather describing its impact as felt through student-debt levels. She argued that fewer young people could afford to go to university to study journalism than previously. Simultaneously, partly because of hiring restrictions over the past few years, instead of hiring young people from smaller papers who had proven themselves – a traditional career path – big papers were only taking hires from university internship programs, usually on contract and not full-time:

> Now if you want to work at the [*Toronto*] *Star*, you better get an internship position out of university; and increasingly if you want to get that internship, you need a master's degree; and increasingly to have that master's degree, you have [to incur] a huge amount of student debt; and increasingly if you have that student debt, you can't afford to work in a newspaper. So what I'm increasingly seeing in my peer group, and this is totally regardless of male or female, is that people in my peer group are opting out. Or they're dropping out. That's the state of the career path from where I sit and I'm ahead of most people my age because I had the luxury of graduating without debt, and I have the luxury of support networks now.

So the only way to begin a newspaper career today, she said, was to be wealthy enough to emerge from a post-graduate program debt-free and to be able to make it through the first few years of relatively low-paid, low-security contracts with lots of support. She told me a story about how she kept running into people who used to work at the *Herald* but who were now doing public relations in Alberta health services. One such woman told her that she had "loved her job but at a certain point working in journalism becomes a luxury."

Another luxury, or at least a potential one, said Gerson, was that women "have the luxury of marrying men who can then carry on more of the financial burden," so that women, generally speaking, felt less pressure to earn higher wages, and this factor might mean more women could decide to stay in journalism, despite having been a generation that was seeing continual layoffs. However, the trend to becoming a freelance journalist, a poorly paid field dominated by women, was scary. It would be like "being an Avon lady part-time." Still, she was not worried about herself: "I'm going to do fine," she predicted, as the "youngest person in the newsroom now for five years running." But down the road, newspapers will not have hired or trained the next generation of managers, creating a leadership gap, she predicted:

> So right now everyone is panicking about the Web and high wages and video and all that. What they're not panicking about and what they're going to start to panic about in the next ten to twenty years is where our next middle managers are going to come from, because they haven't trained enough of us young 'uns to take over that role. So where do you think you're going to get that staff when your next wave retires? They're not thinking long term … So this is where I start to see things fall apart, and where I see this not working in a long-term way. And most people are looking at the career in the next twenty or thirty years and saying, "I don't see how this could work." That being said, for those ten or twenty of us who hang in by our fingernails, we're going to be well-positioned – if we can hang in. But it starts to become a game of chicken for younger journalists.

As Gerson described in more detail how few of her classmates were still in journalism, she added that nobody "stays in a contract when they have a mortgage" and "nobody hangs in when they have a kid." The most talented of her fellow graduates were self-selecting out of journalism altogether because of this perceived lack of long-term prospects. While monetizing the Internet was the current panic, she said several times, the real issue was that papers were "killing the next generation of people who would be taking over, forcing them out," and even though a few minutes earlier she had said she would be fine, she added, "I cannot guarantee that I'll be in journalism."

That wavering was linked to the interplay of her age, gender, and potential parenthood, and the light at the end of the tunnel that shone on the *Herald*'s onsite day-care centre:

> vs: So, if you in five years are thinking, "I'd like to get married, get partnered, have a kid," what would that look like for you in your career?
> JG: I don't know. It's something that, at twenty-six, I'm having to start to think about. The *Calgary Herald* has a day-care program. And I'll admit the first time I walked into the *Herald* and saw the day-care program I

set up my little desk and thought, "Oh good, I can breed one day. That's
fabulous. Great."

VS: That's been there for a long time, too, that day-care centre.

JG: Oh yeah, that's been there for a really long time. And I know a lot of
women in the *Herald* are breeding, it's kind of ridiculous. [*laughs*]

VS: Do you think that's part of it?

JG: Oh, I think that's a huge part of it. Having that there makes a huge
difference. As a woman you look at that and think, "Okay, that's an
employer that accepts maternity leaves are a part of life, and there's
a day care downstairs and little kids run through the parking lot all
day." So that does make this more plausible for women at the *Herald*
I think. The idea of maternity leave, I don't think, would be career-
destroying if I were to stay at the *Herald*.

So the corporate decision to support parents with a day-care centre was
helpful, but the future was also mined with "really thorny issues about
identity and branding and how that works in Canadian journalism,"
which was not a healthy model, as Sarah Petrescu of the *Times Colonist*
described. Gerson said she and other young journalists felt pressure to
develop brands (or public identities) for themselves, to amp up their
Twitter, Facebook, and blog followers in the rush towards a personal-
ity-centric journalism. So while that was interesting and even exciting,
more "branding" could lead to fascinating gender and political identity
issues:

JG: I didn't come into journalism because I wanted to be a brand. Or
necessarily because I wanted to be a columnist, I just enjoy doing
journalism. Now you're telling me that I need to become a public figure
for doing news articles? That starts to get into real issues. Then you start
to put gender politics and gender identity into those issues and you have
another level of very interesting questions.

VS: Such as?

JG: Well, what's it like for a man to develop a brand versus a woman to
develop a brand? Are those different spheres?

VS: What do you think?

JG: Oh, absolutely.

VS: How so?

JG: When a woman develops a brand, she always has to encompass an
element of sexuality or deal with the element of sexuality. A man doesn't,
generally speaking, I don't think. A man can develop a brand about just

his thoughts and a woman can't develop a brand without some element of sexuality. I think that is very difficult for women to do that. Some women do, sure. But I don't think I can think of a single, well-known journalist who at some point hasn't written about some element of her sexuality. I just don't think it really happens.

vs: And by sexuality you don't mean about whether she's gay or straight, but her womanhood?

JG: Her womanhood, some element of sexual practice, some element of motherhood, some element of procreative force. I mean, these issues become an issue and then a question also becomes if you're a brand you also have to have your image out there, you have to have your face out there. Then how you look starts to become far more paramount and that's far more of a pressure for women than I think it is for men.

vs: A guy can get away with being ordinary-looking.

JG: Absolutely.

While Gerson said early in the interview that gender was not an issue, she described here a gendered pressure, connected to motherhood and reproduction, which came to bear on reporters and commentators through social media tools. Here again is that playing with stereotypes on the one hand, the denying of them on the other, and then into the mix comes the detailed expression of how sexism actually might manifest itself on the job.

Unlike other participants, Gerson said she did not go into journalism to change the world or affect the sociopolitical agenda. She got into journalism because, she said, "I just love doing the daily grunt work. And whether or not it makes an impact or change in anything is beyond my ability to control." Her ego, she said, was not tied up in the outcome of stories, but journalism's appeal was that it was never boring, "because when I'm bored I'm dying." Everything from collecting the data to interviewing people to trying to understand something, every single day, was her joy. The process of sating curiosity appealed to her immensely. Being out in the world still seemed far more compelling than management, but, she said, "reporting is a young woman's game and everybody knows that. At a certain point your energy levels come down and your priorities change." She could see herself going in a more writerly as opposed to a more managerial direction, and one day, she said, she would love to oversee young female writers, maybe when she was fifty, as a mentor. Meanwhile, she said, "[I do] not want to sacrifice my career for a kid, I just don't want to. I realize that might be an inevitable reality, but so much of my sense of self is wrapped up in my career I think it would be really hard for me." Taking a part-time position or becoming a copy editor seemed anathema to her, but she was not prepared to say it was the industry's fault she faced these decisions. The question was whether the problem was societal.[3]

In Hamilton, Emma Reilly saw similar conflicts about the industry, family, and the gendered contours of career on the horizon. But as a contract employee, she was more vulnerable than Gerson, feeling that she had to wage a personal daily battle to stay in her job. An ambitious young person, she expanded on the notion of how age-related characteristics dominated her workday and how a female affinity for multitasking would prove effective down the road.

"I have to fight every single day if I want to stay"

Family life and work life were tightly intertwined for Emma Reilly, a twenty-seven-year-old *Hamilton Spectator* reporter. When interviewed, she lived in the west end of Toronto with her husband, commuting forty-five minutes to work on the highway every morning, staying with her parents in Hamilton about once a week if the weather was bad or if she worked late. Her father was a professor of electrical engineering at McMaster University, and her mother was a parish nurse in Hamilton. As a middle child, she said she was typical in that family position, being chatty, attention-seeking, and ambitious. "I want lots of things in life both professionally and personally," she said.[4] At that moment, her career was absorbing her, since it was demanding and intense. She was the city hall reporter, promoted when Nicole MacIntyre, whom we met in the previous chapter, went on maternity leave. She found the city hall beat exciting and important, because Hamiltonians are, she said, particularly engaged in municipal politics.

With an undergraduate degree in English from Queen's University – she "was never very good at math" – and having worked as a copy editor at the Queen's student newspaper, Reilly went on to study journalism at Ryerson (as "there are no English factories that you can go to after university") between 2006 and 2008. She interned at the *Spec* and the Canadian Press newsroom and was hired by the *Spec* for an eight-month contract, but was laid off in 2009. Reilly called being let go from her dream job "totally heartbreaking." For a brief period, she worked as a legislative assistant at Queen's Park, but missed journalism. In the fall of 2009, she was rehired at the *Spec* on contract, and when we spoke, her contract had just been renewed for another year. "I'm relatively safe until October 2011," she said, "but who knows."[5]

Her natural affinity for descriptive journalism was evident in her story, rich with similes, of how she came to it and why she preferred print to broadcasting:

> ER: It was what I was good at and I was so interested in what I was doing.
> .It was like jumping into a swimming pool and finding out you can
> do a perfect front crawl. Or not perfect, but you can move around. I
> remember the summer before I started at the Queen's *Journal*, I was
> reading the *Spectator* more heavily. I wrote a letter to the editor and
> it was published. I was so excited. I don't know what it was about; it
> was just natural, like when you meet someone for the first time and
> you know that you're really going to like this person and you can't
> necessarily explain why. It's a combination of factors that you lock
> into. I enjoyed the process of talking to people. I enjoyed the process
> of writing. I hit a little node of people who were like me, who saw the
> world in a similar way. Who had a bizarre sense of humour, and you
> know what it's like.

Like the other youngest participants, Reilly said she was expected to be technologically savvy and able to multitask. Besides reporting print stories and filing her blog regularly, she had responsibilities to update her Twitter postings constantly and, more recently, to provide online video clips. Only one other reporter, a more senior Tiger Cats (Hamilton's professional football team) reporter had as many "platforms" to fill with content. She said she had been identified as an "early adopter" and, while she enjoyed the role of informally showing others how to use technology, she was frustrated by older reporters who were not jumping into the new media technology and continued just to "write stories." Her youth was an asset, mostly, and a liability, slightly. As cohort member Laura Fraser of the Halifax *Chronicle Herald* will describe later, paternalism crept in:

> ER: That's where age comes into it a lot. That extra sense of "you're young
> so you're technologically savvy, so do this for us and then you can teach
> other people how to do that." And that's not something that's been
> enforced with an iron fist. A lot has been give and take. Some has come
> around naturally. I volunteered to help people with video. I'm happy to
> do that and that's not a responsibility that I begrudge. I like doing it and

I'm happy to do it. So, it's not a negative thing. It's something that I'm conscious of. Not negative all the time, I should say.

vs: So age for you is the bigger factor?

ER: Within the newsroom, but outside as well. I get comments about how young I am all the time. And sometimes I find it funny. Sometimes frustrating. A mayoral candidate who used to be a member of the Tiger Cats came up to me at his press conference and we had talked over the phone many times. And when he met me he said, "Oh, you're still a rookie." And I thought, "Ha, yeah, I get it. You're a former Tiger Cat and I understand, but that doesn't mean that I can't do my job." I think my age is both an asset and a liability because I think [it's] an excuse for people to not take me seriously and that's something that I really don't want. I've learned to almost work it to my advantage because there's this one councillor who is almost paternal in his relationship with me, which you aren't necessarily looking for, but you can maybe spin it to your advantage. And so, it was intimidating to be so young and to have so much responsibility and go out there and work with people who are older than me and more experienced. That was something that I was conscious of and still am.

Like Jen Gerson, Reilly felt tension between her personal ambition and the insecurity of the industry. "I think you'd be hard pressed to find a young person who doesn't feel they have to get their dukes up if they are going to succeed," she said. Journalism required mental stamina and toughness, and so did simply staying employed in it. "I feel like I have to fight every single day if I want to stay," she said, and that fight was worth it for the valuable role that journalists play in informing the public.

Reilly said she preferred to write "a cool neighbourhood story over a dry budget story," but with budgets affecting the whole city, she found herself trying to balance those larger institutional stories with the smaller, human ones. While all journalists tried to be as neutral as possible, she said, a "wide variety of personalities" among those people she wrote about meant that her personal responses towards them had to be carefully monitored. Editors ensured that there was a "buffer" that prevented her feelings "leaching" into stories. With her journalism instructors having inculcated the notion into the students that they must not insert themselves or their opinions into news stories, it was difficult to recognize that this could, and did, happen. With every story, a reporter made choices, and so did the editors who put the headline on it. It may seem like a subtle difference, but synthesizing arguments and positions, as she described, is not the same as writing to try to persuade readers to consider a point of view, as columnists are paid to do. Reporters are not.

Reilly felt that, being on contract, she was "lucky" not to have children, briefly echoing the luck theme of the senior cohort. Her generation, she said, felt pressured to "have it all" as the previous generation did, with that "bring-home-the-bacon-and-fry-it-up-in-the-pan mentality." She saw herself as more focused on work than children at the moment, identifying the old boys' club and how male editors were still "begetting male editors." Reilly described looking down the road five years to when she and her husband would start a family, after focusing on their careers:

> I'm not going to be able to be as devoted to my job as I would like. I think obviously, this has been written about before, maternity leave, part-time, all of that stuff can impede your progression on your career if you're a woman in a way that it doesn't for a man. That's something I'm very conscious of. Looking down that road and wondering how it is going to turn out. And watching other women in the newsroom do it in front of me and seeing how they handle it. It is something that I think about a lot. That's a huge deal in terms of climbing the editorial ladder. But, on the other hand, why stay? Well, because you love it. Because you have a family doesn't mean that you stop loving it or stop wanting to devote your time and energy to it.

Citing other reports, Reilly said it was "obvious" that maternity altered career trajectories. Looking at her mother, mother-in-law, and sister, and how they all thought it important to have a good work and family life, Reilly said she shared this idea, but work was more important at that moment. She listed reasons to be "Zen" about the situation for young women at newspapers, citing factors about which she felt nothing could be done. To go there would be both paralyzing and infuriating:

> If I work hard and push, push, push over the next five years then maybe I'll be in a place where I can afford to take a year off. I definitely have that mentality. Especially in this job, where it's so hard just to get your foot in the door. Once you're in, you don't want to pull it back out again. Whether it's fair for men not to have to deal with that, I don't know. You can't change the fact that women have babies. Perhaps that makes us better journalists because we are able to multitask and nurture and come at it

from a more understanding or open perspective. I'm generalizing here in terms of "quote unquote female characteristics," but it's kind of like my contract job. That I got used to not dwelling on it because if I do, I'm paralyzed. I get angry, I get frustrated. There's nothing I can do about my contract other than work hard and hope. So, again, the fact that women have to take time off work to have kids, there's nothing you can do. That's just it. And I think it's just another level of complexity that you have to deal with as a woman that you don't necessarily have to deal with as a man.

By touching on the levels of "complexity" that women experience because of gender, Reilly called up the concept of how individuals embody multiple identities. From her first days as a journalist, for example, Reilly had been thinking a lot about how to "have a life and do this really demanding job." Even whether to change her last name on marrying was a choice she had to make. She continued using her maiden name for her byline, based on talks with other women in the newsroom in the same situation, for continuity's sake. Being flexible to fit the system seemed uppermost in her approach to newspaper work, along with the sense of power she had as a reporter to influence the sociopolitical agenda at the same time.

Reilly enjoyed being "in the position to set the agenda" for civic politics in Hamilton. She loved to dig around, find something – especially stories where taxpayers find out their money might have been poorly spent – and break that story and then see people talk about the issue, as well as seeing the local TV reporters having to play catch-up. This position was not only a joy, it was a weighty responsibility. Looking ahead, it seemed that the "monster" of technology was going to be a "huge deal for the rest of my career," so she had concerns about having to spend more time on video/broadcast-style journalism, when her real love was reporting in this way for print, and perhaps providing context and analysis. Ultimately, said Reilly, the kind of multitasking that new media technology seemed to require might mean that women would be better suited to it than men. She used the imagery of a tree with many branches to explain this idea, and how women might not be CEOs in businesses because of it. She compared city editor Carla Ammerata's approach to work – as an unofficial top decision-maker by virtue of her multitasking brain – to how her mother organized family life while she had another job:

ER: I think that women are just generally better multitaskers; that's been proven forever. Even my husband, he's good at doing this one thing but then [I] say, "Did you make that vet appointment?" and he goes, "No, I forgot." I have to make sure [he does this, and then I ask], "Did you pay the parking ticket?" "No? Okay, well can you do that tomorrow?" And [I tell him] when you don't do that tomorrow, I'm going to text you in the middle of the day. And then I'm going to buy Christmas cards and write them for my side and make you write them for your side, and all of that stuff will make us better at approaching this multifaceted media of the future. Maybe, even if we are not officially the CEOs we will be the unofficial CEOs of not only the household but of newsrooms in terms of multitasking – I'm picturing branches springing out of your brain and on each twig is a different kernel that you have to be in charge of. And that's how a lot of women approach their homes and maybe that will be the way that women approach their work.

vs: You think of that analogy, you really do see how it has to change because of how it will remain the same if men are at the top and they have women organizing them –

er: Yeah, exactly. You know? That's the funny thing, too.

vs: That supports their continuation in that role.

er: That's something interesting that I'd never really thought of. Maybe it is the women in these [senior but not top] positions who are making a lot of the decisions. And again, that's just something I'm speculating [about].

Even in my household growing up, my mom was the one keeping the house together and going to work, and with me and my husband, it's the same. I'm the one who has the tree branch in my head. And he's very good with stuff like housework, but he doesn't think, "Okay, this, this, this, and this needs to be done."

vs: That domestic to-do list.

er: Exactly. You could make the comparison in terms of newsrooms because Carla is the one who knows, "Emma's working on this story and I've got this meeting" – she's into all of that, right? I'm being presumptuous about what's going on in Carla's brain.

vs: But you can see what she has to do. So she keeps a lot of balls in the air.

er: She sure does. She really, really does.

When I called Reilly in March 2012 to ask her to join me on an industry conference panel in Toronto to discuss these issues, she told me that she had been hired on full-time, and what a relief that was. She also said that speculation had simultaneously risen about when she was going to have a baby (an office pool had begun for the timing), and the news that she and her husband had bought a car prompted a (male) senior editor to ask if it would be easy to outfit it with a car seat. Her reproductive intent was now newsroom gossip, which was off-putting.[6]

Like Reilly in Hamilton, Victoria-based Katie DeRosa found the multitasking aspects of her work a challenging, inevitable feature of being a young journalist. Like Gerson, she found that qualities associated with being female could be an important card to play (or hold) on the job, especially outside the newsroom. While women leaders were nearly invisible to most in this cohort because there were so few, DeRosa had the most to say on the theme of mentorship. She appreciated the support for her own career and helped others coming up behind her.

"This shift towards technology, I don't think it's gender specific"

Katie DeRosa, twenty-six, and I spoke at the back of the crowded Murchie's tea shop on Government Street in Victoria on a winter afternoon. After joining the *Times Colonist* in December 2008, first on a brief internship and then on a year's contract to replace someone on a maternity leave, DeRosa had been hired full-time as the crime reporter. The transition was not seamless, however. At first, then editor-in-chief Lucinda Chodan had told DeRosa no money was in the budget to hire her full-time: but after the *Ottawa Citizen* offered DeRosa a one-year contract, Chodan scraped together enough to hire her. Born in Niagara Falls, and feeling far away from her family there, DeRosa was initially not sure she would take the permanent *TC* job. Instead, she did what she always does in difficult situations:

> That was a decision I had to struggle with, because it was so far away from my family, but it's a full-time position and a lot more security. I talked to a bunch of friends who are journalists, female journalists actually, and they said, "You know, it looks good on your résumé to have a full-time position. Even if you don't stay there forever, it shows that you're not just bouncing around for year-long contracts and [that] someone wants to keep you." And so ... that was a big decision, and I've been here since.[7]

DeRosa said she loved her job, with its office camaraderie and competitiveness with journalists in other media. She appreciated the mentorship and encouragement of her three women bosses (who would all be gone from the *TC* by March 2012). The daughter of a restaurant manager (father) and banker (mother), and a sister of one younger brother, DeRosa said she took a lot of her confidence from a small group of friends she had had since Grade 3. DeRosa, who was single, was about to be a bridesmaid in two of their weddings. Listening to many references to her female mentors, groups of women friends, and her own mentorship of even younger student journalists at Carleton University, I got the impression that DeRosa thrived in a supportive village that was helping to raise her to journalistic heights. And that was happening because enough women were in positions to guide her and each other. These relationships gave her the confidence to try new things, such as fly across the country for a new job, and to hope for – and receive – support and feedback when she wanted to write more than just breaking news.

DeRosa, while acknowledging her own determination, did talk about luck as a factor in her early career gains, but luck was related to being hired during a protracted industry downturn, while the oldest cohort had talked about luck in terms of an ongoing lack of entitlement. "Especially because I'm young, I almost feel really lucky to be where I am right now. I feel that I'm pretty young to have a full-time job compared to other friends I know," she explained. Luck also allowed her to do both hard news and investigative stories; she said some of her female friends who were journalists feared being kept in lifestyle sections rather than being promoted to news. Being on the news side meant she could make the case to her editors (Stephanie Coombs and Lucinda Chodan) to do bigger investigative stories of the kind that would later win her awards, as well as simply being able to develop expertise on her crime beat. That expertise, in turn, gave her the power to choose those stories she felt needed more in-depth reporting. A recent example she gave was a story on the difficulty of charging and prosecuting impaired drivers who are under the influence of drugs rather than alcohol.

As part of a mentoring program at Carleton University, where she, as a fourth-year student, had mentored a second-year student, DeRosa had already seen a tendency among other "young girls" to be timid about asking tough questions of authority figures. She told the younger journalism students that they could "get over that" with time, intelligence, and a lot of research, so there would be no need to use a confrontational approach (as many TV journalists felt they needed to do). She noted another factor regarding women's physical size, which could be a problem or something to exploit, as Gerson had mentioned and as Laura Fraser in Halifax comments on later in this chapter:

> I think women struggle because even from a physical point of view if you're small and you're questioning this big burly police officer or politician, the physical disadvantage sometimes weighs into your mental confidence. So you just literally feel small, and maybe sometimes it comes to your advantage, because you're unassuming so they don't see you as a threat and they relax a little bit, but you have to get over that, you have put yourself on an equal playing field with all the other reporters. And in a scrum I feel that really comes out, because that's when you have to yell over other reporters, and sometimes I leave those scrums feeling frustrated, because I couldn't yell loud enough for someone to hear my question, and maybe my question will still get an answer, but there is something about standing in a scrum with your tape recorder and not getting a question in and you kind of just feel like you leeched off everyone else's questions. And that is a challenge, you have to elbow your way in.

She had one "horror story" attached to her age and gender, which also illustrated the difference between how sexism was manifested when senior participants such as Dalhousie's Kelly Toughill and the *TC*'s Lucinda Chodan (and I) were starting out, and how it can appear subtly today. This story recalled an event during DeRosa's internship at the *St. Catharines Standard* in 2008, before she came to the *TC*.[8] In the following excerpt, DeRosa described how the night reporter took off her byline, removing her name from her story and putting on his own, then at the bottom he put "with files from Katie DeRosa." The "lede" is the first few sentences of a story, which are often updated for breaking news, after the day reporter leaves:

> KD: The most negative experience I had, and I felt it had to do with myself as a female, was when I was at the *St. Catharines Standard*. I spent four hours covering a man who fell off the [Niagara] Escarpment and died. And we had to find out from police if it was a suicide or not, because if it was a suicide we would downplay it; if it was an accident then we would say there was no fence there, how was he there, was he drinking, did he go for a walk and just not see the cliff?
>   So I spent all day talking to people, talking to the eleven-year-old boys who had found the body. I saw the body thirty metres down on the rocks,

and that was the most traumatizing thing I've seen. The night reporter was tasked with calling the police and finding out whether it was a suicide, because we had been working all day and not getting anything from the police.

He took my byline off and put his byline on, and I got a "with files from." Even though all the information was mine, the writing was mine, and all he did was change the lede.

I was furious, because I was a young reporter and that was the biggest news story I had covered at the time, because I was just starting out. And everything counts for your portfolio. I was just livid, and there was no way for it to be reversed, and when I went to that editor about he said, "Oh well, that's just the way [he] is."

vs: So you came out as someone who was easy for him to exploit as opposed to somebody whom he could mentor and share the limelight with?

kd: Exactly. If I was his age or if I was a man, would he have pulled that? Maybe not, so I was furious. And the only thing I got from my editor in the morning story meeting, which [he] wasn't there for, because he was the night reporter, was, "By the way, Katie did most of the work for that story." So he did acknowledge that, but it still didn't feel like enough. And you know I almost look at that as my horror story, and everything else has gotten better from there.

Much admired by more than a few survey participants is veteran sports and court reporter and columnist Christie Blatchford, a talented, hard-working journalist/author who is divorced and without kids, and known for her love of running and dogs. DeRosa is a fan, too, mostly for Blatchford's "no bullshit" way of crime reporting as though she were "writing a novel" and for her toughness and persistence. DeRosa pointed out that Blatchford exemplifies an advantage that women journalists and commentators had over men: she could write flirty, ribald columns that men could not get away with, as they would be accused of "womanizing." Once again, the notion of playing with gender stereotypes – owning them instead of being victimized – appeared.

Still, it was not always easy to do so without being careful. In her own job covering the police beat, DeRosa felt that a big challenge that came with her gender was interacting with her sources in a way that "doesn't come off as flirting" or flattery. While older male reporters might ask police sources out for a drink, DeRosa would stick to coffee and make sure she was not sending a message that might be misinterpreted as romantic interest.

The combination of her gender and unmarried status could be tricky on the job, and her women peers understood that. But the subject was taboo:

> When you're single and you're a female, you think, "Well, you don't want to go out for drinks or out for coffee with this police officer if he's married because there could be a misunderstanding." It's almost this awkward thing that no one talks about. Oftentimes as women we struggle with when to turn on the charm, not [to] loosen someone up but to get them comfortable or get them to joke and maybe get a better interview or get better information than you would otherwise. I don't think it should be construed as using your body or using your sexuality to get a story. I just think it's a characteristic of a female.

Her speculation as to why so few women moved up to senior management in newspapers, notwithstanding her own unusual experience of having three female managers (who have now all moved on), mirrored her peers across the country, touching on the pre-emptive public-relations move many young women graduates take, as noted in the introduction. She saw it as a choice:

> KD: It could be because reporting is seen as so demanding you have to stay late or might have to stay late, or you stay until your story's done or something breaks. Maybe women feel that if they take more responsibility, they're the ones that have to stay late. If they have children or families, that's where they might go into PR, because it's nine to five. In my journalism school I was surprised how many really talented reporters didn't go into journalism, they went into PR, and I wonder if right off the bat –
>
> VS: These reporters were women?
>
> KD: Yes, most people in my class who went into PR were women, so maybe they had this misconception that if you're a reporter you have to do this much overtime, and you're always at the office late. Now that I've worked with the *TC*, for the most part I get out at 5:30, although Stephanie [Coombs] might have a different story. There [have been] quite a few times where three big stories break and she's at the office 'til nine.

vs: What do you think about that? Why should we care if they go into PR and not reporting?

kd: I guess it's their choice. I just was never interested in PR, maybe I'll change my mind, but I find it so much more exciting to do something new every day, and it depends on what kind of PR job I'd have.

DeRosa felt that she could not see leaving journalism, because she loved the rush of doing exclusives from within the collegial news-room. She would not speculate on how marriage and children might affect her career, but did recall how her banker mother would leave work to pick up her kids and then return to work, splitting up her day. That example was partly why DeRosa never expected to work regular hours herself and still needed a reminder from then city editor Stephanie Coombs, to file for overtime when she stayed late to finish a story.

Looking ahead, perhaps when she had turned fifty or so, DeRosa said she might return to Carleton as an instructor. Editing was possible, but she felt she would miss reporting. For DeRosa, the value in "writing a successful story" was being a public educator, making people care about an issue that they might not have known about before, from mental health to police accountability. The only trouble looming for her generation was how to juggle the technological demands, which were accelerating at the same time as damaging, industry-wide cost-cutting. The word "overwhelmed" came up several times:

kd: I've seen everyone embracing this shift towards technology, and I don't think it's gender specific. There are concerns, like how am I supposed to take notes, tape record, and take a video at the same time, so I can feel overwhelmed. I have to take these notes, so when I get back to the office I can upload and put this story on the Web within five minutes. But I've also got to be videotaping and I've got to go edit this video, and I've got to refresh this story I've put on the Web, and find an angle for the next day's paper.

So there's a chance that people will feel overwhelmed, but I think that's a resource thing, you just keeping seeing cuts, cuts, cuts, but you're expecting more of people at the same time. So you're doing more with less, so where is the quality going to suffer? Where is the opportunity for journalists to grow as investigative journalists if we're not given the chance to work for a week, three weeks, or whatever on a story, because we are expected to be chasing breaking news?

vs: And, you notice that the stories that the *TC* has won awards for, and is nominated for, tend to be those investigative stories.

kd: Exactly, exactly. So as a woman who is driven to get those awards and who says, "This is my goal to get nominated for a Webster and this is my goal to get this young journalist award." How do you make sure you are still writing stories that will get those awards, and then embrace the technology at the same time? So I think that is the challenge for women and men and I think that women are just as likely to embrace the technology, but there needs to be some support so you're not overwhelmed.

DeRosa did achieve her goal of being nominated (twice) for a Jack Webster award (British Columbia's highest print journalism honour), and won in the best print reporter category in 2011. More recently (2012), she was awarded the first annual national James Travers Foreign Corresponding Fellowship. She used the time and $25,000 in prize money to investigate the impact of Canada's proposed tougher human smuggling laws on refugee claimants. The judges noted that DeRosa's win of the Webster, her top marks from Carleton's journalism school, and her engaging storytelling skills helped her to win the Travers prize.[9]

Nicole O'Reilly, a *Hamilton Spectator* reporter, also covered crime and was equally busy honing her journalistic craft and teaching others how to use new media technology. She echoed Gerson's and DeRosa's view that using innately female characteristics was an effective strategy for certain interviews, and like Reilly, judged her age to be a major factor in her career. O'Reilly shared the "bring it on" mentality of the others when asked by her editors to work overtime because they knew she was single and without children, but she recognized that her willingness to say yes every time could have its limits.

"If someone needs to stay late because someone's called in sick, it will be me"

Like her *Spectator* colleague Emma Reilly, Nicole O'Reilly, who was twenty-five when interviewed, was born in southern Ontario (Mississauga), graduated from Ryerson University's journalism program, was working precariously (and anxiously) from contract to contract, and was fearful about the future of print journalism generally. And because the two were young white women who had similar last names and sat near each other at work, they both sometimes felt they were considered interchangeable by older editors, just as I and a couple of other "brown-haired girls" in the *Globe* newsroom had felt thirty years earlier.

Single and without children when we met, O'Reilly had the experience, like Gerson, of being raised by a single mom, her father having died when O'Reilly was nine. O'Reilly considered her and her sister's upbringing as middle class, with her mother working in early childhood education. Like so many other participants, she felt the call of writing in high school (on school magazines and yearbooks) and went to Ryerson's journalism school after graduation. Heading into the coursework, she loved the writing process, then soon became enthralled with hard-news reporting and "the digging and uncovering."[10] The notion of privilege arose, not in reference to (the luck of) being white, educated, and middle class, but in terms of being able to tell others' stories and expose official malfeasance:

> NO: It's a real position of privilege. People invite you into their lives and they tell you things that they don't normally tell people [and] invite you into their homes. You're holding police, politicians accountable, government agencies –
> vs: It's so powerful when writing goes out into the community.
> NO: Especially when you feel like you've made a difference or you feel like you've exposed something or given voice to people that would have otherwise not had a voice. That's far more powerful than enjoying the actual way that you write it. Although, writing is enjoyable, too.
> vs: So it's the craft and also the impact?
> NO: Yeah.

While Katie DeRosa and Emma Reilly echoed the luck factor of the oldest group, O'Reilly echoed the common thread of being a voice for the voiceless, which transcended the generations in this study. And along with the others in the youngest group only, she sensed that she would not find gender holding back her career. Journalism school experiences foretold this to her: first, most of her classmates were women, which is typical for journalism schools as noted in the introduction. Second, she said many of Ryerson's top instructors were women. During our one-on-one interview, I asked her why she thought those women might have left daily journalism for teaching, but we moved on to other topics after she said she had not wondered why.[11]

After graduating from Ryerson, O'Reilly interned at the *Globe* and the *Waterloo Region Record*, before working at the *Woodstock Sentinel-Review*. She received a national young journalist award for covering municipal affairs and environmental issues for the *Guelph Mercury*, but that did not prevent the paper from laying her off to cut costs: that memory was making her nervous the day we met, because the *Spec* was offering buyouts for the same reason.

During our interview, O'Reilly shared the view that her age was the primary personal factor that influenced her practice of journalism inside the newsroom, but gender could be at work in the field. She was the crime and security reporter, and described what could happen at a crime scene or dealing with police, as did Laura Fraser in Halifax, Jen Gerson in Calgary, and Katie DeRosa in Victoria; she then turned to how her marital and parenthood status affected her work:

> NO: I would definitely say that my age primarily, but also my gender, affect how people perceive me. It affects how you build relationships with sources, right? I'm a crime reporter and I go to a crime scene. How a police officer is going to react to me being a young, twenty-five-year-old woman is different than the crime reporter whom I took over from, who was a middle-aged man. It's never inappropriate, but they can be flirty with you and you have to make sure that a line isn't crossed, but it's definitely the way you speak with them. You can be tongue in cheek and joke around and they react better to you that way. They are going to be more comfortable with you and honest with you. But within the newsroom I don't feel like I'm treated differently because of my gender, but definitely my age. I think because of my age technology was not as scary for me as it was for some other people in the newsroom. So, it's expected of me and I'm fine with that, I know how to use Twitter or pick up a camera.
>
> VS: Whereas the people who are older, there is less expectation they will pick it up?
>
> NO: It's more they get agitated and upset, "How am I supposed to do all this," and, so in anticipation of that reaction, yeah. I also think that because I'm not married, I don't have kids and my age, and being a junior person in the newsroom, you do have to pay your dues, but if there's someone that has to cover the 6 a.m. shift they will ask me. If someone needs to pick up a weekend last minute, it will be me. If someone needs to stay late because someone's called in

sick, it will be me. If someone needs to get another story thrown at them, it will be me.

vs: And how do you feel about that?

no: I'm okay with it. I feel like I'm at least respected enough that if it was too far, I would be comfortable saying that it is too far … I am happy to be busy. I'd rather have too much to do than too little.

Where members of the most senior cohort resented sexism at work, O'Reilly, like her young counterparts, saw gender as something she could perform ironically and to her advantage, which the narrative analysis literature explains as playing with ambiguities and feminists see as characteristic of third-wave politics. At the same time (unlike Gerson at the *Calgary Herald*), O'Reilly said she felt the old boys' club at the workplace was intact. She also said, however, that gender and motherhood affected women's careers more in the past than today, noting that the paper had strong women in middle-management roles and strong women writers on staff. Still, she acknowledged that at that time at the *Spec*, the publisher, editor-in-chief, and two managing editors were male, with a lot of the mothers in the newsroom working part-time. O'Reilly also said she would feel worried about her career stalling if she had a baby while on contract, but would not worry about returning to her hard-news post if she had a permanent position and got pregnant. But her *Spec* colleague Nicole MacIntyre, a few years older and a new mother, found that maternity caused her to leave her city hall beat (to be succeeded by Emma Reilly) for part-time work before taking on a full-time job in the lifestyle section.

Part of the impact of O'Reilly's journalism was based on the combination of her own skills and the power of technology that allowed her stories to go out on the Internet: she said she was known for her ability to dig, to go through databases, and to provide more context and details in a clearer way than perhaps other reporters could. This meant her stories, which she said gave voice to people who were victimized and gave them a human face, as so many other participants did, could have wider dissemination.

O'Reilly gave one example of an international story she had broken involving human trafficking from Eastern Europe. (She had latched onto it when it was an immigration story, before it involved criminal charges.) The story had gone so far that reporters from Budapest now called her. The only trouble was, she said, that an older, more senior male reporter (whom she liked and respected) had been put on the story with her, and her sense was that this was partly because "my being a young woman really was not safe for me to be going by myself to investigate" criminal activity in Hungary. In other words, if the company decided the story needed to be covered from Eastern Europe, she would not be sent on her own but with the older male reporter. Now that the cases had gone to court, her story had been reported in the national news, and was said to be the largest human trafficking case in Canadian history.[12]

As for her leadership qualities, O'Reilly said that her capacity to train older reporters in new media technology was not any kind of power position; she felt she was not a mentor, just a trainer. But if she did not have power in the newsroom, she did have respect from her peers and bosses, based on knowing when to hold her tongue and when to speak out. Good journalism was what mattered, whether it was online or in print, and good journalism required investigation. O'Reilly said she loved reporting too much to see herself as an editor; rather, she looked forward to becoming a senior writer doing investigative projects in a large daily newsroom.

As a single woman with few perceived strings attached, Laura Fraser said, like O'Reilly, that she was first called for overtime at the Halifax *Chronicle Herald*. And, like O'Reilly, she dwelt on the importance of craft, drawing power from her own free agency to explore that craft within her job and beyond. She experienced the limits and advantages of power associated with physical size, as DeRosa did, but Fraser experienced the complications of having a disability. And her ideas about the power of mentoring went beyond fostering newsroom relationships.

"You can't write about the world if you're stuck in a newsroom"

Scene-setting is important to narrative: where are the characters located, literally and metaphorically? How do their positions affect the action? How does a writer compellingly describe them in their setting? These are crucial matters for fiction writers as well as non-fiction writers such as Laura Fraser, a reporter at the Halifax *Chronicle Herald*. When I interviewed her in a small meeting room beside the empty, quiet newsroom, she was twenty-six, the same age as Jen Gerson and Katie DeRosa, also single and without children. Getting out of that office and into the community to see how people lived was central to her sense of power as a storyteller.

Like so many other participants, Fraser had wanted to write from a young age, but journalism was a flag of convenience at the start. Her real love was fiction: plays, stories, poetry. But to make a living writing fiction seemed unlikely. So the Mississauga-born, middle-class daughter of a teacher-turned-vice-principal (mom) and a hedge fund director (dad) decided to go to journalism school at Ryerson. After graduating in 2007, she came to Halifax, partly because she knew the paper was independent (not part of a chain). During her internship at age twenty-two, Fraser wrote stories about the cost of the Commonwealth Games, based on documents that had been slipped to her. The city eventually abandoned ideas of hosting the Games because of these costs and the *Chronicle Herald* editors were impressed enough to hire her as a summer replacement and then took her on full-time. After three years covering Cape Breton and winning a young journalist award, Fraser asked to return to the newsroom in Halifax, where she was working a night shift in general assignment news.

"What I really want to do is tell great stories," Fraser said, describing in detail one she wrote that involved the Canadian daughter of a woman living in legal limbo in Romania, and how the story had propelled action that could result in the return of the woman's mother to Canada.[13] But in terms of professional development, Fraser said she would just as happily go for a walk in a forest and try to come up with a compelling way to describe a ghostly grove of birch trees: she loved the image she had come up with, that of bony fingers.

For the most part, Fraser said, she did not think of herself as a "young, female journalist," but rather as a journalist. But then she thought more about the issue in advance of our talk, and the issue of her youth emerged, as well as her small physical stature, and how these might be perceived on the job, depending on whether she found herself in the office or out interviewing:

LF: When I thought about it and looked at some of my colleagues who have been in the newsroom for significantly longer, I think at my age and lower experience, where I am still really excited about what I do, I still believe that there is a future with newspapers and I want to be part of making the change. I think that there are people who are a little bit older who are maybe a little more resistant to making that change. Or simply are less excited about what they do and maybe a little more jaded.

VS: So your idea about these personal characteristics for you now, the one that is most meaningful, or the one that as you've thought about, is age.

LF: Is youth.

VS: Is youth. Not gender or anything else.

LF: I'd say the only time I'm concerned about gender is when I go out to a crime scene at night. I do think about that, I admit. You know the other night I went to a stabbing in Dartmouth and with that it's partly gender and partly size. I mean I am only five feet tall and it can be somewhat of a concern. I was out at 11:30 at night a couple weeks ago in a not so great neighbourhood, and there are moments that I am aware that I feel a little bit more vulnerable being a woman. But, at the same time, I still go out and do my job.

VS: Sure. So, for you, the gender stuff is more about how you are out in the world, your smallness, rather than how you are in the newsroom.

LF: Yeah. I don't know if that's just the way that I was raised or the way that I have grown up with other interactions with male figures in my life. Like, I try not to see a major distinction between male and female journalists.

Unlike Gerson, O'Reilly and Reilly, Fraser told a more optimistic story about the industry and her future in it: she hedged her bets, though, having applied to a couple of universities to take a master's program in creative writing (some personal agency emerging here) as well as acknowledging, like the others, that she was thinking about the whole notion of being a parent, and its potential impact on her career.

Fraser saw herself as only loosely aligned to the paper, in that she enjoyed her colleagues and her job made it possible to hone her craft – to write stories, craft scenes and images, create change. Rather than being a newsroom leader, she worked independently for herself and for the reader/public. "I'm not really doing it for the paper, I'm doing it because I think it's important," she said of her choice of stories. She attributed this to her creativity, need for control, and tendency to "push myself far harder than anyone else," echoing a cohort theme of a sense of personal agency being powerful. Embedded in her (fairly typical) response to the question of why so few women were at the top of newsrooms was the downside of being a free agent, when it came to being seen that way by her managers. She was easier for them to move around:

LF: Women are less likely to hold executive positions because of the sort of family and work/life balance. I don't know if it's fair to attribute it to a gender cause; it's just me speaking personally, but I have no desire to be at the top at a newspaper. It's not at all what I want to do. If other women felt the same way I do then perhaps they just want to do an excellent job at whatever position it is that they're holding. I think that there is a lot of pressure on women to be the head of a family in many ways, so it might be preferable to, to let someone else, in some ways, run the newspaper –

vs: Are you single now? I forgot to ask.

LF: Yes. I have thought about it and I think it's hard to be really good at more than one thing. So I feel, and this is just purely from observation, but people, especially as I see friends who are also in the media becoming mothers, it definitely changes their attitude about work. I completely believe in a work/life balance. I think it will be hard to be a great writer, and especially if I want to write a book and be a mom at the same time. And be really good at that. Anyways, that's just stuff I've been thinking about recently.

vs: Well, you're in that age group.

LF: Anyway, we'll see. In terms of how I'm seen in the newsroom, because I am single and don't have children I am definitely the first person always called for OT. When I moved from Cape Breton the discussion was, "So you're unattached, right? Okay, can you be here in a week?" And I said, "I have to move all my physical things." Whereas the person who was moving to Cape Breton had two children and was given a couple [of] months to move. That might just be me attributing things differently, but I do feel there is a little more pressure on me to work holidays because I don't have children and I don't have family here.

vs: So you're seen as more of a free agent.

LF: Yes, definitely. It's just expected that I will work late if something goes overtime. Normally I don't have a problem with that, but just because I don't have children doesn't mean that I don't have other commitments outside of work.

In fact, Fraser was a Sparks leader, which meant that much of her free time was spent with "baby Girl Guides," five- and six-year-old girls who were "the ones who make me think 'all right, maybe I can'" be both a successful writer and a parent.

I asked Fraser if she could comment on what I called a "minor physical disability" I had noticed in her neck and shoulder, about which Fraser did not offer information, whereas she mentioned her small size unprompted. I asked if not mentioning her disability might be related to her expressed values of independence and toughness, which she agreed was a factor. Fraser explained that she was born with a form of congenital scoliosis, and that while her physical health was now generally good, she had many operations growing up and had spent eighteen months in a wheelchair. She explained that her arms were of different lengths and her left thumb was missing, but her disability had "never been a huge issue in the newsroom." That is, until the previous spring. She described the power and limiting forces of disability in the workplace:

LF: I don't know if this is interesting to the study at all, but I broke my rib at work last spring. I was covering a yacht race and they went out during a squall and the boat just suddenly flipped and I was thrown about ten feet and just landed on my back and broke a couple [of] ribs. So since then, work's definitely been more gentle in some ways. But until then, and as long as I reassure people that things are okay then –

VS: And do you find that there's any sense that because of your particular abilities or experiences with your condition that you are asked to report things about people like –

LF: I would say that's probably more of a personal thing. I sometimes go to that. Not too many people that I work with know that I was in a wheelchair but I guess my assignment editor does know now. And he sometimes pushes me towards that a little bit more. I've written probably two stories recently about teenage girls who both through accidents are now in wheelchairs, just because it's easier for them to talk to me.

VS: And you can be ticked off about it, you don't want to be pigeonholed – but on the other hand, you may be able to get more from people.

LF: Yes. Exactly.

VS: So you have to decide whether it's a liability or an asset, eh?

LF: It really does not bother me. I actually prefer it because the stories that bother me the most are stereotypical disabled stories. And so, like you say, I want to look at it as an asset and I'll write the story about the person. It drives me insane to read stories about "Oh look, this person in a wheelchair did this great thing" and I think that, obviously, you can't not mention that someone has a disability because it does make it all the more extraordinary, but sometimes you should still write about the whole person.

VS: I find with a lot of that coverage, people act as if it's a miracle that this person has managed to do whatever. Rather than just be pretty interesting and that's a part of them as opposed to –

LF: Yeah, exactly.

vs: …You can have an ability or a disability, and it can be limiting, which
it might be in some ways, they're not going to let you go out on the next
sailboat story –
LF: No.
vs: You might not volunteer anyway. But also this is an area that you have
power that they don't have, because you're in the position to write that
story.
LF: Yep.

In the place where her disability, stature, age, and gender met, she could
either find power or let herself be pigeonholed. She preferred using
such situations to advance herself. As for the industry, the most important thing it could do to save itself, Fraser said, was to slow things down
a little: to spend more time doing longer stories (not unsurprisingly, her
forte), which would increase readership because it would show them
the newspaper had true community presence. Referring to the importance of place in narrative, she said, "You can't write about the world if
you're stuck in a newsroom."

Expanding the definition of mentorship to encompass and engage
the community, Fraser said she had suggested to management a possible mentoring role for journalists such as herself. They could go into
high schools to mentor readers, and have them come to the newsroom
"and understand what's going on and actually listen to them a little bit
more and have them set the agenda." Like DeRosa and others, she felt
that online journalism was overly focused on "instant news hits." She
could foresee a role for newspapers in fostering more magazine-like,
in-depth features, and perhaps could reduce publishing paper issues to
three times a week, while developing multimedia work for viewing on
a tablet. Women journalists, she felt, were better than men at adapting
to this kind of change, "speaking from personal experience," adding
that perhaps women were well-positioned to come forward with more
creative ideas to improve newspapers, because they had little power to
lose. Men had found a formula that worked for more than a hundred
years for print, and it was dying. That historic concern for profit drove
that model:

And I'm just saying this 'cause, like you say, the majority of people running newsrooms right now are men. I wonder if maybe they stepped back
a little bit and focused ever so slightly less on the profit margin and just
looked at how to continue to make money and be profitable, even if it is
slightly less money. And, just do something differently.

As of this writing, Fraser had been promoted to covering city hall for the *Chronicle Herald*.

Taking up the theme of devotion to craft and personal development, Melissa Martin saw how she could not only hone her writing skills but also could become invested in the next step: promoting herself as a distinctive voice on the platforms offered by the *Winnipeg Free Press*. She went on to do that for nearly two years before being laid off in October of 2012. Rather than moving her to the section that describes those who decided to leave, she remains in this chapter, as she did not choose to depart, but was cut as a cost-saving measure.

"It's possible to brand yourself and still be a good journalist"

I sat down with Melissa Martin in an empty executive meeting room at the *Winnipeg Free Press*, where, at age twenty-nine, she worked as a general assignment reporter. The story of how she got there took three solid pages of single-spaced transcript notes (my interjections and clarifications take only eight lines), recounted by a seemingly natural-born storyteller. Her autobiographical notes on the *Free Press* website display her unusual trajectory and accomplished, self-deprecating style:

> An aspiring media mogul for the post-media mogul world, Melissa Martin is a word mercenary, a closet cat lady, and the best Lady GaGa impersonator in western Canada.
>
> A Winnipeg girl by birth, and a Winnipeg woman by choice, Melissa has long been an advocate for the voice of the Prairies: its sound, its stages, its style.
>
> She launched her haphazard, poorly planned journalistic career at age 17, writing about shows for *Uptown Magazine* that she wasn't old enough to attend. By age 19, she was reviewing concerts and scratching out stories about music, entertainment, and fashion for the *Free Press*.
>
> What followed: a whirlwind of odd jobs and freelance spots, a few years as a sometimes-producer for CBC Radio One, an endless series of very odd nights at the Royal Albert, and a spunky but ultimately fruitless attempt at Red River College's Creative Communications course.
>
> This tumultuous period mercifully ended when the *Free Press* brought her on full time in 2008. She's been literally living her dream ever since.
>
> When not writing, thinking about writing, hating her own writing, or wishing she could write like Salman Rushdie, Melissa's hobbies include trying to find anything else she's good at other than writing and wearing what are, admittedly, pretty awesome clothes.[14]

Martin is the youngest of six children, adopted into a family of "privilege," with her father a professor of psychotherapy and her mother at home until they divorced, then she taught pre-school. Like many other participants, Martin recalled being unusually interested in – and, in her case, she felt gifted in – writing. She felt that writing well was so easy for her as a child that it simply never occurred to her that it was a talent from which she could make a living. She described herself as a "great colour writer," someone who was called on in the newsroom to do stories about events that might seem dull to others but that her editors felt she could make something out of, and she regularly did.[15] A study participant and her former *Free Press* colleague Helen Fallding called Martin "a more brilliant writer than all the rest of us combined."[16]

Yet Martin also expressed a nagging disappointment that she was not successful and felt disillusioned about what she saw as her limited effect on the community. She acknowledged a tendency to self-sabotage, being particularly hard on herself when feedback from readers did not meet her expectations. She did not feel she had necessarily earned the respect she had in the newsroom, and the support from mentors like then editor Margo Goodhand, she predicted, would surely run out some day. (So far, it has not. Goodhand wrote in an email to me much later that Martin was "one of the best writers we had.") If Martin connected these feelings with her self-described position in her adoptive, adoring family as "the baby," whose every act was praised, she did not say so. Her feelings about being adopted were complicated and tough to untangle, and any impact on her journalism, Martin felt, would be subconscious.

During her time as a music reviewer, Martin's own musician's chops were underrated by the male-dominated world of music, she said. She had studied jazz guitar for ten years and played blues guitar semi-professionally, but since "women really still aren't seen as musicians," her opinions as a music reviewer were often dismissed or impugned with a sexual motive:

> You get accused a lot of jealousy or, "you only like him because he's hot," or conversely, "you only hate him because you're not dating him," things like that. It's always assumed to be a sort of groupie relationship, which has never been true for me. So that's very true in music. And it's definitely true in news, I mean, you don't get the groupie thing so much, but it's definitely perceived that, because sometimes your opinion on things isn't as valid, or at least that's what I assume. Guys clearly feel they can play you a lot more than is necessarily fair.

She told a story about working at CBC Radio in Winnipeg in a nearly all-women department and the inherent advantages she saw of being a woman music critic and journalist:

> There were two guys and thirty women. It was ridiculous, it was like a gynocracy, and I talked to my producer and said. "I did not realize it's only women who work in radio." And she started telling me about the CBC and [how] they had instituted in the 1970s a gender inclusion policy, and she said, "What you're seeing now is the result of that." But she said that when she first got hired, her boss had told her that he thought that women made better journalists than men, always. And she said, "Why is that?" And he said that they are better able to both gain the trust [of] the sources and be more sympathetic, more understanding and listen better.
>
> I think that is true and there have been a lot of cases, especially on news, but sometimes in music, too, where I feel like I've been able to do my job more effectively because I've grown up with the way that I am socialized as a female, which is to be less challenging and more consensus-building or more relationship-building. I feel like I'm more effective because I don't threaten people. Especially men. You know, if I'm interviewing a guy, there's not that issue with that. Do you know what I mean? They do feel like they can relate to me more, they can open up to me a little bit more.

As with the other women who were early in their reporting careers, Martin saw gender as being in play outside the newsroom, marking how she dealt with sources. Inside the *Free Press*, with editor-in-chief Goodhand, Martin felt the newsroom offered flexibility for women and men: her main complaint related to a problem she had with how the male-dominated union had handled the situation when she was laid off, since she was the most recently hired. (She would be laid off again in the fall of 2012, long after our interview.) She found the union "hopelessly paternalistic" and non-consultative. The business itself, she noted, had an all-encompassing, high-stress, and unstable aspect to it, the kind of stress that you took home, especially with technology connecting them to the job 24/7. Here she named what seems to be an intrinsic quality of the industry that she could not influence.

Martin recalled organizing a radio show on "women of the *Winnipeg Free Press*" with women colleagues during which they remarked how none of the female reporters had children, while many of the men did. The reporters, they found, were also far younger than the men (the result of a "lost generation" of women journalists described by other participants from the paper) and Martin understood why. Like Gerson

in Calgary and DeRosa in Victoria, Martin had seen a lot of women leap
to government public relations and communications work. "If I had any
inclination to have a child," said Martin, who was married at the time,
"I would get the hell out of here."

When sexist remarks came up about a woman reporter, Martin said,
it was not because those people involved were sexist, but rather it was
an expression of a larger societal problem, as Gerson had suggested.
She also qualified the idea that the playing field at the paper was level
for men and women, describing a subtle gender effect involving male
managers:

> I believe that they're reflecting a cultural bias that they haven't necessarily
> noticed or challenged in themselves. None of them are chauvinists, none
> of them are misogynistic pigs, but they grew up in a society that encour-
> ages and allows them to think this way about someone. They don't think
> that now. So while they did correct that opinion, I think certainly you can
> be met with that response. So it's not fair to say it's completely level. I just
> think it's quite subtle.

Martin, who is white, said she "would like to see more voices from
mothers, especially from a more diverse range," including single Indigenous mothers, adding an element of diversity. When those women
were interviewed, they were "tokenized," expected to be the voice of
all single, Indigenous mothers, she said. Diversity, or the lack of it, was
second on her agenda for change:

> I think I would pass a law that if you didn't really want to do this job and
> care about it and have energy for it, you couldn't be here – number one. I
> think I would go out of my way to hire some people who weren't white.
> And I'd go out of my way to hire people from a much broader cross-section
> of society. Because newsrooms, I think this is true with newspapers, most
> newspapers are still crushingly white.

Despite her feeling that she was not a particularly powerful force in
the paper, Martin recalled a piece she had written on a dying Metis
language: at first she felt it did not get much feedback, but was happy
to learn that a group of Manitoba speakers of that language had seen
the piece. Another story about which she felt rare pride was a departure from the usual kind of reporting, in that she was allowed to follow a survivor of a residential school during a truth and reconciliation

conference. She described it as reportage that recounted this man's experience at the event rather than being a "suffering porn" piece, which she said she hated.

This train of thought led Martin to describe how journalism should be less about trying to find hard answers and more about witnessing and recognizing that questions are often more important than answers. She explained her view that age was the main factor in how print journalism was held back now, as there was a "generation gap" between those who assigned the stories and those who were writing them, between "people who grew up in a digital world and an immediate world and a very self-reflective, consumerist, hyperpackaged and image-heavy world, versus people who didn't." She returned to this idea late in the interview when I asked her to describe in more detail her ideas about what her future would look like in the business.

For Martin, the critical notion to invest in was that "everything is personal now," with branding of personalities essential to newspapers retaining their currency with readers. While Gerson and Reilly had seen a gender double-standard in this area, Martin felt that staking out ground with one's own lifestyle, attitude, and personality would be instrumental to future career success, pointing out that "it's possible to brand yourself and still be a good journalist." Unlike Goodhand and other participants at the *Free Press*, Martin did not comment on whether her blog or other personal aspects of her journalism were repudiated in hurtful, sexist ways by some readers. What mattered to her was to be judged on the quality of the material she produced. Like others in the youngest group, her narratives suggested that she could wield elements of her own identity as she saw fit, taking power and creativity from what might previously have held her back, while still feeling relatively powerless in the newsroom.

Conclusions: "There is a lot of ship to turn around"

These six young women from five newspapers shared similar race, class, and educational privileges as the previous cohorts; where age intersected with these variables continued to be the main area of difference.

Fainter echoes of previous narrative themes emerged, such as external factors – including luck and institutional inflexibility – fuelling their career trajectories. But as this was the youngest group, their narratives positioned them on the most pro-active end of the victim/witness/

agent continuum as identified by Bryman, Teevan, and Bell (2009): they had the least experience and the most time and energy to focus on their developing careers. Members of the youngest cohort perceived themselves as having far more agency to direct their working lives than the other cohorts did, without family demands bifurcating their attention spans. Their work consumed them, both in journalistic practice and in simply remaining on the job in the face of severe cost-cutting measures at their workplaces. They were less like the oldest group, whose members evaluated their careers as a whole for better or worse, and more like the mid-career group, whose members used narratives to think out loud about their frenzied lives which they otherwise had little time to consider, often telling resilience stories. This youngest group went the farthest in theoretical terms to play with stereotypes surrounding age and gender, sometimes performing their identities ironically, as feminists have observed regarding this third-wave generation of Western women. They honoured the same journalistic values as their older counterparts in wanting to make a difference in society and give voice to the voiceless, but expressed no sense of being seen as frauds or outsiders. Male-dominated newsroom culture was not obviously oppressive to them as it had been to the oldest group: those they deemed sexism's stragglers – a burly male cop here, a corporate honcho there – could be finessed through the performance of soft femaleness.

Melissa Martin commented wryly that in the churning waters of Canada's print news business "there is a lot of ship to turn around."[17] Judging by this cohort's responses, its members would be happy to have the opportunity to help set the industry back on course, although Martin herself was later heaved overboard in a layoff. An intriguing contradiction here emerged regarding leadership: women managers were seen by these most junior participants to have better potential than men to lead the kind of change required to make the industry robust again. And those few participants working in women-run newsrooms described connecting with their bosses as mentors and as trusted, respected leaders who knew how to get things done. Yet, at the same time, they did not describe themselves as agents of the kind of *workplace* change that might keep them on the job and contributing to journalistic innovation over the long term, despite their stated sense of personal agency. In general, they could not see their own careers continuing at the pace they currently experienced if they had children, which meant they would be unlikely to help reshape the news culture to help women thrive.

If they were thinking that women other than themselves might lead newspapers to glory, they did not say where those women might come from. Current notions about what constitutes workplace support for mothers – a day-care centre, flexibility in scheduling – were foremost in their vision of the future. Perhaps it would not be so bad to be working mothers; after all, each of their own mothers had been employed outside the home, far more often than described by the older cohorts, and as a result they were already multitasking whizzes. Motherhood was just one more complexity that they, as women, could handle.[18]

Being positioned by their managers as fearless technology users and teachers simply because of their youth was a source of both obligation and oppression. These participants felt managers relied on them to use the many new kinds of media technology best and to instruct older journalists in their use, but at the same time, the general financial panic in newspapers meant their own fledgling careers were constantly in jeopardy. Perhaps not surprisingly then, they spoke less of luck (which, when mentioned, was not associated with class, race or other privileges) and more about strategizing, accommodation, and sheer hard work in their approach to success. With their feet in the door of their dream jobs, they would fight like hell to stay.

While opinions varied on whether the old boys' club inside newspapers had disbanded or was just operating clandestinely, these participants did not see themselves as victims of gender-based discrimination in-house. Still, off the record, one participant told a story about the male editor who had hired her, and who had, she said, "a reputation for hiring young, attractive women." But she noted that she herself had never experienced sexism in the newsroom.

Some of these narrative contradictions and commonly held views came in for review as members of different age cohorts discussed their journalism career challenges in focus groups. What was hidden for some of them suddenly came into sharp relief.

Chapter Five

Of Darkness, Dragons, and Black Holes

The notion that narrative analysis gives priority to individual accounts of events has guided me in the structuring of this book. For that reason, the previous chapters have explored stories that participants told me in one-on-one interviews at each of the five newspapers.

But I also gave participants the opportunity to gather in focus groups to discuss various issues those individual interviews brought to mind, as well as to add any other comments and questions. As narrative-making is a selective process, gathering to compare stories can bring what was not mentioned into the light. This chapter examines dominant themes that arose in those focus groups: aspects of leadership, power/control issues, voice/community impact, workplace frustrations, and generational divides. A key theme throughout the groups and across cohorts was that the participants described, whether played-down or in dramatic terms, two ongoing struggles – one based on their personal positions (age, gender, parenthood status, race, ability) and one emanating from the precarious state of the industry. Accommodating the interplay of these struggles was part of their daily work, as much as doing the journalism was.

Not all participants were able to attend a focus group because of work demands. Kelly Toughill was not included in a group, because she was already head of King's University College journalism program when we spoke. Some participants are not identified so as not to be linked to certain comments they made, and to keep Janet's identity hidden.

The *Spectator*: "What will be left of journalism in twenty-five years?"

The *Spec* focus group, perhaps because the younger cohorts dominated, had the most to say about the mentoring aspect of leadership:

the members needed it. It was also the day after a buyout deadline for which staffers could apply, so weighing career pros and cons was much on their minds. I only knew of one who was considering applying at the time. With two of the youngest participants still on contract and one having difficulties with a new baby, the *Spec* focus group was somewhat tense. It included city editor Carla Ammerata and cityside reporters Emma Reilly, Nicole O'Reilly, and Nicole MacIntyre. In an office meeting room, the participants described how they felt that the individual interviews, held the previous day, were at once cathartic and difficult; they raised issues they had not considered before or thought about, or at least did not voice beyond their immediate peers. In front of their direct supervisor, Ammerata, the three reporters were able to articulate some fears about the future and their generation's attitudes towards the vicissitudes of the workplace. Emma Reilly, who was on contract at the time, spoke forcefully of feeling she could control nothing. Ammerata told them what she had told me, about her own fear of repeating a traditional newsroom management style:

ER: When I think about my career trajectory, I think, "Yes. I would like to be in a position like Carla's at some point. Absolutely." But whether the reality of the industry is going to allow that is another question. So the way I deal with that is to just put my head down. Because it's so beyond my control, it's not even a matter of how well I do my job, it's all these extraneous factors that we've already discussed. You literally just can't think about it. Because if you do, you drive yourself crazy. You think, "What the hell am I doing this for? I'm working so hard and I get nothing." So if I let myself think that way, I can't do my job the way that I am satisfied doing it. There's just darkness, and dragons and black holes.

VS: I see it is. [*To Carla*] How do you respond when you hear that?

CA: I can't imagine what it's like to be Emma's and Nicole's age because I ask myself the very same questions about my career trajectory, and can I actually finish my career in journalism. What will be left of journalism in twenty-five years? So it's a very difficult thing. And because of the economic times, we're in a reactive environment. Even for myself, there's less time for things like professional development, mentoring opportunities. I don't know what is next for me. I told you yesterday, being a city editor was what I always hoped to be, and I'm there. But in terms of what comes next, I don't know. I'm struggling with where I go personally and where the industry is going.[1]

Later, with some interjections and nodding from others, the two also discussed their concern about a kind of competitiveness in the newsroom that was not seen as productive, with Ammerata wanting to draw particular attention to the power of the dominant male culture, and the difference between unhealthy (turf wars) and healthy competition. Even just describing this in the forum of the focus group felt a little dangerous to her, it seemed, since she described the expression of her view as "indiscreet":

CA: We've adopted the male political way to get forward in newsrooms, which is competition not collaboration.

ER: I think that's deliberately propagated by the upper levels of management. That sort of sense that you have to compete and that if you're not competing you're not actually –

CA: And *healthy* competition is a good thing in a newsroom. I'm going to say something. I want to say this. We take our cues from our bosses: at one point we had more managing editors than we do now. And there certainly was a pitched level of competition, to the detriment, I think, of our newsroom at that time. Things have settled somewhat, but I do still think there's a sense, at that level, that it's more about competition and control of their respective areas than, and I'm being indiscreet here, but what is the best thing for the newsroom, right? Collectively.

Vision was also lacking at the *Spectator* because of a lack of resources, said Nicole MacIntyre, causing managers to have to focus on "just getting through the day." The younger reporters said they were less interested in vision as an abstract, wanting instead hands-on leadership, daily guidance, and support that they felt they needed at the start of their careers. After some discussion they began seeing themselves as possibly leading in a different way already, when it came to the areas of training and technology. Ammerata said that yes, they definitely demonstrated leadership in that area. In this way, we can see how a "new story" about work-related orientations could develop from the sharing of the old one, reshaping what they see as being possible for them as leaders.

In terms of personal impact, Reilly and MacIntyre agreed their reporting actually affected the outcome of an election (without describing how), but said they could also see a public backlash against them as reporters, likely caused by people having less trust in institutions generally, including mainstream newspapers. Reilly used an example of personal impact by describing how she wrote a women voters' story during the election, but didn't "get around to do" one on diversity, which seemed to indicate how one seemingly small decision by a reporter could leave a huge range of topics, with diversity at their core, go unreported. Ammerata added that, on thinking more about behaviour patterns inside a shrinking newsroom, changing thinking on diversity "has to be a shift by everybody," and described how she was a member of a community-wide group of leaders looking at diversity in Hamilton. But that was outside the newsroom, which remained overwhelmingly white. She also said she had been in sessions where hiring for diversity was discussed, but had not seen gender equity as an agenda item at a management meeting, echoing the finding that addressing a lack of diversity in newsrooms is low on management's to-do list (Ojo, 2006). "Newsrooms haven't really caught up in a lot of their practices with the rest of the world," said Ammerata.

While many senior women had positioned themselves as victims and witnesses of newsroom sexism, the young participants at the *Spec* felt that they had the individual power to handle whatever "jabs" against women were still happening at the paper, saying in response, "Yeah, throw that at me" and "I am not even going to pay attention to that." Reilly explained it in terms of her understanding of third-wave feminism, its evolution and contradictions:

> We grew up in sort of a post-feminism era. I was born in the early eighties and that was the height of third-wave feminism or whatever. It's almost interesting how there's been a sort of pendulum swing away from feminism. I remember in high school somebody called me a feminist once and I was vaguely insulted and wondered why. It's good to be a feminist.

With two generations of women journalists comparing notes, the *Spec* focus group members saw where they shared ideas about newsroom culture (the idea of an unhealthy competitiveness, for instance) and appreciated each other's angst about the future, in terms of both their own lives and the industry itself, wherever they were in their careers.

At the *Free Press* in Winnipeg, where women dominated the editorial executive ranks, finding a mentor and dealing with a gendered culture were not problems; rather, the collaborative, consultative workplace they created was described almost as an aberration.

Winnipeg Free Press: "There would be a sea of twelve men and me"

The focus group members included participants from all three age groups: Margo Goodhand, Mary Agnes Welch, Melissa Martin (who attended before her individual interview), and Helen Fallding. While some top managers were women, the group members commented on the lack of women elsewhere (in sports and the photo department, for instance). However, the women who were sprinkled around the newsroom were "strong" and showed a "core kind of power," as one younger reporter put it.[2] A question about newsroom leadership prompted one participant to comment on how anomalous the *Free Press* was by practising a "new" leadership style based on communication and collegiality: "I think of newspapers as backwards compared to the rest of the world. Here, it's like exploring the Arctic." As Ammerata had noted in the *Spec* focus group, the newspaper industry in Canada was seen by this participant as a throwback in terms of progressive management techniques. While this focus group differed by the presence of women in the highest editorial office, stories still emerged of the personal and industry-wide struggles that were raging simultaneously as they tried to do their best work.

Editor-in-chief Margo Goodhand compared the working lives of reporters to those of police officers, who also find that dealing with the public can be tough. With 400 to 600 emails a day coming into her computer; with personal abuse heaped on them as individuals by readers who had not even met them; with budgets cut and staff numbers down, she said that the newsroom had to hold itself together as a kind of support group. Recalling how she knew with one job interview the person who should be her deputy, Goodhand illustrated how important it was to her to hire someone people could talk to. One participant commented that many male managers can't or won't do the "talking" work, as that would be perceived as weakness, underscoring the gendered nature of communication in the newsroom. Goodhand reported feeling uneasy in the individual interview, and added how she had wanted to talk more about what she could actually control as editor-in-chief:

> I don't like talking about myself; I'm not used to that. I think it's a control issue maybe, but it's also this, "What is she [VS] hearing, and am I saying the right thing?" I think at this point I feel I've got the paper on my shoulders, too. I don't want to misrepresent the paper. And that's new. I

still came away from it going, "Well did I say – ?" Because I was going to bring up, when we were talking about flexibility in the workplace, what I believe in, ultimately it still has to get past the union. And when Helen tried to go four days a week, I was behind her all the way, but the union felt that what it was, was a management ploy to have people lose full-time jobs. So it was a jobs issue rather than flexibility or even an economics issue.

Melissa Martin, a young reporter without children, described how the lack of younger mothers in the newsroom meant she could not see how creative things such as job-sharing would work. Others in her position said they found parenthood issues "a huge question mark" for them. While men in the office discussed their wives' activities around work and family (such as mommy blogging), those stories were not being told in the *Free Press* pages.[3]

In an exchange about how print journalism was exhausting and unpredictable, Welch offered that the "slightly obsessive nature of journalists" had something to do with the long hours, too; Martin talked about the "adrenaline" factor of rushing to a crime scene. Here, the women seemed to be bonding over the narrative of how journalism is special in its inherent craziness and workaholism, but the discussion also offered hints that they might have the power to change the narrative of journalism, with a better outcome for their work and personal lives.

They also turned their attention to other newsrooms, looking at how others in their situation were handling the work/family negotiations: they talked about the *Toronto Star*, where the group members said "old boys" had been promoted and "really good women are not going anywhere." Things were going backward because of recession fears. While lots of women were working at the CBC, *The National* (the CBC's flagship television newscast) was an exception. Someone joked that with the job description for *The National* they gave out birth control pills.

A few speculated about what would happen if Goodhand left (which she eventually did): the "good stuff" (features, think pieces, policy analysis, and impact) would drop away, but senior management would not recognize the connection between Goodhand's gender and story quality, they surmised. That gave way to stories comparing sexist incidents, including one in which a male manager worried that a woman (the participant who told this story), newly appointed as arts editor, might be too strong a feminist and this lamentable condition would end the glamour and sex of the entertainment section. Here, narrative analysis reminds us of how we position others, as well as ourselves, in terms of our victimhood, accommodations, and agency.

The topic of leadership was discussed in a way that I found fascinating, since the women did not automatically start flattering their top editor, Goodhand, despite their obvious respect for and comfort with her as they sat with her in her office. Instead, Welch and Fallding were singled out as newsroom leaders. Welch was identified for her "backbone" and because she was the president of an industry professional group, the Canadian Association of Journalists. Her beat of public policy meant she was strong and independent, someone who saw the big picture. Assistant city editor Fallding, who later left the paper, was lauded for being a combination of "hard-ass" and supportive, as well as hard-working and extremely bright and fair-minded. Women leaders were seen as less ego-driven (which may be why they did not fawn over Goodhand) and did not practice the authoritative, single-minded approach that men favoured. Female leaders were seen as more creative and collaborative. Men, they speculated, might see that as weak, however.

When sweeping newsroom changes were needed, Goodhand was praised for making "the tough decisions" that her male predecessors did not. She was a mentor, someone to whom a reporter could say "this place drives me crazy" and she would talk that through with them. Goodhand and Fallding recalled how important each one had been to the other in gender terms:

HF: When I first came on city desk, I felt that you were supportive in a news meeting or whatever, if I was nervous, you'd go, "Helen, what do you think?" I don't know if that was conscious.

MG: Helen, I was so glad to have another woman at that boardroom! We had so few, for so many years I was the only woman. There would be a sea of twelve men and me. I was the entertainment editor; I was the girl, right? I got almost used to it. So when Helen came in, holy shit.

HF: But I think you managed to increase my credibility with the guys by looking to me or propping me up.

MG: You always had something to say and it was always worthwhile. I wasn't trying to prop you, I was just glad you were there. I remember one time we had a "women's issue" come up and I was the only woman there, and [the male manager] called [a colleague] in, who's a lovely woman: she designs pages though. He looked out at the newsroom and he couldn't find a woman [journalist] to bring into the meeting to discuss this issue ... I thought it was a low moment.[4]

Today, the focus group agreed, a critical mass of women existed at the paper so that mentorship went up, down, and across the newsroom, as well as over to Red River College, site of the local journalism school, where women reporters and editors were often speakers. But even so, they felt that this was "not a new paradigm" and that the men journalists were "waiting for this to be all over [so] we can get back to being a paper." (Well they might say that: the *Times Colonist* went from having three women in the top three editorial positions to none, and both Fallding and Goodhand have left the Winnipeg paper, leaving men in ten of thirteen newsroom management positions as of mid-2014.)[5] In the meantime, they were living with personal "branding," no longer the anonymous reporters, but high-profile tweeters and bloggers, doing live chats about whatever issue they were covering. As well as being the targets of what they described as misogyny in anonymous comments online, participants felt somewhat positive about opportunities to analyse and even editorialize more, based on having to feed various media platforms. The more broadcast-oriented the platform, the more gender and personality came into play, they felt.

At the *Calgary Herald*, stories were told that highlighted blatant sexism experienced by the older women, as they described in individual interviews, and weighed the impact of new industry-wide uncertainties that the young faced, continuing the theme of intersecting influences. And there was a rare frank acknowledgment of the pure thrill of power. At the *Herald*, you could (gently) poke a stick at authority inside the office, as well as call the powerful to account on the outside.

Calgary Herald: "I didn't know I'd have such a desire for power"

After a long discussion about the evolving nature of competition among and within news media – was it an evolution, a crisis or a rebirth? – the *Calgary Herald* focus group, including Monica Zurowski, Jen Gerson, and Paula Arab, began to discuss how women print journalists today, at least the younger ones, felt that the issues for them were less about gender and more about the insecurity of being young inside the industry chaos. Managing editor Zurowski posited that this could lead to newsroom managers finally having to deal with such issues as flex time and working from home. With so few reporters, editors, and columnists left, senior managers would not remain long in a position to insist that online work be done in traditional ways.

The younger women were able to hear first-hand stories about blatant sexism of the kind that they were not experiencing: a more senior participant, who had previously covered business news at a Toronto paper, told how she would not go "out drinking with the boys" and so her sources, who drank with the reporters, would not take her seriously.[6] Her solution was, she said, to "flirt my ass off," reminding us of the use of narrative to situate/justify/legitimate behaviour in the face of tension between oneself and cultural norms. Reporting, she noted, required her to demonstrate "male traits" such as being tough, assertive, and tenacious. And she added that with friends, she had to learn how to return to behaviours that were more socially acceptable for women, describing an act of constant self-revision.

Men still had the advantage of being taken more seriously, this participant added. Their egos could get in the way, however, so that women had an advantage in that they were less afraid to ask "am I missing anything?" of a source or an editor. This comment bore on a notion that Kelly Toughill mentioned in her individual interview (and will be described further in the next chapter), that newsroom culture did not allow any public displays of journalists learning: one was expected to know things, never to admit ignorance, and suppress fear. The culture of factual correctness is also deeply ingrained, for the important reason of ensuring as much accuracy as possible: if a journalist errs, her/his standard response is to say, "I have to go kill myself right now," as one focus group participant put it.

The definition of mentorship was fluid for this focus group, which gathered in an editorial meeting room. Mentorship was seen as formal and informal, with agreement that it was important for younger journalists to see women doing well in roles typically reserved for men. For a true mentoring relationship to work, the younger person could not just "suck up" to the manager, the rapport had to be genuine.

Underscoring a key theme of being social advocates, the participants described the power of their voices to tell others' stories, to write about social justice issues, and to use, as then columnist Paula Arab put it, "your own discretion and what moves you" as guidelines for topic choice. Arab emphasized the importance of one's "authentic voice" as a powerful tool but one that was difficult to tap into and "believe in." This was easier for her to wield, as she was a columnist. Jen Gerson, as a relatively recently hired reporter, joked that being "at the bottom of the totem pole is a fun place to be" because it allowed her to challenge those in authority both inside and outside the office, with the caveat that she was still learning how to use this tool with care and not "be a jerk." She felt that technological demands put her in a sometimes scary position from which to experiment with social media (such as Twitter) in a way that might get her into trouble, especially with her wry, potentially misunderstood, sense of humour. Her boss, Zurowski, noted with amused understatement (and amid some laughter) that hearing about Gerson's potentially inappropriate tweets was "fine" and that managers were working on how to vet tweets (for taste, libel, and so on), but the number of tweets was growing too fast for them to keep up. Asked to describe the impact of power in her senior job as managing editor, Zurowski, then forty-nine, replied, smiling, "Briefly, it's great," to the sound of uproarious and appreciative laughter. "When I was in my twenties, I would have said I didn't know I'd have such a desire for power," she continued, and then gave a detailed explanation of how she had learned to ask for what she needed from reporters and editors as neutrally as possible, and, she hoped, with a sense of empowering her staff. Here was a rare open expression of a senior woman journalist's desire for power, with a gendered twist of including others in its appropriate use.

One participant told a cautionary tale: a friend, another woman journalist in another city, was let go from her contract after dating a "much, much older" editor. She said she knew of many other such examples that showed a continuing double standard of what happens when newsroom staffers date one another, especially across the rigid hierarchy, where older men have power. It was precisely young women's contract status – they didn't even have to be fired, just not have their contracts renewed – that made them so vulnerable. She described the men involved as "predatory" because they went after impressionable interns, who would then "fade away."

At the *Times Colonist* focus group, the extent of that lingering sexism was seen in a larger context, at the corporate level, even as women celebrated their gains. They ran the joint (even if it turned out to be briefly), and having the freedom and authority to hire was a powerful way to make change. Too bad not much hiring was going on.

The *Times Colonist*: "Still a very male-oriented power structure"

On a day-to-day level, what constitutes a gendered workplace? For some participants in the *Times Colonist* focus group, which took place in the evening at the home of a participant, the newsroom was not

particularly gender-influenced. The group included then editor-in-chief
Lucinda Chodan, then city editor Stephanie Coombs, then online editor
Denise Helm, Petrescu, and reporter Katie DeRosa. Coombs, who we
met in chapter 3, reiterated her view, expressed in the individual interview, that her youth was more of an issue than gender as she negotiated
the workplace. As she had supervised people who had been reporters
and editors before Coombs was even born, gaining respect by doing
her job and respecting staff was the key challenge she felt she had met.

As the most senior manager, Chodan (who had just announced she
would be leaving the *TC* for the larger *Edmonton Journal*) could look
back and see what changes had occurred, and what was still problematic from her generational perspective. Her position at the top of the
paper gave her a closer connection to the chain's new owners and its
board, who were all men:

> I'm so much of a different generation than all of the other people here,
> except you [*gesturing to VS*]. Some of the things that Vivian and I talked
> about earlier were what it was like being a young woman twenty-five
> years ago coming into the journalism profession, and how much it has
> changed, in some ways, since then. But still, I find, barriers or, not barriers,
> really, as much as indices of different treatment of the generation of power
> holders who are older than me, who are predominantly men. So, for me, as
> I'm changing from a leadership role in a small newspaper to a leadership
> role in one of the larger newspapers in Canada, it is interesting.
>
> In the time since we've talked, our company has changed ownership,
> we have announced a senior executive team who've announced a board
> of all males, and [*clears throat*] it is impossible for me not to see that col-
> oured through a gender lens. Because that is the environment that I began
> my career in. It did affect my career in terms of the kinds of mentoring I
> received, and the career path I took, and the treatment I was afforded at a
> very senior table with older men, who were not as enlightened as some of
> the people that we have the great pleasure to work with.
>
> So I would say that my recent experiences at a senior level, becoming
> more senior, have reinforced my feeling that there is still a very male-ori-
> ented power structure, where it's very helpful if we can talk about sup-
> ports. That is the kind of environment in which I will continue to have to
> find a way to move ahead.

As a woman who came up through management ranks at the same
time as Chodan, I found this a powerful statement. As women in our

late fifties who had experienced overt sexism, Chodan and I shared the impact of her story, unlike the younger generation for whom blatant sexism was not imbued with personal memories. The more junior women immediately went back to what they experienced day to day. For them, without having the sense of being face to face with gender discrimination, the glass ceiling, whenever it might noiselessly slide over them, seemed an abstraction. As DeRosa explained, "The corporate side, the male dominance, I think that is still an issue. But in day-to-day function, does it really affect your work? I haven't found that it has."

Chodan gave an example to make the invisible, visible. She suggested how gendered decision-making was possibly at play, when cash-strapped newspapers (she mentioned a few) cut costs everywhere except the travel budget for covering professional (male) sports teams. The discussion moved to why women or men journalists were more predominant in what could be seen as gendered sections of the paper, such as arts, business, and sports. But Chodan was not entirely persuasive. Coombs argued that it was her choice not to write on certain topics:

> But I would ask, are women wanting to do those jobs and being denied them? Or do women not have the interest to do them? Because I think that's the crux of it, is whether women are being denied a job because they're a woman, or if women are saying, "I'm not interested in doing that." Because I frankly am not interested in writing about business, I'm not interested in writing about sports, and I'm not interested in being an editorial writer, an opinion writer. Those are things that don't interest me.

As the most senior editor at the *TC* – and the person who hired, among others, Coombs, DeRosa, and Petrescu, and who promoted Denise Helm – Chodan explained how hiring fit into her management role: nothing else was more important for long-term success. To explain her process, she described several of her hires and how their personal circumstances were not an issue, when they might have been had she used standard (male) hiring criteria. She also used a reminiscence of an event involving a newspaper-chain-wide spelling bee, in which the updates for the bee were threatened by technological problems, and Stephanie Coombs's response:

> LC: I would say that I always pick the best person for the job, because the older I get and the more senior I get, the more I realize that hiring decisions are number one, the most crucial decisions you make when

you run anything. Number two, they are lifetime decisions. They have a life that goes on and on and on. And that's really something I didn't realize as a younger person, and I think that this is slightly different, too. But having said that, I also think that, having chosen the best person for the job, I have not been deflected by things that other people might have been deflected by.

vs: Such as?

LC: Denise is someone with a young daughter. It never would have occurred to me, having worked with her for a couple of years before I offered her the online editor job that she wouldn't figure out a way to make it work. And it has not been an issue. She has never made it be an issue and has always been available, able to accommodate that. In the case of Stephanie, I turned down several wizened men. What convinced me was, remember that night when you were doing the Can Spell spelling bee?

sc: Yes, oh god. Almost poked my eyes out.

LC: She was working at [the *Citizen*], and I was minding the shop at the *TC* and I could see that the whole system had broken down, and so Stephanie was giving updates every ten or less minutes. I can't remember why it broke down, but I just thought, "There is this tremendously bright person on a tight deadline who is making this thing work. Single-handedly." So I wrote a note to the Canwest news service. And [someone] told me, "Actually Stephanie got shit for doing that because she wasn't supposed to be doing it." I just thought, "What a bunch of fucking morons." So, in spite of a lot of pressure to hire somebody else, I thought, "This person is the best person for the job." When I met her in Ottawa, my only question about it was also her age. When I met her I thought, "Oh god, she's a teenager."

For Chodan, this anecdote illustrated how perhaps, if she had been a traditional manager, she would not have hired a young woman but would have yielded to pressure from above to hire somebody else (perhaps one of the wizened men?), who might not have figured out how to circumvent a national-chain-wide technological disaster and then accept being berated for it.

Conversation about leadership focused on the egalitarian nature of the *TC*, where it was felt that mostly managers and staff worked hard together, with constant communication being the essential ingredient to promoting a sense of positive energy, similar to the *Winnipeg Free Press*. Chodan said that it interested her to hear the others talk about things that she believed in, such as respect, communication (including regular performance reviews and goal-setting), and collegiality. These very things were missing from the newsrooms she began in. Interestingly, the participants later spoke of how these same values (but not identified as such by them) were dominant in the *TC*'s use of its new online capabilities. Coombs described using social media in a respectful, professional way to promote "community-building, relationship-building, and seeking out news." Columnist Petrescu used her own fashion blog for community-building, too, to get ideas for columns, find models, and allow interaction with readers. Even though the Twitter account represented a small part of the *TC*'s readership, it was worth building on, which meant saying "thank you" to those who left comments. Hearing about the power, positive and negative, of personal branding online, Chodan said that she was probably "more careful about my personal brand than almost anyone I know." She explained that she wanted the readers "to feel that there is somebody who's impartial and judicious and taking the concerns of every single reader to heart." The other reason for her discretion was that she had been a victim of a stalker in Edmonton, and someone in Victoria had slashed her tires, and she had had to take out a restraining order on the person. So Chodan was "struggling with how to manage [social media use] in a way that was appropriate. She did answer nearly every reader email, however, so they felt that a real person was at the other end. This anecdote marked clearly the often difficult interplay of personal vulnerability and professional expectations.

Chodan did not see any change in how papers approached the development of managers, the DeRosas and Petrescus of the future, which would effectively continue the traditional way of thinking about leadership and who makes a good leader: "I think newspapers are the same as they've always been. They devote virtually no time and energy to developing managers and helping people with their own professional development." She said she would be taking her practice of conducting performance management sessions to the *Journal*, and was curious as to whether they would continue at the *TC* under her successor. That successor was Denise Helm, and she has already left print journalism.

At the Halifax *Chronicle Herald*, the luxury of comparison between staff and management views didn't exist, since the paper had no women managers. Notwithstanding a lack of role models that the other papers had, the participants still felt they had influence in the community and gradually came to feel, through their discussion, that this gave them power. The qualities they had as women who were young or in mid-career, as parents or a person with disabilities, as a black woman journalist: all these things could be problematic, but also empowering. And in their sharing of stories, information came to light that prompted the group to question management's behaviours.

The *Chronicle Herald*: "We can challenge the status quo"

Discussion about leadership had a tone of resignation as the focus group in Halifax began. Only three participants were able to attend the event, held in the same small meeting room as the individual sessions: reporters Sherri Borden Colley and Laura Fraser, and Patricia Brooks Arenburg, who alternated between reporting and copy-editing on the night desk. The three women did not feel they would see a change in the newsroom hierarchy over their working lives, and said they were not seen as leaders in the newsroom by managers, even if they were seen as leaders, mentors, or advisers outside the paper. Borden Colley, who, in her individual interview spoke of quiet determination to combat racism, did begin to speak of hope in other areas where a difference could be made: having fought back against insensitive treatment at the paper when her newborn baby had died, she said that "maybe the next woman who loses a baby won't get a call three weeks after asking her when she is coming back."[7] And even if changes were not coming to the *Herald*, they could hope for change in the larger professional world of work, and "even talking together was therapeutic," she said. Later in the conversation, she indicated that she had actually blazed a trail by being the first person to return to work gradually after her maternity leave. And in response to a colleague who said she did not feel her stories changed the news agenda, Borden Colley said the work they did as women could challenge the status quo, thereby indicating that for her, her racial and gendered background and position (and presumably others characteristics) could be used to inform good journalism and keep her there:

> Another thing that keeps me here is, as women, we definitely add a more sensitive approach to stories. We bring a different perspective because of our experiences as women who face discrimination out in society. You know, we can call wrong "wrong" through our writing. We can say it through someone else's voice. We can challenge the status quo. There's

some fluffy stories that I just don't think should be in the paper because they don't make a difference, but you know, when I go looking for story ideas, I want to tell a story that either educates people on historical things that may have been forgotten in Nova Scotia or I want to write a story that has an impact. At the end of the day, I want my story to have made a difference. And that's another reason that keeps me here. Because as I mentioned yesterday, there's so many stories that have not been told yet and I'm going to remain here until all of those stories are told.

That prompted the others to offer examples of stories that they felt had made a difference in the lives of ordinary people – again, a key theme throughout the narratives in all cohorts. After several stories were described, the reporters agreed that they did have a lot of power, but did not realize it. It also meant a great deal to handle a news story with sensitivity and understanding, such as when a reporter had to go to interview the family of a young person killed in an accident. To reflect and describe that person who had been lost to family and community was an important duty. The victims were once babies whose mothers had dreams for them, said Borden Colley. And that idea, they agreed, was a particularly female perspective.

Laura Fraser, the reporter who had been reticent about mentioning her physical disabilities in the individual interview, told a story about how one of the male managers upset her by calling her "his daughter" and that he was her "Nova Scotia father." As her colleagues interjected in both supporting and teasing ways, Fraser continued telling her story. Interjections from others are in parenthesis and italics; the Xs stand for the names of male reporters:

LF: I called in sick one day, when I was really, really sick. I was like, "Oh, I don't feel well, I'm sorry, I'm going to stay home today." He was like, "Oh, I can hear it in your voice. You just crawl back under those covers and curl up and go to bed." *(Gosh!)* And I remember thinking, "You would never say that to XXX or XXX, you would never." And he said that he was a "little jealous" that my dad was coming to the Atlantic Journalism Awards. *(When you think about it, would he say that to XXX?)*

VS: Is there some aspect of your physical vulnerability, your smallness, is that a part of it, maybe?

LF: I would definitely think that's part of it, *(Oh my god)* but whenever I get sick, whenever I get hurt, this particular person calls me every day, and I had thought at first *(Wow…)* he was concerned about me returning to work. But I think it's the genuine concern about, I think it definitely is, he sort of sees me as this smaller, more vulnerable *(And where you don't have family here ...)* That's a huge part of it for him. *(That must be it.)* But would he do that to one of the male interns? *(He wouldn't, he wouldn't. They wouldn't. They wouldn't.)*

Hearing this story seemed to reveal to the women how fatherly concern from a manager was not necessarily appropriate. But as they were hearing this information for the first time, they also discussed reasons that the manager might realize he differentiated his reporters based on their gender, age, and size. After all, the focus group participants had just started to consider among themselves how his words could be perceived as paternalistic. Fraser continued to describe the uneasy feeling she had about a person she liked, saying he had two voices: the dad voice and the professional voice, and what she wanted was "one homogeneous, professional interaction."

How they each navigated the workplace power structures was not initially connected to any sense of how they might show leadership through their daily journalistic actions. But when Fraser commented that she was not a leader and still felt "junior" in the newsroom, the others told her emphatically that she had "paid your dues" and "proven yourself." Borden Colley described an occasion when an assigning editor had given her a story to write about a woman delivering a thirteen-pound baby, and the editor had done so because Borden Colley was a mother. She insisted that the editor give the story to a male reporter, which he did after some argument, and the story ended up going on the front page. Borden Colley said she had made her argument for personal reasons, rather than out of a sense of being a leader or to challenge the idea that only mothers could write about babies. She joked that had she known the story would have gone on A1, she would not have insisted that a man write it.

Without any women in management, the *Herald* focus group members agreed that there seemed to be no room for advancement, but they still saw themselves as having power to influence the community through their journalism, and that was important. Fraser and Borden Colley assured Brooks Arenburg, who was on the night desk shift every other week, that she had power to affect the news through assigning stories. Fraser also said she could "exercise her power to leave" if the company did not see her as an asset, and that was why she did not worry about having actual newsroom power. If she consistently was not allowed to serve the public the way she wanted through her writing, she had the "ultimate power" to hand in her notice and move on. The participants to be examined next did just that.

Conclusions

In the focus groups, participants at all career stages told "war stories" that seemed to indicate a preference for remaining in the field of journalism doing still-important work, while feeling frustrated by what they saw as inevitable inequalities, and despite no sense of having any control over their futures in the industry. They were working hard to impress the leaders of an industry that won't acknowledge, let alone accommodate, their gendered, age-related needs. They saw themselves reproducing the culture that holds them back, but seemed unable or unwilling to call it to account. Part of this may be due to the nightmare conditions of their dream jobs: barely hanging on to yearly contracts, working over multiple media platforms, teaching technology to older staff, handling family responsibilities along with their careers, managing with dwindling resources, and so on. Given that they were deeply embedded in their demanding daily tasks of doing journalism with a social justice intent, they had little opportunity to analyse critically their own stories about their career situations. Given the opportunity to do so in these groups, they questioned some of the meta-narratives that they worked under and saw that they could be false, or at least contestable.

In one group, several early-career women who had previously thought the newsroom was generally gender neutral, said they were now seeing how differently male newsroom interns were treated, as the male interns had been given hard-news (crime) stories to cover when they, the women, had not. In many cases, younger participants described how having the individual interviews made them appreciate how much had changed for women journalists, how they took for granted that they could do any hard-news beat as well as any man. Along with some aspects of their own privilege, the historic role and difficult circumstances of women who preceded them had been invisible to them. Sharing stories revealed to the women that they did have potential and real power, but did not yet realize it. In Halifax, for example, the women spoke feelingly of their own power to write for the community "good." As they talked, the participants appeared to see glimpses of how it is possible to internalize gendered norms as they negotiated work/family domains.

In her focus group, Nicole O'Reilly said she had much new information to process about her individual interview experience. She had found it surprisingly difficult:

> NO: We were talking about how all my professors were women, and you [VS] said, "Why do you think all your professors were women?" And it was like a light bulb going off. "Oh yeah, that's probably why they were women, because they weren't working in newsrooms any more. Because they were having trouble moving up." I guess I just never thought of it before.
> VS: It may not be true for all of them, but that's certainly my experience as a journalism instructor, and I think for a lot of other women, too.
> NO: To me, they were strong women who were great professors. I never thought their career had led them there for other reasons. If you're not advancing, if you reach a ceiling in the newsroom, and you have a family, you want more time with them.[8]

In this way, the group heard how, generationally speaking, perhaps not as much had changed as they thought in terms of the impact of parenthood on a journalism career. The group discussion also allowed many young women to speak candidly to those senior participants in leadership or "power over" roles, who could make or break their futures, indicating to me a high level of comfort and trust. (The exception was Halifax, where no women managers existed.) For example, Emily Reilly of the *Hamilton Spectator* said, in the presence of her boss, city editor Carla Ammerata, at a time when Reilly was on a contract, that her journalism future seemed like a forbidding place of "darkness, dragons, and black holes."[9] In front of their managers, younger journalists spoke feelingly of their frustrations and vulnerability, even describing how they had been pitted against one another by managers not present. Even if they survived in the industry in the short term, they would endure only to have to "choose" between career and family later on.

These expressions of powerlessness dominated many of the focus groups, whether from the top leaders who felt they could make few changes because of dwindling resources, to contract-level reporters who felt they had barely a toehold in an unforgiving industry. Only Monica Zurowski in Calgary talked frankly about enjoying her power, while Laura Fraser in Halifax said her power rested in a choice to leave if she felt the paper was not giving her what she needed. Those younger women maintained that their youth was often more important a factor in their careers than gender, but continued to see the motherhood/ family issues as defining. They did not connect their forced march towards "choosing" between work and family as a gender issue. In one group, tension arose when younger women described what they saw as a swing away from feminism in Western culture, and how they worried about being seen as "strident" or "whiny." At least one senior participant found that idea troublesome and even appalling. But they eventually agreed that the younger women did not want to be seen as gender victims (echoing the narrative use of positioning); rather, they felt they were so strong they could "handle" sexism, so go ahead, and "throw that at me," effectively reflecting theories of differences between second- and third-wave feminisms.

Even where women held more than one of the top editorial posts, for example at the *Free Press* and *Times Colonist*, the focus groups did not see that situation as marking a trend in the industry towards encouraging female leadership. They were smaller-market anomalies, female-led islands in a testosterone sea. As Ammerata noted in her focus group at a largely male-managed newsroom, "we take our cues from our bosses."[10] Those cues included long hours and encouraging unproductive competitiveness.

The focus groups and individuals who left their jobs were related in a significant way: personal/professional intersections and gendered leadership qualities were key themes in focus groups, which were dominated by younger participants; and the women who left the business – all but one in the oldest generation – cited these themes in terms of their own career fulfilment, both accomplished and left undone.

While one who left said she craved personal decompression, the others exuded a sense that not too many career years remained in which to achieve the heights they had been working towards, and newspapers were no longer conducive to the kind of goals they wanted to accomplish before retiring – or being bought out. The majority of those who left were in the most senior group, and appeared to have abandoned their careers after refusing to internalize further newsroom discourses that younger participants were embracing with trepidation, or accepting with regret and anxiety. If they stayed, it meant being able to continue to fight for themselves, their stories, and their communities, despite industry frustrations and personal exhaustion. If they left, it would be about accepting what appeared to be a sad truth: newspapers were no longer the best place for a skilled communicator to make a difference in the world and where she could finish her long, productive career with pride.

Six Who Walked Away: Frustrations and New Beginnings

Young reporter Laura Fraser told the members of her focus group in Halifax that she could "exercise her power to leave" if her employer did not see her as an asset. If she consistently was not allowed to serve the public the way she wanted through her writing, she had the "ultimate power" to hand in her notice and move on.[1] So far, Fraser – promoted to be city hall reporter for Halifax's *Chronicle Herald* – has decided to stay, as have most others I interviewed. But six have moved on, nearly a quarter of the participant group. To continue to make a difference in the world – and regain a sense of personal equilibrium – they left their newsrooms. Resistance, accommodation, challenging meta-narratives and gendered forms of communication, acting as witnesses and voices, experiencing victimhood: all of these experiences, over time, seem to have pointed these journalists to the door, judging by the narratives they offered me.

Five women have left their newspapers since participating in the study: Paula Arab, columnist for the *Calgary Herald*; editor-in-chief Margo Goodhand of the *Winnipeg Free Press*; acting editor-in-chief Denise Helm, formerly at the *Times Colonist*; Assistant City Editor Helen Fallding, formerly at the *Winnipeg Free Press*; and Janet, who asked to be not identified. A sixth participant, Kelly Toughill, left the *Toronto Star* long before our interview and a seventh, Melissa Martin of the *Winnipeg Free Press*, was forced out through layoffs and then rehired.[2]

Unbeknownst to me, Janet had already decided to leave before the day I interviewed her. Fallding told me she was leaning towards leaving the *Free Press* at the time of the interview and Goodhand acknowledged that she saw her job as having a natural life of no more than five years. If Helm was planning to leave the *TC* when we talked, she gave no hint. Arab, she said, was (like others) in her "dream job" but could see a different future. Whether they indicated they were leaving at the time I interviewed them or not, the five who were yet to leave still spoke of newspapers as places where good work could still be done, but the possibilities were dwindling.

For Toughill, Helm, and Fallding, universities were places where good things could still happen, too: Toughill had become the director of the journalism program at the University of King's College in Halifax; Helm now manages media relations at the University of Victoria; and Fallding runs the Centre for Human Rights Research at the University of Manitoba. Janet, who was older than the others, left full-time paid work, which was causing her increasing frustration, to focus on free-lancing and her family, which included adopted children. Goodhand had several projects in mind and began writing a history of women's shelters in Canada. Arab started her own communication consulting company.

As with many senior participants, Toughill negotiated the children/career paradigm in print journalism with her husband's help. But she left newspapers in order to influence journalism in ways she felt no resource-starved, ham-strung publisher could. Her leadership model demanded visionaries, but what she saw happening in newspapers across the country was just sad, as other participants would find after her.

"My father expected me to be President of the United States"

Kelly Toughill's office in an old King's College building in Halifax was warm on a fall morning, so we had the window open, and the sound of students below filled the air. Eventually, so we could hear each other clearly above their calls and laughter, Toughill shut the window.

Clear communication was the key to her approach to effective leadership; communications as a career was in her bones. Born in Washington, DC, in 1959 to "upper-middle-class" parents, Toughill said her childhood was fairly chaotic, with her mother, a TV news executive, leaving her father, a journalist-turned-congressional-aide, for a fisherman in California.[3] Toughill went to boarding school on scholarship, lived for a time in Mexico, and attended university in Massachusetts before switching to a journalism program at San Francisco State University. She met her husband at nineteen, and credited him for being in a support role for most of their marriage. Without him, including his conveniently being Canadian so she could work here, Toughill said, she would not have been able to do what she has done.

"My father," she smiled, "expected me to be President of the United States." So it was not surprising to hear of her many accomplishments, which included working at a daily newspaper in Florida before putting in twenty years at the *Toronto Star*, where she started in general assignment (replacing a reporter on maternity leave), cycled briefly through the lifestyle section, and went on to cover the HIV/AIDS epidemic full-time, the first Canadian reporter to do so, and winning a National Newspaper Award for her work. She had one more NNA nomination.

At the *Star*, Toughill covered health, Queen's Park (the Ontario legislature), served on the editorial board, and led the paper's Halifax bureau. She turned down an offer for the Washington, DC, bureau, a plum post, because of the long hours and toll that would take on her family. Along the way she earned an MBA from Queen's University. Her final job at the *Star* was as deputy executive editor in charge of newsroom personnel, which involved a weekly commute from Halifax to Toronto. But six months and one titanic management shuffle later, she left the job, realizing her protectors were gone, and that if she were going to influence the next generation of journalists, she could do it "a helluva lot better" at King's than at the *Star*.

Toughill, fifty-one at the time, was the only participant who was no longer in daily journalism before we met. I had decided to interview her because of her unique position as a former newspaper executive with a long journalism career who was now training new journalists for the rigours of the newsroom, or, more likely, the rigours of being their own bosses. She was helping to develop two streams of journalism study; in one, young journalists, schooled in everything from writing and interviewing to videography and running their own business, could make their way into the new multimedia world as journalist/entrepreneurs; the other stream offered investigative skill development. Her career experiences and position as a female mentor made her a pivotal figure for this study, giving her a long view forward and back and a synthesizing perspective. Indeed, a year after we first talked, we met again and she offered a compelling insight about the power of shame in newsrooms, particularly when it came to journalists' fear of being seen to learn something, and to make mistakes while doing so. She saw how the "I don't want to look stupid" discourse had bullied journalists for years, particularly women, and was thankful that now it was being challenged by techno-friendly young reporters.[4] As more of the older participants – they were all in their late or mid-late career years as journalists – began to leave their newspapers after the interviews were held, her story took on larger importance in the study, as a kind of foreshadowing of the others. In particular, new ways of serving society were apparently on the minds of those who left, but accomplished without further loss of self.

That feeling of needing greater personal agency in her work led much of Toughill's career trajectory. Having read her work and talked to her on the phone, I knew Toughill could tell a great story about those seminal events. Here she described her first day at the *Star* in 1986:

KT: There was [an] editor who was somewhat infamous. And he was an asshole. My first day at work I came in and XXX was then the city editor, and he said, "That guy over there is your boss. Go talk to him." So, I didn't have a desk or a phone. I knew nothing about the place whatsoever. I went over and said, "Hi, I'm Kelly Toughill. I'm the new reporter." He said, "Oh, yeah. Toughill." Then he looked up and he said, "So, Toughill, you've heard of Flannery O'Connor right? *A Good Man Is Hard to Find*." And I said, "Yeah." And he said, "Do you think a hard man is good to find?" That was my first conversation in the newsroom with my boss. It kind of set the tone.

VS: Do you remember what you did? Were you shocked or, "Oh, that's newsrooms"?

KT: No, I was stunned. That level of overt sexism was quite surprising to me. But I was on contract and I was a big girl so I said, "Oh, gee, I haven't really thought about it because I haven't been looking for one."

VS: Would you say that tone was pervasive or just random sorts of guys were like that?

KT: Well, XXX had huge power over the general assignment pool. He liked to play favourites. He was profoundly sexist and homophobic. [*pause*] What's her name? The woman who swam all five Great Lakes?

VS: Um ... Cathy somebody?[5]

KT: The reason I can't remember her name is that the only way he ever referred to her was the "dyke mermaid." So that atmosphere was certainly condoned by all sorts of people. That did change considerably over time. Partly through women pushing back.

VS: Mmm hmm. That's the way it happens, yeah.

In this example, Toughill handles the tension between herself and the dominant structure, as represented by her homophobic, sexist boss, by playing along despite being stunned, since she was a powerless contract worker. Her challenge to that behaviour came later: Toughill recalled part of the resistance came from the establishment (by two women feature writers) in the late 1980s of a so-called women's caucus of reporters and editors (including a recruited Toughill), which addressed issues of content and newsroom equity. She didn't recall the details, but noted that the caucus benefited the women involved, as their numbers gave them clout. One well-known male journalist told her he was "clearly afraid" of the caucus, and that made her feel that it "was kind of nice to realize there was a sense you couldn't fuck around with us [women] quite as much as in the past because there was an organization."

Toughill told many stories about life as a young woman journalist, including how she was nearly fired for writing a story that infuriated a *Star* board member, but was kept on because her boss (mistakenly) thought Toughill's husband was unemployed. "I was a woman who needed to be taken care of," in her boss's view, she recalled.

Several times she mentioned how important it was to break ground in her reports. She first thought she would not like the dull repetition at the Ontario legislature (Queen's Park), for instance, but quickly found how to enjoy it:

> I discovered there were all sorts of stories at Queen's Park that nobody was doing but the *Star* was happy to put them on the front page. I was again in a position where I was doing lots of stories that nobody else was doing and I really liked that because I was not interested in the political stuff. I was interested in the policy stuff. So, if it had anything to do with health, education, or welfare, the rest of the bureau didn't care about it. So all of the people stories, how people were affected [by] what was going on at Queen's Park, my bureau didn't care. They cared about who was up incrementally and the polls and the inside jockeying in cabinet and all that other stuff that I didn't care about.

Toughill supports the notion here that women reporters tend to feel their best work is based in reporting social issues such as health and welfare, as Beam (2008) argued. Central to Toughill's concept of her success in this area was how she defined vision, which was the idea that she usefully zigged where other journalists zagged. As a younger reporter imagining herself as a senior newsroom manager, she could see a loss of control and independence, and hence, a loss of personal vision. Now, as journalism school director, she described a clear vision of how the new curriculum ought to go and the path to its creation. In newspapers, especially inside of the "Medici court" of the *Star*, Toughill saw limits to a hierarchical management early on:

> When I was pregnant with my first child, I remember XXX, who was then our editor-in-chief, taking me out to lunch and saying, "Well, do you want to come into management when you come back?" I said, "Not really." And he said, "Don't you want to be editor-in-chief someday?" And I said, "Not really." And he said, "Why? Why don't you?" And I said, "Why would I want to? I can have so much more influence, frankly, as a really good reporter than I am going to have as an editor-in-chief who will last maybe three years and then get kicked to the curb."

She was motivated to exercise power doing what she called "my own journalism," that of the reporter with direct access to the readers, influencing their interests and priorities. Toughill reasoned – with *good* reason – that in the cut-throat business of news, her tenure as editor-in-chief would be short, with a nasty and brutish end. Interestingly, this event took place when she was pregnant, which is not usually a time when women are assumed by their most senior managers to be eyeing the top job, as stories in this book illustrate. This editor-in-chief appeared to understand that successful careers are built over time and many experiences. Or perhaps he toyed with her because he figured she'd quit, as so many other women did and do.

Now, as the head of a journalism program, Toughill was in a different place, "in a significant leadership position." She noted that the leadership structure at the university meant she was constantly in meetings with "women of power," along with men, giving me the list of names. Her excitement was palpable as she described the group that was restructuring the journalism program, how the team members involved communicated well, describing communication in gendered terms. We compared the discourses of academia and journalism, with Toughill first describing her curriculum development meetings:

> KT: It is the most constructive group I have ever been part of. We talk about, "Okay, what are the obstacles? How do we resolve people's interests and then how do we find a solution?" And there is no jockeying over who has dominance. I really think it's a gender issue. These are

the most satisfying meetings I've ever been in. There are substantial disagreements about what is going to be done but it's not personal and it's not ego-driven and it always seems to be about the work, not about the people around the table. And maybe some of that is journalism versus academia, although academics are not known for having really small egos either.

vs: When I think of journalism and academia, there is a social justice/social service component to both. Obviously, the newspaper is a profit-driven company but the work that journalism does is around social justice and particularly for crusading papers like the *Star*. But the academy has a social-justice orientation in my view. Because of the work they do and because they are public bodies spending public money.

kt: Yeah. I'm always very conscious of having to translate what I said at the *Star* in any news meeting. You know, I didn't use the same language constructs in a news meeting that I would use at my kitchen table.

vs: How so?

kt: I haven't analysed it specifically, but I was always far more careful and conscious of what I had to say in any news meeting. There was a barrier to communication and those were meetings of almost all men. I am just not finding that in these meetings. I'm finding that people understand what I am saying. I was used to having to repeat myself three times. First time just to get heard, you know? And the second time to get the ideas across, and the third time to do the convincing. And now I only have to say it once.

Her story about deafness at meetings offered an explanation as to why an intelligent, energetic, and ambitious woman might exit print journalism despite understanding – and relishing – the idea that her role as a reporter gave her the power to influence social policy. You might leave because you had to explain an idea three times to your bosses, day after day, trying to cut through another language understood by those men at the management table who decide what stories run and where resources go. She acknowledged, with humour, the substantial size of the academic ego, but was experiencing a different kind of communication in meetings with her university colleagues, one that she felt allowed each person to speak once and be heard.[6]

Her message for her young journalism students (60 per cent of the student body in her program was female) was that the journalism school power dynamic had changed – "the women in my program do not have less power in any way than the men, if anything it is the opposite" – and that the management structure she encountered as a young journalist was now essentially in chaos. Therefore young reporters had to be "really aggressive" in order to "survive the newsroom politics," and would stay only if they understood the work they were doing was significant, ideas that the youngest cohort in my study confirmed through stories of their experiences. She pulled together the notion of how technological flux provided the space for diversity to take root in a print newsroom culture that allowed only white, educated, (at least) middle-class men, reminding me of how many decades print newsrooms operated without diversity, compared to more recently created broadcast newsrooms:

> Women definitely have more opportunity now because the entire industry is in flux. Any time you have this level of chaos there are fresh opportunities. So, when I went into the *Star*, I went into a place with a very calcified hierarchy that had been around for a very long time, and the basic theory is that you hire and promote people that look like you and sound like you and feel like you. And if you are a woman or a person of colour or somebody that didn't grow up educated and from [the] middle class, that put up huge barriers in the newsroom that were self-perpetuating.
>
> But things are being blown up pretty dramatically right now. So I think there's all sorts of opportunity, in terms of how widely news gathering is spread across the population now. This whole new function of managing those inputs didn't exist before and that's a big part of what journalism education needs to figure out how to teach. But you look at the hierarchy on TV news programs and it was far friendlier to women than newspapers, and that's because those structures were created in the 1950s and 1960s, not the 1880s.

The challenge, as Toughill saw it, was to turn natural observers – the journalist's classic role – into managers of their own brand, with the skills to market themselves in this new, fractured world of news-gathering and dissemination, as well as acquiring journalistic skills. The trick was not only to report stories that mattered but also to "think about how those stories fit into the media landscape, and where the money is coming from," meaning journalists needed to discern how to get paid, including studying tax law, incorporation, and advertising. Her approach aligned with her credo of journalism, which was to have the confidence and skills to report stories others did not. We agreed young women would not find that confidence by reading or writing for women's magazines, which cultivated what Toughill called an "attitude of cheerful self-loathing." Freelancing for such magazines, sadly, is what many young women writers end up doing.

She told me why she stayed in journalism so long, a turning-point tale that also launched us into a pessimistic musing on how mainstream newsrooms could suffer even more as the ground under their sclerotic feet trembled and women sought career happiness elsewhere:

KT: There was a really pivotal moment for me. I'd been at the *Star* a year, or eighteen months, and I had every crap general assignment that you could possibly be given and I was given another one. I think it was literally like a cat show or dog show. There was a day when I was thinking, "I can't do this job for anybody but myself. I cannot try to please these people in this newsroom. If I do that, I will not survive. That will be a soul-sucking experience that will destroy me as a journalist and the only thing I can do is take every single one of these assignments and find something that excites me, and I don't care what the angle was that I was given," and that changed everything at the *Star*. And that's very hard to do as a manager. You know? So I could work with a lot of independence within a wildly sexist organization as a reporter, but it would've been difficult as a manager.

VS: You almost paint a picture, or maybe I'm inferring too much, of how the hierarchies of newspapers will be slow to change if the bright young things, who you are training here, and I'm hiring as an editor, decide to do other things because the landscape is changing [outside of mainstream newsrooms]. It's almost as if –

KT: There are opportunities now that didn't exist before.

VS: So if women take those other opportunities, the newspapers become, by definition, more irrelevant and more calcified and more dead.

KT: It's sad. A lot of what's happening in the newsroom right now is sad.

While Toughill still saw jobs at newspapers and radio stations in particular as being good training grounds for journalists, the days were gone when a reporter could win a National Newspaper Award, be given a trip to Brazil as a bonus, have the freedom (or chutzpah) to charter a plane into the Amazon without checking with managers first, and write about the environmental impact of Canadian dams in Brazil and the treatment of the people there. Toughill did all that, but nobody could today, probably not even Toughill. The resources have dwindled, and with them, many possibilities for doing groundbreaking

work. Whatever emerging journalists can accomplish, her stories suggested, will come from what an enterprising person can create and
sell in the jumble of stalls that make up the marketplace of new
media.

Janet had many similar career experiences that led her to conclude,
as Toughill had, that capitulation to the dominant culture was not an
option. For Janet, however, speaking truth to power was becoming
increasingly infuriating. First gender and now age were becoming
marks of perceived inferiority, and she felt powerless to stop it. She
was too tired to fight anymore.

"He golfs with the managing editor!
I can't compete with that"

At Janet's office, we met in the cafeteria, but at her request we moved
to a small, private lounge adjacent to the women's washroom. For personal reasons, she asked to be anonymous. She wanted to vet any detail
that she felt might identify her, since only five papers were involved.[7]
Janet focused on her passion for social justice clashing with the injustices of a newsroom where management perpetuated sexist behaviour
and coverage. She felt frustrated by younger women journalists who
didn't seem to see how complicit they were in allowing the situation
to fester.

A typical senior-level participant demographically, Janet was in her
fifties, a white Canadian, had a liberal arts degree, and had grown up
in a middle-class household with two parents and siblings. A multi-
award-winning reporter with a passion for social justice, she had been
reporting for more than twenty-five years and, unlike many in her age
cohort, did not describe luck as influencing her career.

Janet recalled details of long-ago sexist incidents (such as male editors sending women reporters across the newsroom to get something
so that the men could watch them move) with frustration and anger
still apparent. She described going into managing editors' offices over
the years to voice concerns about the lack of women editors in news
meetings and how "twelve white guys, balding, paunchy, go in there
to decide what to put in our paper," and all they seemed interested in
was the courts, crime, and city hall, plus local male sports teams.[8] Even
their hobbies excluded her. Of one male reporter held in high regard by
management, she cried out: "He golfs with the managing editor! I can't
compete with that."

Janet said years of protest earned her the reputation of being "a troublemaker" and "the office fembo." However, in the mid-1990s, one manager finally asked Janet and a few other women to document their concerns about the lack of women managers. This resulted in a report that was supported by some male colleagues, but other men in the newsroom responded by calling the women involved "the thought police," she said. A committee to study the news pages for male bias was struck, including men and women, but it soon collapsed in disarray. Ultimately, only one woman was promoted to mid-management, and, according to Janet, this woman felt the hostility of the men who saw her as being promoted solely because of her gender.

Janet recalled having always had a difficult time persuading editors to run her stories about social justice matters; even when her beat was called "diversity," the problems persisted. When we met, she had four stories from the diversity beat sitting in "overset," the electronic folder where newspaper editors keep stories they have decided can wait for a rainy day. Often, partly to feel the security of a full pantry, they never let that day come. Said Janet:

> I have a personality where I'root for the underdog. It's a really good trait to have on social issues. Because I'm good at interviewing people who are homeless, bipolar, abused women, kids who've been sexually molested, those are my people. I often joke about that but they are. And I love them. I want to tell their stories because their voices are not being heard. That's my personality. And now my beat is also diversity, so for the last year, I've been covering diversity. And again, I was thrilled! Because I wanted to tell the stories of people who come here from Pakistan and Rwanda, and everything else. But it's the same thing, I can't get their stories in the paper.

Janet felt her best work put a spotlight on social issues, as more women reporters than men have said they do in the literature. Toughill had said the same. Janet explained that the issues she covered were still considered "soft news" so that most of her stories about social justice issues, people's "tragedies and triumphs," ended up in the lifestyle section, alongside the "lipsticks and recipes and fashion and a whole page on celebrities." She said her career had stalled because she negotiated an eight-to-four shift so she could be home for her children after school. The "optics" were bad, because others stayed until 6 p.m. But of course, they were not in the office when she arrived at 8 a.m. Otherwise, said

Janet, the paper was not flexible about childcare. She blamed "the male culture. Definitely, absolutely long hours. Lack of flexibility and even issues around going part-time and [taking] time off and taking your kids to doctors' appointments."

Janet saw the future of journalism as a mixed bag for women because they were "better multitaskers" than men, which meant they would be seen by managers as capable of blogging, tweeting, taping video, and reporting simultaneously for twelve hours a day. As for her own career, Janet said that the sexism she has experienced was now intersecting with ageism.

Soon after my interview with Janet, she left her newspaper. She had become "too tired to fight" anymore. The next time I saw her, nearly a year after our first interview, Janet looked like a new person: twenty pounds lighter, her face brighter, and exuding good health. She said she had felt her anger and bitterness disappearing as she had more time for her family and personal writing projects. Still, she thought a lot about workplace issues for women, such as being sidelined during and after maternity leaves and "the acceptance that comes with that."[9] And she was concerned about the "whole push to get boomers out" of newspapers and other workplaces. This rankled, because boomers "come with a lot of context and background, and knowledge and everything that's been really disregarded."

When I asked Janet whether she thought that news media reflected reality in society or played a part in creating it and perpetuating stereotypes, her response started an exchange that ended with Janet making an astute observation about the double standard of newsgathering, wherein reporters exuded power when out on the job, but when they returned to the oppressive cultural atmosphere of the office, they wilted. For women journalists, this meant a continual reinforcement of their historically unequal status, particularly as they became mothers and as they aged:

J: I've heard women say at meetings, that it's a 24/7 business, and that's what they always fall back on and that's why we can't change, and that's why we have to work fourteen-hour days if you're the senior editor. I just don't buy it. If you look at new, progressive businesses, like I've heard the way the Google office works, there's a 24/7 business. They bring their dogs to work, we are still locked into the old, industrial revolution of the 1920s; hard work means you're a good person. We're still locked into that! We could be working at home, there's telecommuting, so I don't buy that.

So many people used to say to me, "I can't believe you're dealing with all that stuff now, newspapers are supposed to be thought of as so progressive, because you write about that stuff, like sexual harassment." And I went, "Oh no!"

vs: That brings in a central issue that I want to write about.

j: Like can it change?

vs: Women I've interviewed often express the notion that you've identified, that that's the way it is, that's "the way the culture works," and we have to negotiate ways to fit into that, right? Or be sidelined, or leave.

j: Right, right.

vs: At the same time they don't talk about themselves in power terms but they say, "I give voice to people who don't have a voice." Or "I can affect how people vote because of what I write about city hall. I can bring out issues."

j: So a very powerful job.

vs: So they describe themselves in the job as being powerful. But if you say, "So if you were to take that power and apply it to this [equality] work, or to – "

j: To make change in the office or the newsroom.

vs: Yeah, why is there such a disconnect there?

j: And what do they say it is?

vs: They –

j: They're scared.

vs: Some are, and some don't see it.

j: Keep your head down, don't make waves.

vs: Right, yeah, and they also see it as a larger societal thing, like we're just reflecting society, the idea that women have to do the mothering, and all that kind of stuff. So why do you think that disconnect is still so powerful?

j: When I started here, there was a real kickass guy, everybody loved him, and he said to me, "Why is it management always expects you people to be tigers out in the community and wimps in the office?" I remember thinking that is so true! We are in a job where you are expected to be extroverted, like you walk into a meeting with 200 people, and you might have to go on stage, you're going around talking to people –

vs: Yeah, push your microphone into somebody powerful's face.

j: Yeah, you have to be assertive, aggressive, and also phoning people and insisting they talk to you. There are all sorts of components of our business that require you to be [a] very assertive and passionate person. And you're absolutely right, we come back to the office and we're all supposed to be these "yes" men and "yes" women. And that's a huge, huge source of frustration for people.

Kelly Toughill had had the insight about journalists' tendency not to want to appear vulnerable by learning something new (like blogging) in view of colleagues who might snicker. Janet hit on a related notion that journalists had a strong, crusading face in public and a weak, appeasing side in the office, which was echoed by Nicole MacIntyre at the *Spectator*. The male-dominated newsroom culture seemed to demand a narrative that fit the strong, silent hero, a man who cannot be seen to acquire any skills but magically had them, and who questioned the powers-that-be in public office fearlessly, never showing disloyalty to the culture from which he had sprung, fully formed. Women journalists went along with the good guys/bad guys approach, the conflict paradigm, suppressing their own views or voting with their feet, said Janet. She came up with other possible ways of conducting business, including running the city desk in a more relaxed way. Otherwise, women leave the business:

> Yeah, there's breaking news, but a lot of it is just smoke and mirrors. It's that old-school, macho thinking of "got to get the news out" [*claps hands*]. Well, technology has made it quite possible for us to do things differently. Working from home, and more flex time, more benefits for part-timers, there should be all that sort of thing.

Another thing still bothered Janet, and that was the idea, expressed to her by a few of the younger women in her focus group held months earlier, that she "paid the price" for her forthright criticisms by being sidelined, never to reach management. Janet did not see herself that way. She mentioned this in both of our interviews, nearly a year apart. How could those other women journalists have seen her as sacrificing her career options, when the only other choice was to censor herself and not to speak honestly about the situation in the newsroom for women? This story of sustained resistance showed how she might ultimately become tired enough to retreat, and give priority to her family and her own writing.

At the focus group meeting that she and other participants attended, Janet ardently took on the interviewer role from time to time, asking the younger women if they still saw a glass ceiling, as there were no top female managers, and commented on their vulnerability as contract employees. Janet acknowledged that before this discussion, she had not thought of the younger women as newsroom leaders in terms of their informal roles as technology teachers. Janet dismissed the notion that older reporters could not handle new technologies well, noting that she had had a laptop for years and was still not recognized as an office "early adopter." Technological understanding was something Janet felt older reporters had and could develop, if trained and encouraged. She was still vehement about the newspaper's "macho" editorial culture being "absolutely entrenched" in the late twentieth-century media discourse that defined feminists as "victims and whiny man-haters" and that the newsroom was "blinding in its whiteness."

Similar themes of tiring in the face of a persistently male-dominant culture ran through Helen Fallding's story, along with a sense that mentorship by women made all the difference in her wanting to stay. But even that was no longer enough.

"Newspapers are structured in a way to squeeze people to death"

A proud and self-confessed "shit disturber," Helen Fallding was fifty and the assistant city editor of the *Winnipeg Free Press* when we spoke. She told me about how, when she was starting in newspapers, an interviewer at the *Ottawa Citizen* looked at her résumé, which included feminist organizing and running women's centres in Victoria and Toronto, and asked if Fallding thought her interest in social justice would be "a problem" in the newsroom. "My answer at the time," she told me with a laugh in the *Free Press* cafeteria on a winter afternoon, "was that 'I don't expect you'll be hiring me any time soon to write your editorials.'"[10]

Fallding wasn't hired for the reporting job that day fifteen years ago, either. Like Janet and Toughill and the others, Fallding was committed to promoting social justice through her work, but had recently felt that she had hit a wall. Hers consisted mainly of white male baby boomers who were getting in the way of her continuing to make an impact.

The youngest of three girls, Fallding was born in Australia to a biologist mother and sociologist father, who also was a published poet. They moved around the world, which she said programmed her to be adventurous and "totally flexible about where I lived." They settled in Waterloo, Ontario. By nineteen, she was part way through a biology degree when she began to experience sexism at the University of Guelph, so became involved in feminist organizing on campus. She stayed for some years in the Yukon after moving north for a summer job. Fallding turned to journalism in her early thirties to satisfy her social justice itch, which had been put in place by her mother. Her mother, she said, "was one of those women who broke every barrier there was and she raised her three girls to think we could do anything. We would run across other people who tried to stop us and it pissed me off."

Fallding had taken time to consider my questions before we met: her responses were nuanced, thoughtful, and succinct. The words "justice" and "injustice" and "social justice" came up often as she explained her approach to journalism as a reporter and in how she assigned stories as an assistant city editor. Her position put her between staff and management. On the one hand, she assigned reporters and handled copy and their problems as a sister union member, and on the other, she influenced managers, who counted on her to help with their decision-making. Reporter Mary Agnes Welch called Fallding the newsroom's moral centre and an astute judge of its politics. Her biggest problem, Fallding said, was a dearth of reporters to assign.

The initial mention of a characteristic that might affect her career came when I asked Fallding about her first reporting job at the *Free Press*, which she joined in 1998, when she was recommended by a friend who worked at the paper. She was hired as the Brandon correspondent:

> HF: I'm a lesbian and I don't think they would have hired me for that job if they'd known ... I was strategic and didn't mention anything about my partner until my probation period was over. But in some ways, it was my big journalism break to get into a bigger paper, and I just don't think it would have happened –
>
> VS: Well, sexuality is off limits in terms of hiring, but you felt that even if they had known somehow?
>
> HF: You know there are so many factors in hiring. They wouldn't have to say anything. Lots of people applied, somebody else gets the job. And Brandon was fine.

Institutional hypocrisy on the issue of same-sex rights showed up early. After being hired, Fallding said she had to threaten the paper with a human rights challenge in order to get benefits for her partner. The paper had previously taken an editorial position in favour of same-sex benefits, but it would not extend them to its own staff, based on an argument, she recalled, that the paper at that time had an American-based owner. It took months for her to gain those rights, with support from the union. She was the only participant who told me that she was homosexual. If others were, they did not say so. I did not ask that question of anyone. But sexuality seemed otherwise not defining for Fallding at work, just one part of her identity that also had its advantages:

HF: Once everybody got over that [*laughs*], that's been a non-issue in terms of my work life. It's been an advantage in an odd way in terms of some sources that I work with.

vs: How so?

HF: I had an Aboriginal leader give me his personal cell phone number and call me all the time with scoops, and he said he was doing that because I understood what it was like to be a minority. And he just thought that I listened to him in a different way and he thought that's what it was about.

Gender, for example, was more important in her sense of how she did her journalistic work. Fallding went from covering Brandon to becoming a legislative reporter, during which time she found that, like Toughill, she was not interested in covering politics the traditional way:

HF: I felt like I had to learn to be interested in horse-race style politics. I'm a political person but not in that way. I'm interested in issues and I think women tend to be more the "how does this affect me, how does this affect the kids at school, how does this affect the food bank," than "does Mr. X have more power than Mr. Y right now?"

vs: The minutiae of jockeying and that kind of stuff.

HF: Which has totally fascinated whoever I'd been reporting to, so I felt like I had to develop, I had to steer myself in the direction that didn't interest me and I wasn't sure interested our readers, but it interested my guy editor. I can do it, it's just I'm not sure that's the direction the paper needs to be going in.

vs: There's this idea of holding our government leaders to account and that piece of journalism is important, but that still gets all the attention in terms of the horse race. The "who's on first today, who's up in the polls today," reading the tea leaves of who has power, as opposed to "what are they doing with it"?

HF: And my sense is that the political reporters who came before me, what fascinated them was power, and what fascinates me [are] issues.

vs: Do you think that the being-fascinated-by-the-power approach to political reporting has an impact on how society organizes, or how society responds in terms of a political agenda, in terms of a social agenda?

HF: I think it's part of why people tune out, why readers tune out. We don't get great readership on our political reporting, and all those people who don't vote. I think if you're not into that, it's like if you're not into football, if you're not into that particular game, it doesn't interest you and that has frightening implications for people's disengagement from politics. Because we're not making clear to them the connection between their everyday life or [their] children's aspirations and what's going on politically.

Her observations on how leaders' decisions affected work life were pointed: she had been hired after the *Free Press*'s "lost generation" of women was finally noted (a large group of women had left the previous decade, largely due to family and newspaper-culture clashes), and then she felt that perhaps it was only because management thought she was younger than she was. "There was a whole history of women coming back from maternity leave and saying, 'I'm wondering if I could work part-time for a couple of years because my kids are little?' and they'd be like, 'No. If you want to work part-time go to McDonalds.'" The fact that the number of racialized minorities was close to zero in the newsroom of more than 100 people shocked her. She felt the newsroom was "highly racist" and that sexism had only diminished because of Margo Goodhand's leadership: she no longer felt she had to ration her opinions on sexism as before, when she feared being "slotted as the feminist to be ignored," as Janet had felt. With women in the top jobs, Fallding said, she could do things like write "twenty-five stories on water and sewer issues in the First Nations. But that would not have happened without [a senior editor] and Margo because they thought it was important and I think the guys that preceded them would have gone, 'Well, Indians don't buy the paper.'" Male managers' assumptions affected her in her role as an assigning editor, too:

Most of us have had abortions or have friends who have. So we know what we're talking about and most of the guys I'm surrounded by have more of a sense of it as a theoretical issue. I have to remind them, "Probably one in every three women here has had an abortion and probably even higher because career women, a lot of them probably wouldn't be in this job if they'd had an unwanted pregnancy that they'd carried through with." So stop thinking of it as a marginal or religion issue, this is the real life of regular women, and that's the way that we need to approach it. Not make some weird assumption about the kind of women who have abortions being not the kind of women who read our paper. About it being some unethical fringe ... "Guess what guys? It's a mainstream reproductive health issue."

To the extent Fallding felt she succeeded, it was "because women absolutely every step of the way" helped her. That mentorship continued,
with a lot of "sisterhood in this organization at this moment and I certainly try to do that for younger women coming up." But she also saw
pretty student interns getting more attention from the male editors. She
found herself watching who got help from "the guys" and who actually
needed help, feeding "story ideas to the smart ones so they'll have a
better chance." Even a shit-disturber has to work the system discreetly
sometimes.

Fallding told me she was being recruited for a university job and
not to tell anybody. I didn't, just as I kept similar secrets about other
participants. She was leaning towards taking the post, since her partner was tired of her long, unpredictable hours – they did not have
children – and the new emphasis on web-driven news meant assigning more breaking-news stories and less issues-related journalism.
The newsroom was shrinking, so her worst days revolved around
not having enough reporters to assign. As a commercial enterprise,
"newspapers are structured in a way to squeeze people to death"
and all she wanted was to keep doing "some good in the world."
Fallding was able to carry on doing that as she did take a leave to
become manager of the Centre for Human Rights Research at the
University of Manitoba soon after. In the fall of 2012, she officially
left via a voluntary buyout.[11]

Like Fallding and Toughill, Denise Helm of the *Times Colonist*
switched to a university job after a long career in journalism. But she
did not speak of any such plan or idea when we spoke, focusing on
journalism as her "calling." If talking about the importance of "personal
growth" and doing "work of purpose" was a hint that she had topped
out at the newspaper in that regard, I missed it completely.

Mainstream Media Lacks Diversity, but
Still Can Change Society for the Better

Denise Helm, as online news director for the *TC*, described how she
was responsible for bringing more readers into the daily's Web pages
and related that to the industry's need for diversity in its newsrooms.
Newsroom diversity, or lack of it, was an issue for her, as was leading collegially and by example. Helm felt she needed to have personal
satisfaction and growth, as well as a sense of purpose in her work, and

spoke of how personal subjectivity could constructively be brought to bear on journalism:

> I think journalism is more of a vocation than a job. I presume, because it was true for me, perhaps not for a lot of people, but journalism is a calling and I've always seen it as a calling. I feel that there's an amount of community service and community purpose to it and to me that is a very rewarding, the most rewarding part of the job.[12]

She described how she was born into a middle-class family in Vancouver, the fourth of six kids, part of a household where newspapers were important. Like many participants, she had been a strong English student in high school. Growing up, she had felt a little bit like an outsider, not a rebel like Fallding but a curious observer, which turned out to be a good fit for journalism. Helm's mother was a homemaker and her father was the executive director of a network of neighbourhood houses on the Lower Mainland, overseeing an organization that did a lot of community-based work and what she considered "work of purpose."

Her interest in media didn't come into play until Helm took a solo travel break to Europe in 1980 before completing her third year of an undergraduate degree in international relations from the University of British Columbia. She was interested in social issues, and storytelling and journalism, but didn't know if she was "hard-nosed and hard-headed enough" for newspapers. But with the European trip having widened her world view, and after a stint of volunteering in Nigeria, she excitedly took a certificate course in journalism at Langara College in Vancouver.

After working at a number of papers around British Columbia, Helm began thinking about being married and having a family, and also wanted to be closer to her own family. She began at the *TC* in 1991, thinking she would stay only a few years, but was there twenty years later, having been a reporter, columnist, press gallery reporter, assistant city editor, city editor, and online news director.[13] She had always believed, and still did, that journalism was worthy work: "Media can help people make decisions about their lives and can help change for the better your community and your society," she said. Being a middle child, said Helm, was partly why she made a better observer/reporter than commentator: she was better at empathizing and seeing all sides of an argument than trying to persuade people to a point of view. That notion of the singular perspective of mainstream media was troubling to her, with personal attributes both keeping certain people out of news-rooms and keeping current journalists from getting good interviews:

> DH: I would say the mainstream media do not reflect the demographics because I don't think you see working-class, marginalized people. When I look, for instance, at British Columbia newsrooms, it's white, middle class, and the advertisers are aimed at that same white, middle class. I suppose my appearance and gender and middle-class upbringing allow me entrance into certain news-gathering situations that someone who would be more extreme in their appearance or personality might not have access to. Being, appearing, and looking part of that "safe" demographic [reminds me] of when I was at the press gallery. There was a fellow who tried to get accredited who dressed oddly and he obviously had an agenda and he was not allowed to get credentialed. They were worried that he was ... he would not maybe respect the ...
>
> VS: Code? [*laughs*]
>
> DH: The code or whatever. I think those same characteristics can be a drawback if you are trying to do some of the reporting that frankly isn't done. Is that making sense?
>
> VS: Tell me more about what you mean. How can they be a drawback?
>
> DH: I think you have to be more skilled as an interviewer in situations where you are dealing with minorities or marginalized people. If you come across as a white, middle-class person, if you're trying to really get at the stories of someone who's homeless or a streetworker or a new immigrant or someone who might, rightly or wrongly, assume that you could have no idea what it's like to be in their shoes. You might not be able to build that kind of rapport that gets beyond the surface of an interview.

Mainstream media reporters were "part of the establishment" and rather than the mainstream expanding to include minorities, those minority groups were creating and watching their own media, Helm explained, citing a TV network being watched by Indigenous peoples, and Asians on the Lower Mainland working for their own media but not reporting for the *Vancouver Sun* or *Province*. That was a problem, because ethnic media silos meant less understanding among people and lost opportunities for a more civil and informed society.

Over Helm's nearly thirty-year career, issues of age and gender had changed. When she was younger and single, she recalled, she tried fitting in with the guys, hanging out with other journalists ("a drinking crowd"), partying and so on. After marrying in her thirties and having her daughter four days before turning forty-two (her daughter was eight at the time of the interview, Helm was fifty) she saw how having a child "filled the well up again" after a gruelling day. Even as online editor, which meant she worked an earlier shift than she had as city editor, and understanding the capacity of technology to lengthen her day, she did not take the job home unless she was the editor on call. She needed, and got, rejuvenation time with her family. Her husband's schedule was more flexible, so he did more of the emergency childcare work.

Helm did not mind that, as a senior editor, she no longer ate and breathed journalism. She commented, in a foreshadowing I missed, how work at a non-profit group might, now that she was a parent, give her "that sense of purpose" and of contribution and personal achievement. But at the *TC*, she saw having a child as bringing her a closer, different connection to the community, and adding to the kinds of subjectivity that she said enriched the job at the paper every day.

Since coming to the *TC*, Helm had seen parity for women journalists: there was no ghetto for them, no prestige beats for men. That might not be true at other newspapers, she felt, where women might only get so far and the boys' network would kick in. Then, at a certain age, the women would keep their heads down or look for something else, depending on their ambitions. The *TC*, as a kind of "destination" paper where staffers stayed, meant the atmosphere was unusually collegial, allowing even unconventional women reporters like Jody Paterson to move up the ladder.[14] Paterson broke ground for women like Lucinda Chodan, someone Helm felt was a great mentor, firm but supportive of staff. Helm mused on how women leaders in newspapers had an easier time in smaller, more collegial newsrooms. Perhaps it was her way of wondering where she could go in journalism next to find a similar culture:

> To use stereotypes, a woman's attention to the social dynamic, and [the] interpersonal, and I don't want to say human, but human side of things, is a different type of management style. I would say there's probably other senior editors-in-chief elsewhere who perhaps … [are] more manlike, right? [And] who are dealing with a higher ratio of men. So in a newsroom this size, it's probably easier for a female manager, I also think it depends on the culture of the newsroom and how collegial it is, because I think that [*pause*] a stereotype is that women tend to be a bit more consensus-building

and, if the ongoing culture in a certain newsroom is more confrontational
and dictatorial, I think a woman might feel less compelled to join those
ranks.

She was careful to note that the women's leadership attributes she
described were stereotypical, but seemed at the same time to see them
as having some truth. Her own style as a manager, as she described
it, was informed, but not dictated, by her personal life: she'd let an
employee go home to nurse a sick child, just as she would let someone go early to look after a sick mother. People had to do their jobs,
but hard workers earned flexibility. For Helm, the story was that leadership had gendered elements, and paying attention to that might
influence how domains of work and home could be more easily
negotiated.

A great day for Helm was to see her staff engaged and enthusiastic,
supporting them with constructive feedback and improving her own
work with some kind of professional development: perhaps a webi-
nar or reading a good article about online technology. As the editor of
online news, Helm relied on the technology running smoothly to have
peace of mind. To have someone comment on – or even notice – that
she might have done a good job was also part of a great day, and offering
praise was something she said she practised with her own staff. A bad
day involved technology that went wrong, being forced into "response
mode," dealing with crises rather than in control of her work agenda.
Being sleep deprived because of her daughter made things difficult, as
did office confrontations; getting into turf wars and power plays was
not her style.

Charged with developing the *TC*'s Web presence, Helm had joined
what began as a male-dominated club of Web editors across the
chain's (Canwest at the time) Western Canadian papers. It evolved
into a group of eighteen, including nine women, whose members held
regular conference calls. A shift had occurred so that the men, who
had been seen at first to be more tech savvy, were being joined by
women like Helm who were no longer nervous about the technology
and brought new ideas – and confidence – to the table. This would
enrich the news agenda, Helm felt, as well as help bring more flexibility to the workplace. It was a turning-point story in which she
expressed hope that enough women would "stick with it to cause

that change," because leadership could still easily remain reserved for men if all that women journalists won was flexibility for their childbearing years.

Harkening back to her international roots, and with a recognition of privilege, Helm was the most globally minded participant in imagining where big change in print journalism would come from, besides the drive of technology: "I am still, at the end of the day, a fifty-year-old, middle-class woman in a Western country, and I am not even sure it's going to come from a Western country. Maybe China, maybe some place unexpected," she explained. To Helm, the best word to describe what was coming next for the industry was "liberation," set loose from the traditions that held it back. I wondered later if it was her own "liberation" she meant.

In early 2012, Helm left her post as acting editor-in-chief to manage media relations for the University of Victoria. The once women-dominated *TC* masthead returned to (white, middle-aged) men as editor-in-chief, city and news editors, sports editor, business editor, and lifestyle editor. So in the end, she did not stick with it, as she hoped other women would. Margo Goodhand, one of the few at the top of the newspaper industry's editorial hierarchy, was also heading out the door.

"That's haunted me forever, that idea that we can't be leaders and be female"

When Margo Goodhand received my request to talk about why women stay in newspapers, she said she felt grateful to be asked, and thought, "Well, that's great someone is doing it."[15] I was grateful, too. She had a terrible cold the wintry day I arrived in her large office at the *Winnipeg Free Press*, but she was still up for the interview, which was conducted in comfort at a coffee table. We talked about how much has changed for women and yet nothing had, which prompted her to remark on a recent issue of the *Ryersonian*, a media magazine produced by Ryerson University's journalism students. On the cover was a drawing of the three editors-in-chief of the *Toronto Star*, the *Globe and Mail*, and the *National Post*, respectively, three white men in suits, striding (of course) under the headline "Never Say Die":

MG: Yeah, I get the *Ryersonian*. I always think one of those young college students is going to do something on this ridiculous situation we have with women in management in the newspapers, but instead I get – well, the one that really threw me off was the one where they have John Stackhouse and Doug Kelly and the new guy at the *Star*, Michael Cooke, walking down the street. These men in their trench coats like the three men of the apocalypse and how they were changing the newspaper industry in Canada, and I thought, "This is just so old school."

VS: Really, and that's in the *Ryersonian*?

MG: That's in a place where there are a lot of female journalists and you wonder what they're thinking when they look to that kind of a paradigm and go, "Where am I going to be and where do I fit in?"

In a way, Goodhand, then fifty-three, had been trying to figure out the answers to those questions since she started in journalism. She was born to a feminist homemaker mother who voted NDP and a surgeon father who voted Tory. Goodhand was the middle of five kids and was raised in Winnipeg, where she got a BA in political science and English. She left to travel to Europe and only came to the idea of journalism when a younger brother died. She suddenly recalled it was something that had appealed to her as a child, so she signed up for a journalism course at Langara College in Vancouver after his funeral, and it was "like a light went on" for her:

The first day I was sitting there and it was the most amazing experience and I went, "Well, this is it, this is what I want to do and be" and it fit into every personal characteristic that I have, every personality quirk that I have. You know, you're relatively introspective but you like to be a part of seeing how history is made. You care about people and issues. You're politically bent; you have a passion about making a difference. You get to meet interesting people and the whole thing was just a tremendous turn on – and then you get to write stories.

Goodhand didn't wait to graduate from the one-year course before taking a job at a Vancouver weekly where she had interned, then moved to the *Medicine Hat News* in 1985. She quickly became the paper's first female news editor because she says she "couldn't stand having the city editor change my leads any more. I got pissed off." That meant an early end to her reporting days, which she mildly regretted, but since then she had written a couple of columns and continued to do so as editor-in-chief of the *Free Press*. She recounted that history and didn't wait for me to ask the next question, because she knew that I was familiar with the barrier: "How did I get here? I worked my way up. When I had my kids – you know what that's like – I worked nights and my husband worked days so we didn't have to put the kids in day care."

Unlike others, most notably in her senior cohort, Goodhand said nothing about luck: she told resilience stories. Her several years on the night copy-editing desk, during which she worked until 2:30 a.m., were terrible, she said, a horrible job of cutting stories. In those early days of her marriage and her career at the *Free Press*, she had two sets of grandparents to help with the kids. When her journalist-husband started working from home, and when the youngest boy was in kindergarten, she felt she could go full-time and then into management. (One editor, she recalled with a laugh, told her when she turned down an earlier offer for a management job due to family and childcare concerns that "that was 'what nannies were for.' I thought, 'this is a man who has had four marriages.' He had no idea.")

Her career took her from a post as an assistant city editor to an assignment of editing Pan Am Games stories, then to features editor, entertainment editor, deputy editor, and finally editor-in-chief. I noted that most women rise through the arts sections, which are traditionally female. She replied with a reflection on the nature of women and leadership in newspapers:

MG: Yeah, they wouldn't give me the city editor's job. I applied twice and I got turned down twice and the second time I was told I was too nice to be a city editor and I'll never forgive them for that. Most of those guys are gone, but that era was "my way or the highway." It was very hierarchical and I'm not like that. I'm a fairly collaborative person and the whole idea about being too nice, I thought, "That's just crap." I think they didn't understand that women's leadership skills are so different than men's. You know, there is just so totally different a style and what they perceive as weak is actually pretty strong. We get the job done; we just get it done in a different way.

VS: Can you articulate what some of that difference looks like?

MG: [Traditionally] it's looked on as weak if you ask people's opinion, like you don't know your own opinion? Or that you don't trust your own opinion. I mean, a better decision is made if you consult with people and talk to people. In this business, you're not allowed to be, or you are questioned as being, weak or not decisive enough. We [women] always make a decision. I hope it's as informed as possible, and as inclusive as

possible. What I've had happen a couple of times, certainly when I was
starting out was that "Oh you're too nice." I'm not that nice. [*laughs*] I
would like to be known as fair and I'd like to be known as creative, and
certainly nurturing is too loaded a word, but I do resent the fact that nice
guys don't finish first.

vs: It's also that sort of code word for "you're too female."

MG: Can a leader lead and inspire and make something, make a difference,
and not be completely top-down? I think so. I think you can create an
environment where – in the new newsroom especially is that it's not
a top-down thing, and I don't think the new generation would put up
with that crap either. But it's still, that was very old school and it exists
in a way today. There's a real military hierarchy – those really old school
guys who go, "It has to come down, you have to *make* that reporter do
that. Make that story and make this," and I don't want to work at a
newsroom like that.

Here, Goodhand describes vividly the dominant forces that perpetuate
sexist norms. And when reflecting on the impact of her personal qualities on her work, she was the only participant in this cohort to express
a sense of history, to say how much she has benefited from being on
the "coattails" of "really great female journalists and advocates," while
the feminist in her (nurtured by her mother) was constantly sad and
outraged. She had seen many female journalists come and go over the
years because they "couldn't handle the atmosphere" as she described
it in the exchange above, or said "it just wasn't worth it." And the problem did not stop there. I had not asked about diversity yet but she said
that hiring freezes and immovable baby boomers caused the "stuck"
problem that was common among the cohorts. She did not name racism, but hinted at it in a story about a big dinner party for an Aboriginal
scholar:

MG: I'm very aware of the fact that there's no diversity in my newsroom,
that we need Aboriginal voices, that we don't represent the Filipino
community. There are so many things that I really feel badly about and
passionate about.

vs: In terms of the diversity aspect, beyond gender, when you get talking
about ethnicity – is that frustration part of – is that a cultural, structural,
systemic problem?

MG: It's just sheer money. I don't know, my staff will not go. I've got a
certain amount of people – my head count can't go up and no one's

leaving, so I can't even make a change. My next hire is going to be what I want it to be, but I haven't been allowed to hire anybody for years. In fact, I had to lay three people off last year in the middle of the recession, so I get frustrated by that.

The whole city is like that too. I was at a very posh dinner, raising money for an Aboriginal scholarship, and I looked around the room and the only Aboriginal person was the one accepting the scholarship. I thought, "The day this place is half and half or has more – is the day that this city is healed." I think it's a travesty that we try to pretend that everything's okay and it's not. There are a lot of issues that I do wish I had the power to address and, at this point, I'm still stuck.

She mentioned the paper did focus on issues, citing stories about a lack of running water in First Nations communities such as Island Lake and about tuberculosis in Lac Brochet and elsewhere, and that the online deputy managing editor was Metis. Also, one of the reporters, Alexandra Paul (whose story is in chapter 2), had Indigenous status. Goodhand added she created a scholarship for an Aboriginal journalist to come to the newsroom for several weeks to be trained and mentored. She shrugged, it always seemed to be a tough workaround, and she did not have the power to fight the status quo as she wanted. She seemed to feel thwarted by the authority that resided solely with the company, while making a case for the way women tend to accomplish things efficiently by pooling their skills and talents, rather than working top-down. In effect, she described a coping strategy, when what Goodhand wanted to do was lead change.

A great day for Goodhand was when everyone was charged up by a story, or when they tried something new, like live-streaming civic election coverage, which was so good (and original) that even the candidates were watching it live. This "rich, textural experience" was a light-bulb moment for Goodhand, enabling a 138-year-old newspaper to do "this incredibly cool stuff." She was proud of the crusading role the paper played in areas such as social justice for children. And she had figured out a novel way to fund reporting that required travel money (especially about the environment and Manitoba's north) by applying for Canadian Institutes of Health Research grants, which provided "independent, hands-off, no-strings-attached funding" for important projects. Taking this money also disqualifies a paper from being considered for a National Newspaper Award (NNA), which is the Oscar of Canadian print journalism. I was amazed to hear of these grants being available to the media, and impressed that Goodhand and her staff were willing to tell these stories without hope of recognition from their peers and competitors. A bad day at work involved a poorly reported or sensationalized story, and increasingly, what she called anonymous "'shame-on-you' comments" that could be shockingly rude and sexist.[16] She cited, among other things, how stories circulated that she bought coffee for the men in the office.

As to why women were so few in number in senior newspaper roles, Goodhand described how "ambitious and fabulous" young women were, but then they had a "real problem when they hit the marriage and the babies." At that point "something has to give," she said, "and often I think women just go 'it's not worth it' and my heart breaks." If only they could see how great the rewards are – advocating for the community and for change – then more might remain, she said. She recalled the era in the mid-1990s, when so many women left the paper (Goodhand can still name them and did) that it was "a whole generation gone." Others called this "the lost generation" at the paper. That created gaps in coverage on social issues and trends, as well as eliminating candidates for important positions such as editorial writer. (Only one of the *Free Press*'s four editorial writers was a woman.) But she cited a troubling, wider viciousness, and how she had been haunted by the notion that women couldn't be leaders as they are currently defined in journalism and politics:

Judy Wasylycia-Leis was in our office and she's a mayoral candidate and she said she'd never had such a rough campaign. She'd never been exposed to as much sexism and aggressive hostility and held up to ridicule. I looked at her and I thought, "That's why women don't expose themselves to leadership roles," because if you put yourself out there, they're criticizing your clothes, they're criticizing the tone of your voice, the way you talk – you know, it's "shrill," it's always shrill – your management style, your leadership qualities.

That's the one that's haunted me forever, that idea that we can't be leaders and be female, or be leaders and have a different style than the guy from the *Spiderman* newsroom, you know? That's what they think is a leader and what they think is a newsman.

Politicians are the same way. They have to be testosterone-fuelled, aggressive. They have to go on the attack, and as soon as a woman does that, she loses her credibility because women are not perceived – they're not allowed to act like that. We're constantly assessed and found wanting for any ambitions to be in a leadership role.

I think that's where I've been finding, these last couple of weeks, you do have some rough days, and you go, "Do I really – is it really worth it to me to stay here and accept the kind of public pillorying?"

For these senior participants who left, this comment illustrates the extent to which the personal situation intersecting with the professional challenges had become too much. Journalism was supposed to be about people and stories, she concluded, not about being a punching bag.

Thinking ahead, Goodhand noted she had always said that she would stay on the job no longer than five years, and was in the middle of year three when we met. She was still finding reasons to be optimistic. For example, she recalled a simple meeting over coffee with someone who mentioned how a *Free Press* editorial had caused a certain influential person to call Winnipeg's mayor and resolve a pressing social issue. "So I think that the paper has a tremendous ability to make a change if we want to. We have tremendous power to put forward ideas, to discuss issues. I don't think we realize the power that we do have." She did worry, however, that with newsroom numbers cut, and the number and diversity of voices dwindling, that "police blotter" news was overdone. She saw the online paper as the more creative, collaborative place for young journalists to shine. The Web culture, she felt, would change the newsroom, because it was driven by a generation that wouldn't tolerate the male-dominated, militaristic culture of the past. She laughed that, because the newsroom was "cool in the summer and warm in winter," older workers stayed on and stood between her and a few good hires.

Goodhand, while saying she had never had a female mentor nor been (formally) asked to be one, still changed things incrementally with every editorial decision she made. When I spoke to other women in the newsroom, they clearly admired her collaborative leadership and news sense and appreciated that she was a woman editor-in-chief with a woman deputy editor working beside her. Like the others who have left the industry, she described years of clashing with the dominant culture, her rise through the hierarchy marked by personal contortions to fit the expected norms, and how her position of authority was not a position of power. She was caught, unable to right historic wrongs, such as hiring for diversity. But there were many highs, too, which she enumerated in a letter to the *Free Press* staff before she left on 30 July 2012. Goodhand named the paper's many successes since she had started as a "frazzled mom," most recently an award-winning series on immigration and an all-Africa edition, and then wrote:

> I've really loved this job, and you people are like family. One big, dys-functional, fabulously creative family. And I will miss you. But I am really happy, I know how lucky I am to be able to leave on my own terms, and on good terms. If the choice is to die at your desk or to go when people think you're too old or have lost your touch, this is how I want to go.[17]

She "just kept getting the chance to work my way up," she wrote, reflect-ing again on the idea among the oldest cohort that such advancement was amazing and inexplicable, while at the same time she underscored how hard she had to work, which was especially difficult during the years her kids were young. When the industry began finding new ways to reduce resources – and therefore possibilities for change – Goodhand decided to get out. The only luck she cited was about making a clean getaway.

The *Calgary Herald*'s Paula Arab, like Goodhand, decried the lack of diversity in newsrooms. As an immigrant's daughter, she experienced a Halifax childhood that determined her lifelong commitment to expos-ing social unjustices.

"I don't think any newsroom in Canada is completely diverse"

A young Paula Arab found the criminal courts in Halifax instrumental in her wanting to become a journalist. As a child of a Lebanese-born father and a mother of Lebanese heritage, Arab went to the courts with her mother, who worked as an Arabic-English interpreter. She loved what she called "the subculture, the excitement" of the courts. Her father, who emigrated from Lebanon at age nineteen (her mother was born in Canada, and her grandparents were pivotal in the establish-ment of the Lebanese community in Halifax), was a businessman who was deeply involved in community issues. In her home, education was seen as the key to success, along with language and cultural learning: Arabic lessons and folk dancing were part of Arab's childhood. Her cultural background and gender (as a woman with a cultural heritage descended from a country that oppresses the voice of women, as she described it later)[18] informed her social justice approach, which she positioned as at odds to white, middle-class journalism. She saw a lack of diversity inside the *Calgary Herald*, and in other newsrooms, as resulting from a lack of access to journalism schools, which are the typical gateways to a newspaper career. She herself graduated in 1991 from Ryerson's journalism program after studying liberal arts and journalism at the University of King's College:

> PA: The individual personality is so much wrapped up in journalism because we filter information differently, and that's why a diverse newsroom leads to a diverse product, because someone with a different identity is not going to see a story or is not going to be interested in a story that I – as a woman, daughter of an immigrant, [with a] strong social justice background – would be. At the same time I'm not interested in the story that somebody, like a white, middle-class, private school journalist might be interested in.
>
> VS: Do you think the *Herald* is a diverse newsroom?
>
> PA: No. I don't think any newsroom in Canada is completely diverse, because you need money to become a journalist; you need money to go to school, to go to four years of university. And at Ryerson's program, the last year you have to do a mentorship and it's unpaid … So I think that's where the problem starts, is what we're saying you have to do to become a journalist.
>
> VS: So it becomes an exclusive club in that sense.
>
> PA: Well yeah. You have to be able to afford it. I don't think you can get a job anymore without having a journalism degree. Not for what you learn, but just for the foot in the door. When I was in journalism school the director didn't have a degree, because in his generation, no one had a degree. But it's becoming more competitive, I mean it's really hard to be more diverse when there aren't more efforts being made to go into those diverse communities and encourage them to be journalists.

With her having a last name of Arab, she said, some readers assumed she was Muslim. But she is a Catholic who did not feel that her religion was her identity. She didn't feel like a "token anything; at least I hope I am not." Because she was both a columnist and an editorial writer, Arab felt that she did have influence and authority in the community. As an editorial writer, she helped broadcast the *Herald*'s stance on matters of public interest; as a columnist, she had a more personal relationship with readers, who often contacted her to tell Arab she had inspired them. She decided to write about local affairs after attending an editorial writers' conference, describing it as a turning point, one of those pivotal moments that individuals experience that seem to redefine their position in the larger societal structures in which they operate:

> It was all editorial writers in the U.S., this was in 2007, and they were all talking about how local opinion is what's going to save local newspapers. When I pick up the phone I am more likely to get someone at city hall as Paula Arab, columnist at the *Calgary Herald*, than I am as Paula Arab, taxpayer, and, ever since that conference, I've really focused my writing on urban issues because I think that's what people want.

Arab gave an example of how she was bringing a quality of being attuned to diversity to bear on such local issues that would otherwise be ignored. The issue began when the Alberta government cut funding for gender reassignment surgery. She explained:

> It was a tiny amount in the grand scale of a $5-billion budget and no one wrote about it; I was the only one. It's such a minority that no one would care, and to be able to write a column on that and to shame the government, to make them accountable. There was no justification for that cut, other than it was easy to make, they thought they could get away with it. It was a group of people that were so different, so far from the mainstream that nobody was going to rise to their defence that they almost got away with it.

The column generated buzz, the province eventually relented, she said, and "rethought" the cut. For her, to give people who needed financing for their surgery this platform was, she said, "very much who I am, and I don't know if that's because I am a woman or if that's just why I went into journalism. I just want to be able to be the voice for the voiceless," as so many other participants said they did. In this instance, she expresses gender as the possible motivating factor rather than any identification with minority groups because of her racial background.

Her early career coincided with a recession, so Arab struggled through a series of short-term reporting jobs with stops along the way in Quebec, to learn French, and in Winnipeg, to help start Canwest's wire service, before arriving at the *Calgary Herald* in 2004. She began on the assignment desk for eighteen months, and was promoted to the editorial board, where she remained. Editorial board members have high status, as they have the writing and analytic skills to craft the editorials that represent the publisher's view on any subject of public interest. (They also work coveted day shifts.) In 2008, she began a weekly column, opining on any topic she chose.

When we spoke, Arab was forty-two and single with no children. This footloose state, she felt, had allowed her to move when work demanded it, but left her feeling rootless, too. And today, she said, she looked around the newsroom at other women her age with families and didn't "see them being very happy" in what she saw as an inflexible newsroom:

vs: Why is that?

pa: They seem to sacrifice so much. The strong women journalists when I was coming up the ranks looked to me like Christie Blatchford. I don't feel I sacrificed anything for my job other than I haven't put down roots, but I feel if I had a family, would I have necessarily had a conflict in balancing my priorities? Do you know what I mean?

vs: So you mean, if circumstances had said you were going to have a husband, kids, whatever, you would have found a way to balance that?

pa: Yes, at least that was always my idea, that I would have balanced that, but I have noticed places like the *Herald* are not very open to job-sharing and flexibility.

Arab said she did know of some women who have job-shared and found good day care (onsite and off), but the problem of women's unhappiness was more of a newsroom "mindset":

pa: It's more this mindset that you have to be seen to be valued. I don't know where that comes from. I don't know if they assume if you're working from home you're not doing any work, or what. In journalism, we should be redefining what the office looks like because we have a deadline every day, so it's pretty easy to measure if you are doing your work or not. You're either producing or you're not, and with wireless, why do we have to physically be in here? I feel that newsrooms are not as progressive as you would think they should be. And with women that makes a big deal, a big difference.

vs: Why are newsrooms not as progressive as you think they would be?

pa: Well because journalism is all about challenging the establishment and the established way of doing things, right? But, yet, they just don't like change.

vs: Why's that?

pa: Maybe that hierarchy, that patriarchal culture, was established to get stuff done.

As other participants had commented, Arab viewed newsrooms as less progressive than their status as social barometers might indicate. Here, it seemed that the hard work needed to "get stuff done" had, over time, turned into a long-hours-for-show culture that everyone took part in, reproducing cultural norms. To disrupt that culture with, for instance, a run to the day-care centre or by working from home, was career-limiting. A hierarchical mentality still existed in newsrooms, Arab said, with employees feeling disempowered because "someone above them can always come and override them or discourage them." Women, in her view, felt this keenly. Not driven by a need to have titles, they were lower on the hierarchy, and even where things looked equal on the surface, men were generally taken more seriously:

> It's how you present yourself, right? So if I have twenty facts lined up I go into meetings with a very different voice of authority than if I don't. Whereas my male colleague can go in there with that same voice of authority without having done any research whatsoever, because he's a man and used to having that voice of authority. I just notice when a guy says something in the room it gets taken way more seriously. It's not challenged the way it is when the women in the room say something. So I'm not sure how much of that is the way he says it versus he's a man and he has an assumed authority that comes with being a man.

However, over the years, Arab said, she has sought and enjoyed the help of many mentors, male and female. Now that she was pretty much in her "dream job," she did have ideas about turning to teaching next, even being part of redefining "journalism in the electronic age." In the summer of 2012, Arab acted on those ideas, leaving the *Herald* dream job to start her own communications consulting company.

Conclusions

To leave the *Globe* job I (mostly) loved in 1994, one that paid well and that I believed contributed to public education, was extremely difficult. The decision was agonizing, took months to make, and took a toll on my emotional well-being, which, in turn, affected my family. I can understand how difficult it must have been for these women to decide to leave, even though I was at least a decade younger than most of them when I quit daily print journalism. Unlike me, the participants who left their newspapers did not have children under five still at home (although two had older children). And because I was only forty-one when I left, I felt that I did not get a chance to show what I could accomplish over the long term in a senior management position. Something was wrong with me, I thought, not them. If to leave Canada's respected national newspaper constitutes a defection, surely one who chooses to leave must be defective.

Those study participants who left did not appear to feel that way. While some may have pointed to luck as a sizeable factor in how their careers progressed, these older participants took pride in their staff's accomplishments, their own social-activist inclinations, non-institutional story approaches, and inclusive management practices. After years of accommodation, they looked around at where they were "stuck" and understood that they did not fail the system: it was the other way around. And the devil they knew was becoming more desperate for survival, in a frenzied spiral of cost-cutting, technological upheaval, and diminishing readership. Dreams about hiring for diversity would not be realized soon if ever; a deep communication gap between them and male leaders could not be bridged; and their power bases were eroding without financial support. Burned-out and frustrated as the women journalists reported feeling in Reinardy's 2009 study, these participants left daily print journalism to try other ways to make a difference.

It appears that after years of accommodation and resistance, women journalists who left were no longer able or willing to suppress or adapt their complex selves (particularly gender, age, sexuality, and ethnic background) in service to the promotion of the values that their newspapers represented. They had each spent decades positioning themselves in relation to the male-dominant forces of the newsroom, which required them to obey or engage in stressful struggle with overt and covert biased practices. Their narratives described being silenced, bullied, harassed, and discounted as Elmore (2009) describes in her "Turning Points and Turnover among Female Journalists: Communicating Resistance and Repression." Their acts of resistance were often covert (such as Fallding's quiet assistance to the otherwise ignored women interns) or foiled by industry downsizing calls. They counted successes in the commonly cited role of serving community and being a voice for the voiceless, telling the stories of those whose qualities of difference (class, race) effectively kept them from telling their own stories.

Much more than gender is at play when women print journalists in Canada decide to leave the jobs they love. While those senior participants who remained spoke of luck in their continuing careers, the leavers did not. The wholeness that their narratives might normally have expressed at that point in their long careers had unravelled.

For them, the luck story ran out. It was time for a turning point, a bit of bold personal agency, a happier ending.

Chapter Seven

Conclusions: Taking Control of the Narrative

By the time I finished the manuscript for this book, more than one-quarter of the participants did what I had done years earlier, by one means or another. They had left their newsroom jobs – what they called their dream jobs – either by quitting or through a buyout. The few women who had made it to top editor positions and were staying on did not seem to have the kind of working life that beckoned to the youngest ones. The contours of all their career paths were obscured by the precarious state of Canadian newspapers and executives' fixation with monetizing digital media technology. And with their heads bent over the endless process of producing news across multiple platforms, the participants focused, not surprisingly, on what they experienced as individuals, not on what unseen forces might be hidden from them and influencing their lives. As for that single, corporately run onsite day-care centre at the *Calgary Herald*? It closed at the end of April 2014, when Postmedia put the Calgary Herald Building up for sale. As the workforce aged and numbers declined, only one editorial employee was using it.[1]

The earliest days of women occasionally daring to enter strictly male newsrooms are long gone in Canada. But the stories told by the women journalists in these pages reveal that an overt hostility towards a few has been replaced by a systemically reproduced inequality that ends the careers of many women who manage to enter the field and that limits the progress of those few who stay and seek to make change through their work.

Throughout my exploration of stories of women journalists' career triumphs and challenges, I looked particularly for clues as to how the women described navigating the power structures of their industry and the embedded – and often hidden to them – discriminatory practices of the newsroom over their careers. When well-educated, socially minded women drop out of print journalism, it is a pressing problem for a country that depends on a free press for socio-economic and cultural health: democracy is weakened when women's contributions are treated as less important than men's by its agenda-setting mass media (Ross and Carter, 2011).

Using narrative analysis – specifically, examining storytelling thematically – I took earlier findings that gender on its own does not appear to determine these women's newsroom experiences and production as cultural "outsiders" and asked if other kinds of diversity, in relation to gender, might be at work. The answer? Yes, other social characteristics come into play during women's newspaper careers. Most important, they do so *over time*, particularly as expressed in narratives that reveal how the most senior participants combine their multiple identities and external workplace and social values into a coherent whole as lucky professionals, while the younger cohort members describe experimenting with and exploiting various aspects of their identities and the larger societal influences to survive in a tough, "macho" environment.

These journalists' career paths appear influenced in multiple, fluid, and often hidden ways by other characteristics as they intersect with gender. Assumptions about these characteristics, such as age, race, parenthood status, and class, further complicate the shaping of participants' experiences in their workplaces, offering them ways to either reinforce or resist the traditional newsroom culture. The participants took up navigating these confused seas in ways that often left them frustrated and angry, but ultimately most felt they were "survivors" who made a difference in the sociopolitical agenda through their journalism. They are, or were, voices for the voiceless, as long as they hung in.

Key generational differences appeared in the participants' stories. Generally speaking, senior participants saw themselves as *lucky survivors* in these frustratingly gendered newsrooms; those in mid-career were *self-sacrificing, hard workers* who needed, but were not getting, workplace flexibility; and the most junior ones presented themselves as *individual strategists*, capable of handling whatever routine injustices were thrown at them. They wanted to stay in the business long enough to "choose" between careers and parenthood, with their technological proficiency as a lifeline.

The luck factor was seen as powerful, and had to do with what the older participants saw as sheer serendipity of circumstance. They were just lucky to have got that summer internship or that promotion at the right time in order to keep their careers moving. A sense of being entitled to those positions through their own hard work and strategizing was not often part of their storytelling, as it was with the younger groups, reflecting what feminist theorists often characterize as generational differences between second- and third-wave feminisms. These differences are, in turn, complicated by "the lived messiness of contemporary life" (Snyder, 2008, p. 193).

Members of the oldest generation also tended to position themselves as longer-term victims of gender bias, either personal or institutional, reflecting the ubiquity of sexual harassment that women experience in the workplace generally (Forrest, 1993). The mid-career cohort described hearing about or witnessing such incidents and the youngest members more often talked about their own agency in playing with sexism, which they felt they could exploit to their own advantage. The less time in the news game they had spent, the less sexism was an obvious issue to them.

Other themes spanned the cohorts. Having children or deciding whether or not to have them was pivotal in all the journalists' career trajectories, or judged as pivotal in those of other women, whether they were new recruits, in mid-career or nearing traditional retirement age: the men in the newsroom weren't seen to think about parenthood as an issue. Also, despite the structural and cultural constraints, the participants' passion for their journalistic work, being voices for the voiceless, remained strong, even in the face of deep, personal family struggles and stressful industrial upheavals on both the financial and technological fronts.

In the focus groups, participants could better identify and question meta-narratives that might cast them as outsiders, given the opportunity to compare stories across the generations and having had the issues brought to mind in the individual interviews. Also, where their own stories dominated in one-on-one interviews, the format of discussion across age ranges brought out the theme of leadership, both in a gendered quality – as women, leadership was seen as more collegial than top-down – and in terms of the existing and pending gaps in the kind of female leadership the women felt would improve news production and their personal lives. Certainly, as a witness to and driver of each of the conversations about their working lives, I could see plainly that the women were hungry for more: more sharing of work stories together and with male peers in an open forum; more discussion of leadership and mentorship; and more confidence in their own positions as valuable workers whose opinions counted and who could influence managers' thinking about how newspapers operate. Many simply did not see themselves becoming "leaders," even though many were, unofficially.

They explored the context of their working lives in the focus groups in lively conversations, re-examining their positions more clearly within the complex system of the "macho" newsroom and larger society. Young women who took perceived equality for granted found themselves challenged. Sharing stories revealed to them the potential and real power they had, that they had not previously considered as such. Focus group talk solidified the notion that in terms of parenthood affecting working lives, nothing had changed much for women over generations in newsrooms. Participants seemed to feel powerless when it came to articulating their own workplace needs for flexibility, and they generally conceded an inevitability about gender roles on the job and at home, enmeshed as they were in the endless daily tasks demanded of them. I trust that with their growing appreciation of power and its uses, the participants and others like them will find ways to question this fundamental inequity publicly.

And why not ask that of them? After all, the overwhelming majority of participants largely defined their own work as being standard-bearers for those who they said could not speak for themselves. As overwhelmingly white, middle-class, well-educated, and able-bodied women, the participants are still privileged, while experiencing discrimination through gender, parenthood status, and age. Only a few participants described an even greater, more complicated sense of difference because of their race or ethnicity (two), their disability (one), class origins (two), or sexuality (one), with those markers giving them an added sense of personal responsibility to be social advocates in whatever ways seemed available to them. All but two participants expressed certitude about feeling called to tell others' stories, and in so doing they helped in some small way to improve others' lives. Paula Arab at the *Calgary Herald*, for example, felt her column was instrumental in publicly shaming the government into reinstating support for transgendered people. What had been done to them was hidden, and she revealed it.

My research confirms several trends revealed in other studies. For example, women journalists do consider leaving their jobs not only when they have had children, but in advance of becoming mothers, as Melissa Martin, and others, said they would do. Women in leadership positions (such as Carla Ammerata) do feel pressure to adopt male leadership discourses (long hours, competitiveness) as they rise in the ranks. And, perhaps most telling, in terms of perpetuating certain elitist social values that tend to be universalized by newspapers, as Williams, Manvell, and Bornstein (2006) have suggested, elite women such as my participants repeat and reinforce the "choice" myth of women having to choose between work and family, a myth that echoes seemingly without end.

The participants perpetuated and reinforced many gendered myths, questioned them silently, and suppressed their opinions about them, and they also offered open resistance. In Janet's case, her women colleagues said she had paid a price for that resistance and had become saddled with the label of "office fembo."[2]

I posit that the traditional male discourses in newspapers that slap on those kinds of labels have a normalizing effect and that women align themselves with those discourses or resist as Janet and others did. The stories my participants told support this theory: as Leslie McCall (1992) found, women tend to internalize the male/female opposition as they work out how to navigate the responsibilities of paid work and family, congratulating themselves on their ability to juggle frantically rather than throwing balls into other hands or simply letting them drop.

Back in the Headlines Again

This false binary of how women must juggle careers and families erupts, dormant-volcano-like, in more lives than mine and the women who participated in my research. Witness, for example, the media attention paid to the news that Marissa Mayer, when she was newly announced CEO of Yahoo, was six months pregnant when hired. The story caused a deluge of stories, commentaries, and frenzied Tweets across the Western world.[3] Most wondered how she could "do it all," and even how she dared, while others insisted she be a role model for all womankind, her multimillion-dollar personal wealth aside. Some bloggers, like salon.com's Rebecca Traister, found the intensity of the reactions "kind of depressing, as if they had hired a yeti" (in Timson, 2012, L3). *Financial Times* columnist Lucy Kellaway (2012) opined in the opening of her column that nothing had changed for mothers at work despite decades of research, and that the situation was a "continuing, fluid game of survival, the rules of which are unclear, shifting and different for everyone." This forces women into endlessly judging each other for their "wrong" decisions, caught inside what American feminist historian Sally Kitch calls the societal decision that something about being a woman and giving birth is inherently inferior. And, I would add, apparently has nothing to do with men.

A quote from the Yahoo CEO herself shows how she internalized lessons of accommodation to a male-dominated (high-tech) industry well and how eager she was to pass them on to other mothers/managers-to-be. "My advice is to take control of the narrative," said Mayer. "Reveal the pregnancy sooner and, at the same time, clearly communicate your preparedness and competence for the next role" (as quoted in Eichler, 2012, B15).

Of what narrative is Mayer asking women to take control? She is telling millions of people in the working population that at the highest levels, they should continue to fall into line with the meta-narrative that suits male-dominated systems of industry, which essentially says this: don't let human reproduction get in the way of our profits. The participants in this study, who were trained to query and challenge, and who generally saw themselves as social justice advocates, enacted this storyline with every apology for rushing off to the day-care centre and every unspoken objection to a sexist story and every missed family pizza night.

Still, the story of women's work experiences flares up in the news because women are slowly moving up workplace ranks and the urgency for solutions rises. One obvious answer – men need to be equal partners at home – is taking decades to be taken seriously by more than just a few brave stay-at-home dads. In her 2013 bestselling book *Lean In: Women, Work and the Will to Lead*, Facebook chief operating officer Sheryl Sandberg urges women professionals to "lean in" to their careers with passion and fearlessness, demanding support when they need it. What much of the mainstream press missed – or perhaps avoided – in its coverage of the book's release was Sandberg's clear and sustained exhortation to men to "lean in" equally to the domestic sphere. Shortly after her book was released, journalists Katty Kay and Claire Shipman (2014) identified a lack of confidence – which many of my participants expressed – as being key to women's stalled progress in the workplace. Writing in the April 2014 issue of *The Atlantic* about their book on the subject, they described how they saw this first in their own lives as journalists: "Katty got a degree from a top university, speaks several languages and yet had spent her life convinced that she wasn't intelligent enough to compete for the most prestigious jobs in journalism" (para. 6) – Kay is the anchor of BBC World News America – and "Claire … had a habit of telling people she was 'just lucky' – in the right place at the right time – when asked how she became a CNN correspondent in Moscow while still in her 20s" (para. 7). How familiar these stories sounded to the ones I had been hearing across the country! And their prescription was familiar, too: with hard work, women can close the gap. Men, it seems, are not required to stop overestimating their abilities to succeed: women need to stop underestimating theirs. What could be simpler?

Reflexivity Revisited

Back in the *Globe* newsroom on that hot August day in 1987, when the publisher marvelled at how my pregnant belly and I were still there, it might have been helpful to have been aware of the complexities I was able to tease out of researching this book. Like the younger participants, I was in my dream job with little idea of what lay ahead. Of course frustrations and outrages abounded at work, but I relished the challenges of helping sustain Canada's most respected newspaper, creating stories of national interest and importance (usually business and politics, of course) with my colleagues. I had an experienced and understanding mentor in the *Globe*'s Shirley Sharzer, and yet I could also see how she was being continually sidelined, not quite in the inside circle, always near the top of the editorial ranks but never without a "deputy" or "assistant" in her title. In the midst of all that I got married one chilly November day and then faced that turning point where what felt like a personal choice seemed to launch me down a socially determined and narrow path, one that sends followers far into the wilderness.

Over the next few years everything changed, first with one child, then two. One day I found myself speeding home from work at noon in downtown Toronto traffic, screaming and honking at every car, because the frightened nanny had called to say our son had grabbed an electric cord and pulled the television down on his head. (This was the 1980s; TV sets were heavy.) A few hours later, with my son treated in the ER and the crisis over, I pulled society's meta-narrative about "good" mothers down on my own head. Why *was* I still there in that newsroom? Why were any of us women still there, mothers or not, sideswiped, sidelined, and feeling guilty for not keeping up, let alone getting ahead? Were the panic attacks I began to experience related to the growing lack of confidence I felt? Those questions, coming out of my experience and that of so many others, drove this book. And by developing more awareness of my own many privileges, I have come to see that the project gleaned more meaning than it would have, had I stayed with gender as my sole criterion for why women stay or leave. I have begun to see what was previously invisible to me, hunkered down as I was in my own story of why I loved my job, why I left, and how the panic attacks ended. Who enters print journalism – and who is likely to succeed on the inside – is about gender and more. I recall a meeting where several white women managers at the *Globe* met a group of black women activists and we felt the heat of their disdain for our defence of the paper's coverage, or lack of it. I remember another management meeting in which we were asked to discuss a proposal to run a series on "black crime" in the city, based on ideas apparently gleaned from a dinner party. We decided in the end to do a few stories on criminal connections between Jamaica and Toronto instead, after a meeting with local black leaders. In that meeting, only one editor – Ann Rauhala – dared to question openly what unspoken attitudes might be informing the paper's decision to run this series. She is also one of the few women who made it to the level of department head (foreign editor) in the early 1990s. She left to work at the CBC, then to teach at Ryerson's school of journalism.

I think of these experiences and feel the shame of not understanding how much exercising my own privilege could hold others back. I fancied myself a liberal, even accepted the label as an office feminist/ apologist for all the times I called sexism and discrimination into question in headlines, news coverage, columns, and workplace structures. The *Globe* day-care study I worked on never went anywhere, as I and the others in the office who cared about it were, not surprisingly, pregnant, and became invisible once we went on maternity leave. Management would not even distribute the questionnaire about what day care we might want; the union did.

All of our workplace experiences are profoundly affected by others' absences, invisibilities, and exclusions. This even applies to those who come before us. For instance, the groundbreaking work of previous generations of women journalists was, for me and most of the participants, invisible (or at least rarely mentioned) as a factor in making our careers possible. Continual departures of other women journalists created contemporaneous absences. Participants spoke of women colleagues they knew who had left newspapers once they had children or the newsroom culture got to them, as I had done: Margo Goodhand and others sadly described an entire lost generation of women at the *Winnipeg Free Press*. (By mid-2014, just nine of forty-three reporters, columnists, and managers at the paper were women. In order to reach gender parity, the next twenty-five hires would have to be female. As one ex-staffer pointed out to me off the record, "Can you imagine how long it will take before a newspaper can hire twenty-five people?") These are big gaps, where female mentorship and role models could have developed but did not, and certain kinds of stories (e.g., about child care or the impacts of poverty on families) were not reported. Few women were left to demonstrate the kind of leadership for which the participants seemed to yearn, involving more flexibility, collegiality, understanding, and diversity. As it was, junior and mid-level participants could not see themselves in senior leadership roles; most mid-career women did not want to go beyond their current mid-management roles into corporate decision-making; and senior participants were exhaustedly trying to replicate the only leadership model they could see, the one that the men enacted. Another invisible group rarely considered by managers as important in the workplace – children at home with fathers or nannies or in day-care centres – had a profound impact on their mothers' experiences in the workplace, as the women were torn between the urgency of their perceived maternal duties and joys, and their work responsibilities and challenges. As Nicole MacIntyre of the *Hamilton Spectator* said, she could be either a good mother or a good journalist, but not both. Halifax reporter Patricia Brooks Arenburg drove herself crazy wondering if her son would be proud of her for her work or would he think she just wasn't there? These powerful beliefs about children at home pit women against the possibilities of their own futures in newsrooms.

Other powerful unseen forces can keep the status quo in place. Those of us who hold these publicly oriented jobs, partly because of our privilege, can be de facto placeholders for those people we characterize as invisible and "voiceless." By taking on a classic hero/standard-bearer role to speak for those deemed to be powerless, the participants – and others like them, men and women both, me included – can be seen as part of the wall of privilege that holds back members of many marginalized communities from telling their own stories as paid journalists and commentators in newspapers. As it is, Canada remains an extremely diverse society in which mainstream media do not begin to reflect the extent of race, ethnicity, class, gender, religion, sexuality, ability, and age diversity within our culture.

At least, however, the women's positive attitudes towards those they said they spoke for ran counter to the more common mainstream media storyline about Indigenous peoples and other racialized groups and non-elite classes, which is that they are social problems, irrelevant or inferior. Sherri Borden Colley in Halifax, for instance, was proud to tell stories about individuals' successes in the local black community, of which she is a member. Borden Colley, unlike many other participants, could tell those stories with authenticity, just as Laura Fraser could write about the experiences of disabled people from her position as a person who had used a wheelchair. Alexandra Paul, who had married into her Indigenous status, used her position at the *Winnipeg Free Press* to try to bridge the divide between Indigenous and non-Indigenous communities. Janet did her best to bring the stories of marginalized people into her paper.

The demographic and social characteristics of reporters and the stories that they create and admire are connected. The vast majority of participants had a sense of the need to go beyond their own privilege and said they used their positions to help those they deemed voiceless. Despite seeing the exodus and sidelining of women like themselves, and the free fall of newspapers' financial stability, participants of all career stages often ascribed to themselves an almost messianic sense of personal influence over the course of social justice. It didn't matter whether they were fledgling reporters or highly placed senior editorial decision-makers: the participants felt they could, and did, influence social policy from the community to the country. But they did not say the same about discourses and practices at their workplaces. Their journalistic practice gave them the power to disrupt authority's narratives on the page, but inside the newsroom, they felt little power to challenge the workplace narrative that privileges traditional male-dominant leadership. In this way, the participants told stories that were subversive, while at the same time felt that they were personally "stuck."

Janet, who left her paper, summed up how a more diverse workplace could affect the sociopolitical agenda: "What filters through your own life experience is what ends up in the paper," she said. Those facts and events, sifted through an industry whose practitioners, particularly at the highest, most powerful levels, are white, middle- (and upper-) class, well-educated, middle-aged men, become what they decide is news.[4] Whether participants were aware of their own gender-based negotiations or not, many participants challenged the male news agenda, writing about gender, class, ability, and race-based issues and even demanding men tackle "women's issues," as Borden Colley did. The *Hamilton Spectator*'s Emma Reilly recalled in a focus group that she had written a story about women voters but had not "gotten around" to doing one on diversity in the electorate. This realization hit her during a discussion of how personal characteristics affected news judgment. Much later,[5] she told the same story to about fifty journalists and students, and at least one male publisher, offering them an opportunity to judge their own decisions about which stories to cover and why, as she had now done.

This book, I hope, goes some way to enhancing our understanding of the importance of these personal variables, and how they combine with gender, over time, to create for women print journalists enough reason to quit the newsroom or to carry on in the few numbers that they do. This group of participants was significant in its resistance to outsider status: decades of working in a high-stress, male-dominated workplace did not cause these skilled women to flee, although some considered it and members of the most senior cohort members did leave.

Feminist researchers have a valuable role to play in exploring why and how newspapers can provide more inclusive coverage, with difference as a central marker, so as to help build a stronger democracy (Byerly and Ross, 2008). This book will stand, I hope, as part of the body of knowledge that helps the industry move towards that goal. It also raises the question of whether leaders in the small-c conservative Canadian newspaper industry avoid, deny, or remain unaware of the damage that the lack of diversity in their newsrooms can cause in terms of the profitability they so desperately seek. Much recent research finds that companies with women well-represented on its boards and management teams do better financially than those who do not. In one large recent study, for example, Cristian Dezso and David Gaddis Ross (2012), using fifteen years of data on 1,500 American corporations, discovered the positive effect on firm performance (and middle-management women's motivation) when women are represented in management. Specifically, a given firm "generates on average one percent (or over $40 million) more economic value with at least one woman on its top management team than without any women on its top management team and also enjoys superior accounting performance" (Dezso and Ross, 2012, p. 1084). Why the resistance then, to making gender, and other diversities, a priority in print newsrooms? The answer may lie in what happens psychologically to male managers when the entrenched cultural discourses that keep women and racialized people outside of senior business ranks are threatened. They're unhappy. "Diversity in gender and race has deleterious effects on the psychological commitment, absenteeism, and intention to stay of men working in operating units, suggesting that gender diversity may reduce the overall motivation of male managers," say Dezso and Ross (2012, p. 1085). In other words, it may seem easier to senior managers to lose more women than men from the workplace. Morale, and all that.

For the record, at least, the *New York Times* (a historically sexist daily, as we learned in chapter 1) recognizes that it should look inside its own editorial offices to address the problem of lack of diversity, which was linked in a University of Nevada study showing that far more male sources than female (3.4 to 1) are being quoted in the paper's front-page stories. "This situation illustrates the importance of pushing for a more diverse newsroom – in gender, race and ethnicity, background, religion and other factors – which remains a priority for us," said Phil Corbett, the associate managing editor for standards, in an article published by the Poynter Institute, an American journalism education website. He also said that a diversity quota "seems like a blunt instrument that could create as many problems as it solves" (Layton & Shepard, 2013). (A website called whowritesfor.com now counts NYTimes.com front-page bylines by gender daily.) And, in unrelated news or not, the *Times'* only female executive editor to date, Jill Abramson, was fired in May 2014 after fewer than three years at the helm. Dean Baquet replaced her, the first African-American in the top editorial job. A few weeks after that story broke, the *Washington Post* followed up with a piece written by Nikki Usher (2014) and headlined "It's not just Jill Abramson: Women everywhere are getting pushed out of journalism." The cause according to Usher: male domination of the worlds of programming and related technologies, where journalism is increasing its hiring, and of venture-backed, for-profit start-ups. The result? An incomplete and less diverse news agenda. In an essay called "Editing While Female," American journalist Susan Glasser (2014) wrote after Abramson's departure: "There are shockingly few women at the top anywhere in America, and it's a deficit that is especially pronounced in journalism, where women leaders remain outliers, category-defying outliers who almost invariably still face a comeuppance" (para. 6).

Where to Go From Here?

As well as offering fertile ground for more research – we need to ask male journalists these same questions, for a start – a number of important implications for future practice in the industry arise out of this project. The high level of interest shown at a recent (April 2012) national industry panel on this project indicates to me that Canadian women print journalists hunger for more discussion on the issues raised and, more importantly, want action to make their lives as journalists less stressed and more rewarding, especially as technological demands increase. The participants' stories of workplace inflexibility and newsroom cultural inequities deserve to be told to a wider audience, including industry leaders. Awareness of this project would increase their understanding of women journalists' work experiences and how reviewing and altering work practices might improve the retention of not only women journalists but also attract more diverse kinds of employees in general. (According to Bell's 2014 article, "Hiring with Diversity in Mind" in the *Columbia Journalism Review*, digital news media start-ups have insular hiring practices that equal traditional media's dismal track record in hiring with diversity in mind [see also Oputu, 2014].) A focus on developing future leaders, which the *Hamilton Spectator* has taken up, could be adopted, with difference as a central aspect of defining leadership potential. Because of that program and her own tenacity, Nicole MacIntyre became a *Spec* assignment editor, earning industry notice for innovative assigning.

The current industry rhetoric about strategic risk-taking to regain financial ground should expand, given that instability is the new normal anyway. Editorial leaders need to take a smarter risk by stepping outside their own narrative comfort zones, encouraging new work practices to give all employees more flexibility and control over their own work flow, including rewarding those who take maximum paternity leave. That would be something to write about proudly, rather than endlessly whining that newspapers are dying and nobody knows what to do about it except to shutter papers (the *Kamloops Daily News* is a recent corpse; it closed its doors in January 2014 after eighty years of publishing), lay people off, and not publish on holidays or Mondays.

If increasing diversity in newsrooms is as important as participants indicated it is, the industry could reach out to racialized, ethnic, and other communities; promote journalism in under-represented communities as an important career; and work with journalism schools to seek out a wider range of students. Exchanges with journalists in the "ethnic press" would open many eyes to how wider diversity would broaden the definition of what is really making news in Canada. Media companies could also fund scholarships for low-income students at journalism schools, doing for other potential journalists what Dalhousie's program for black and Indigenous Nova Scotians did for journalist Sherri Borden Colley: it started her career.

Borden Colley (2013) wrote and sent me her first column – readers may recall she told me she could not imagine writing a column because she, as a reporter, had never done so. It is a passionate, personal piece written on the death of her friend and social activist, Burnley (Rocky) Jones. Wrote Borden Colley of his impact on marginalized Nova Scotians: "He was a pioneer who fought for the rights of those who could not fight or could not speak for themselves." She also wrote about her father, who, at ninety, still calls himself "coloured" and how growing up in New Glasgow he could not eat in white restaurants or get a haircut in barbershops.

I hope that women in print journalism, particularly those aspiring to or holding management positions, read this book to increase their own understanding of what complex factors influence their personal development within their newsrooms, as well as to assess their relationship to the workplace and the public whose interests they hope to engage. Professional women in general might also glean insights into how their own workplace insecurities are held in place, as everyone shares and reproduces damaging myths about women and their ability to lead.

I also hope that for the general reader, this volume sheds light on the idea that promotion and wide dissemination of different accounts of the world and a wider witnessing could lead to greater understanding and better public policy, potentially improving all of our lives – and not, incidentally, the bottom line of a major international industry that informs us about our world, yet is mired in financial despair. Public policymakers at all levels of government could be better informed if this book were to play a part in helping the news agenda evolve as a mechanism to promote informed citizenship as widely as possible across Canada's entire population.

Finally, a wish for those women journalists who told me their stories and agreed to take their inside voices outside with their names attached. I hope they see their participation in this study as empowering, adding to the force of their own career experiences and the legacy of those who went before them, ready to lead change through the current upheaval in journalistic practice. I think in particular of Emma Reilly, the young *Spectator* reporter who looked ahead and saw darkness, dragons, and black holes ahead in her career, who is on maternity leave at this writing. I think, too, of Margo Goodhand, the *Winnipeg Free Press* editor-in-chief who left journalism at the top of her career feeling discouraged, haunted by how women in print journalism could never be seen as leaders. She is part of what makes this no longer a given: after spending time away to write a book about the history of women's shelters in Canada, Goodhand returned to daily newspapering. She is now the editor-in-chief of the *Edmonton Journal*, and she wrote to me that, while she is still frustrated and challenged by dealing with a business in decline, her gratitude for doing such rewarding work with a talented newsroom outweighs the downside. Goodhand might be heartened to learn of a new meta-analysis published by the American Psychological Association that shows stereotypes that tie leadership to masculinity are slowly dissolving in the United States and Canada. Echoing the "confidence gap" theory, the study's authors found that men rated themselves as far more effective leaders than women rated themselves (Paustian-Underdahl, Walker, & Woehr, 2014). Goodhand has replaced Lucinda Chodan, who moved to the same post at the *Montreal Gazette*. Chodan has also taken on a new, larger role as a regional vice-president for Postmedia, overseeing editorial operations at the chain's papers in Ottawa and Windsor and co-leading national online developments. Chodan wrote to me that she is (mostly) kidding about being part of "a cabal of competent motivated women [ready] to take over the world." Meanwhile, at the *National Post*, Anne Marie Owens, who was not in this study, has been named editor-in-chief. Likewise, Cathrin Bradbury has become vice-president and editor-in chief of Metro English Canada, Torstar's chain of free dailies in Eastern Canada.

At the very least, these women, and hundreds of other women print journalists across the country, through their leadership and through their stories, are well positioned to question publicly and loudly the current narrative about what it means to be a journalist. Their stories have helped me to understand my own experience in newspapers, and I hope they will encourage others to continue their contributions to society's ongoing struggle for equality and social justice.

Notes

1. Introduction

1 Similar cultural effects can be seen in broadcast journalism. For example, Barber and Levitan (2012–13) found that in coverage of the 2011 Canadian federal election, female reporters were just as likely to interview male experts as male reporters were. The researchers found a dearth of women interviewed during an important time of national discourse, women accounting for less than one-fifth of interview clips analysed.

2. Senior Women Print Journalists

1 E. Barnard, personal communication, 15 November 2010, Halifax. All direct quotations in the following discussion are taken from this individual interview, as is the case for all direct quotations in this chapter.
2 Members of the most senior cohort who have left daily print journalism (one did so before the study began) are described in chapter 5.
3 The paper did have a female publisher. Sarah Dennis inherited the position from her late father, the first woman in the family dynasty to own the largest-circulation daily in the Atlantic provinces.
4 A. Paul, personal communication, 22 November 2010, Winnipeg.
5 P. Lee, personal communication, 14 November 2010, Halifax.
6 Lee has since become a web editor, giving her "that control that I so dearly seem to need" and is doing a freelance TV blog. Two managers she spoke of were fired, she said. (P. Lee, personal communication, 8 April 2013.)
7 P. Sword, personal communication, 23 November 2010, Halifax.

8 Unifor, Canada's largest private sector union, now represents unionized journalists across the country.

9 M. Steeves, personal communication, 18 November 2010, Hamilton.

10 M. Zurowski, personal communication, 18 January 2011, Calgary.

11 M. Zurowski, personal communication, 9 April 2013.

12 On the way out, I was shown a quiet corner for newsroom staffers to retreat to, named in honour of Michelle Lang, a *Herald* reporter who died in 2009 while covering the war in Afghanistan.

13 L. Chodan, personal communication, 30 June 2008, Victoria.

14 Chodan now serves as the *Gazette*'s editor-in-chief.

15 The only woman who identified herself as a lesbian will be described in chapter 5, as she was among those who have left journalism.

3. Mid-Career Participants

1 L. Corbella, personal communication, 18 January 2011, Calgary.

2 Two members of this cohort, Denise Helm and Paula Arab, left daily print journalism after the interviews. They will be discussed in chapter 8.

3 L. Corbella, personal communication, 14 March 2013, Calgary.

4 C. Ammerata, personal communication, 18 November 2010, Hamilton.

5 S. Borden Colley, personal communication, 15 November 2010, Halifax.

6 P. Brooks Arenburg, personal communication, 15 November 2010, Halifax.

7 This is similar to the experience of *Vancouver Sun* reporter Kim Bolan, who described at a Canadian Association of Journalism convention I attended in Vancouver in 2009 the criticism she has received from readers who thought that as a mother, she should not cover such crimes, as mentioned in chapter 1.

8 N. MacIntyre, personal communication, 15 November 2010, Hamilton.

9 N. MacIntyre, personal communication, 5 October 2011, Hamilton.

10 Ibid.

11 Ibid.

12 As I write this, the news is full of how Marissa Mayer, the newly appointed CEO of Yahoo, was hired when pregnant with her first child – gasp! – reigniting heated media debates about women and work/life balance.

13 Twenty years earlier, I was doing the same thing. My co-op day-care centre, where I was vice-president, charged $1 for every minute after 6 p.m. that parents were late.

14 S. Petrescu, personal communication, 11 January 2011, Victoria.

15 Arianna Huffington, "How to Succeed? Get More Sleep," TEDWomen (December 2010), retrieved 15 May 2012, from http://www.ted.com/talks/arianna_huffington_how_to_succeed_get_more_sleep?language=en

16 Petrescu was hired by Lucinda Chodan and her immediate boss was Stephanie Coombs, who left to work with Chodan in Edmonton. Petrescu worked with the editor in charge of the website, Denise Helm, who left later to become manager of Media Relations for the University of Victoria. Chodan, Coombs, and Helm are participants in this study. Within a few months over 2011 to 2012, white men replaced the all-white-female top tier at the *TC*. The sports and business editors were also white men. The publisher (who once had me fired and rehired from my freelance column and consulting work) survived the *TC* when it was sold to Glacier Media, then retired in early 2013.

17 S. Petrescu, personal communication, 14 March 2013, Victoria.

18 S. Coombs, personal communication, 14 January 2011, Victoria.

19 S. Coombs, personal communication, 14 March 2013, Victoria.

20 M. Welch, personal communication, 23 November 2010, Winnipeg.

4. For the Youngest Journalists, It's "a Game of Chicken"

1 J. Gerson, personal communication, 17 January 2011, Calgary.

2 The exception was Melissa Martin, then of the *Winnipeg Free Press*, who started her career in freelance entertainment reporting as a former musician.

3 Gerson has since left the *Herald* to work as Alberta correspondent for the *National Post*. In an email, she said, "The game of chicken continues." J. Gerson, personal communication, 14 March 2013, Calgary.

4 E. Reilly, personal communication, 18 November 2010, Hamilton.

5 Reilly was eventually hired as a full-time employee.

6 Reilly joined the panel along with Margo Goodhand and Kelly Toughill, both in this study; Marci Ien, the co-host of *Canada AM*, offered a broadcaster's perspective; and Patricia Graham, then vice-president of digital development for Postmedia's Pacific News Group, participated as one of the most highly placed women in Canadian print journalism. Graham left Postmedia and is now the Ombudswoman for Brunswick News Inc. in Saint John.

7 K. DeRosa, personal communication, 12 January 2011, Victoria.

8 When I worked at the *Standard*, from 1977 to 1980, I was in the Women's Department, behind the washrooms. Some composing room staffers (men) often tried to embarrass me when I went downstairs to watch type and

photos being put on pages. This was the era of nude photos of women on composing-room walls, the *Globe* included.

9 Canadian Journalism Project, "Katie DeRosa Named First James Travers Fellowship Recipient" (2012), retrieved 16 May 2012, from http://j-source.ca/article/katie-derosa-named-first-james-travers-fellowship-recipient

10 N. O'Reilly, personal communication, 18 November 2010, Hamilton.

11 O'Reilly did return to the topic in the focus group the next day, which will be discussed in chapter 5.

12 N. O'Reilly, "Human Trafficking Case Puts Spotlight on Refugee System," *Hamilton Spectator*, retrieved 15 April 2012, from human-trafficking-case-puts-spotlight-on-refugee-system

13 L. Fraser, personal communication, 15 November 2010, Halifax.

14 Her biography was retrieved from the *Winnipeg Free Press* website on 2 April 2012, but it is no longer posted. A portion of her biography can still be found at Muck Rack, http://muckrack.com/link/9ONd/martin-melissa-winnipeg-free-press

15 M. Martin, personal communication, 23 November 2010, Winnipeg.

16 H. Fallding, personal communication, 11 October 2012, Winnipeg.

17 M. Martin, personal communication, 23 November 2010, Winnipeg.

18 In fact, if it weren't for maternity leaves, Katie DeRosa and Nicole O'Reilly likely wouldn't have been hired at all, and Emma Reilly might have had to wait a lot longer to be promoted.

5. Of Darkness, Dragons, and Black Holes

1 C. Ammerata, M. MacIntyre, N. O'Reilly, and E. Reilly, personal communication, 23 November 2010, Hamilton.

2 H. Fallding, M. Goodhand, M. Martin, and M. Welch, personal communication, 23 November 2010, Winnipeg.

3 At a Canadian Newspaper Association panel on my research that was held in Toronto on 27 April 2012, and which I chaired, Margo Goodhand told the audience that in the previous eight years, seven babies had been born to *Free Press* editorial employees. All were the babies' fathers.

4 The woman was apparently not a journalist, but a clerk.

5 H. Fallding, personal communication, 15 April 2014, Winnipeg.

6 P. Arab, J. Gerson, and M. Zurowski, personal communication, 18 January 2011, Calgary.

7 S. Borden Colley, P. Brooks Arenburg, and L. Fraser, personal communication, 16 November 2010, Halifax.
8 N. O'Reilly, personal communication, 19 November 2010, Hamilton.
9 E. Reilly, personal communication, 19 November 2010, Hamilton.
10 C. Ammerata, personal communication, 19 November 2010, Hamilton.

6. Six Who Walked Away

1 L. Fraser, personal communication, 16 November 2010, Halifax.
2 Because she did not choose to leave her job, Melissa Martin remains in chapter 4 with her cohort.
3 K. Toughill, personal communication, 16 November 2010, Halifax.
4 K. Toughill, personal communication, 12 January 2012, Victoria.
5 It was Vicki Keith in 1988.
6 Toughill elaborated on this newsroom communication problem at the previously mentioned industry conference in Toronto, in April 2012, during a panel I convened to air the issues my research raises. She, Emma Reilly, and Margo Goodhand, plus two others not in the study, participated.
7 The ethical review covered this concern.
8 "Janet," personal communication, late in 2010.
9 "Janet," personal communication, late in 2011.
10 H. Fallding, personal communication, 22 November 2010, Winnipeg.
11 Fallding said in an email (personal communication, 13 March 2013) that, while she missed the irreverence of newsroom culture and the influence she had as a writer, her work/life balance has improved dramatically.
12 D. Helm, personal communication, 14 January 2011, Victoria.
13 Helm would go on to finish her career at the *Times Colonist* as the acting editor-in-chief, after Chodan left.
14 Paterson went from reporter to city editor to managing editor to columnist, and then left journalism. She received an honorary PhD for her community activism and journalism work from the University of Victoria and spent two years as a volunteer communications worker in Honduras.
15 M. Goodhand, personal communication, 22 November 2010, Winnipeg.
16 Women journalists have begun to comment publicly on this widespread problem of being the target of sexist and violent harassment online, including, most recently, Amy Wallace in the *New York Times* (2014) and Amanda Hess in the *Pacific Standard* (2014a.)

17 Internal memo from Margo Goodhand to staff at the *Winnipeg Free Press*, Winnipeg, 15 June 2012.
18 P. Arab, personal communication, 25 March 2013.

7. Conclusions

1 E. Anderson, vice-president, human resources, *Calgary Herald*, personal communication, 22 September 2014, Calgary.
2 "Janet," personal communication, late 2010.
3 A sample headline from the *Times Colonist* on 19 July 2012, page D7, was "The CEO Is Pregnant: Yahoo's New Chief Reignites Can-We-Have-It-All Debate." *Financial Times* management columnist Lucy Kellaway found more than 4,000 newspaper articles written about Mayer as of 19 July 2012 when her column "Jobs, Motherhood and Varieties of Wrong" was published (Kellaway, 2012).
4 An example: a sixty-something white male industry veteran named Lou Clancy has been brought out of retirement (after a forty-five-year career mostly at the *Toronto Sun* and *Toronto Star*) to run PostMedia Network Inc.'s new Hamilton editing facility, where stories destined for all the chain's dailies will be chosen, laid out, and edited. Clancy and his associates will decide what national and foreign news will go on the front page of all the member dailies, limiting input from local editors. See "Postmedia Sheds Costs with Shift to Hamilton," *Globe and Mail*, 15 August 2012, B1. The then *Globe* media reporter, Steve Ladurantaye, wrote in the *Globe* of 18 August 2012, page B3, that Postmedia CEO Paul Godfrey told him, "It's not that we want to do this: we have to do this." Clancy, said Godfrey, is "the guy in charge" who will ultimately make the front-page decisions for the entire chain (debt: more than $480 million), including the *Montreal Gazette* and the *Vancouver Sun*.
5 Reilly spoke during a Canadian Newspaper Association panel on 27 April 2012, in Toronto, for which I was the moderator. The topic was based on the findings of this project: three of the participants were on the panel.

References

Abrams, L. (2010). *Oral history theory*. New York: Routledge.

Aldridge, M. (2001). Confessional culture, masculinity and emotional work. *Journalism, 2*(1), 91–108. http://jou.sagepub.com.ezproxy.library.uvic.ca/content/2/1/91.full.pdf+html

Allen, C. (2006). Narrative research. *Nursing Research, 13*(3), 4–6.

Altheide, D.L. (1985). *Media power*. Beverly Hills, CA: Sage.

Archer Mann, S., & Huffman, D.J. (2005). The decentering of second wave feminism and the rise of the third wave. *Science and Society, 69*(1), 56–91. http://dx.doi.org/10.1521/siso.69.1.56.56799

Association for Education in Journalism and Mass Communication (AEJMC). (2010). Women in the newsroom: Burned out and fed up. Online Live Chat. 21 January.

Association for Women's Rights in Development (AWID). (2004). *Intersectionality: A tool for gender and economic justice. Women's Rights and Economic Change. No. 9.* Toronto: AWID.

Atkinson, P., & Delamont, S. (2006). Rescuing narrative from qualitative research. *Narrative Inquiry, 16*(1), 164–72. http://dx.doi.org/10.1075/ni.16.1.21atk

Bamberg, M. (2003). Positioning with Davie Hogan – Stories, tellings and identities. In C. Daiute & C. Lightfoot (Eds.), *Narrative analysis: Studying the development of individuals in society* (pp. 135–57). London: Sage.

Barber, M., & Levitan, J. (2012–13). Not seen, not heard: Gender representation on Canadian television news during the lead-up to the 2011 federal election. *International Journal of Diverse Identities, 12*(2), 1–8.

Barber, M., & Rauhala, A. (2005). The Canadian news directors study: Demographics and political leanings of television decision-makers. *Canadian Journal of Communication*, 30(2), 281–92.

Barber, M., & Rauhala, A. (2008). *A portrait of women as newsroom leaders: A Canadian perspective.* Paper presented at the Gender, Journalism and the Press Conference, Rennes, France.

Bateson, M. (1989). *Composing a life.* New York: Harper Collins.

Beam, R. (2008). The social characteristics of U.S. journalists and their "best work." *Journalism Practice*, 2(1), 1–14. http://dx.doi.org/10.1080/17512780701768428

Beers, D. (2006). The public sphere and online, independent journalism. *Canadian Journal of Education*, 29(1), 109–30. http://dx.doi.org/10.2307/20054149

Bell, E. (2014). Diversity – or lack thereof – in journalism startups. *Columbia Journalism Review* (18 March). Retrieved 20 March 2014, from http://www.cjr.org/minority_reports/diversity_response.php?page=all

Benson, R. (2005). American journalism and the politics of diversity. *Media Culture & Society*, 27(1), 5–20. http://dx.doi.org/10.1177/0163443705047031

Biklen, S.K., & Casella, R. (2007). *A practical guide to the qualitative dissertation.* New York: Teachers College Press.

Booth, W.C., Colomb, G.G., & Williams, J.M. (2008). *The craft of research* (3rd ed.). Chicago: University of Chicago Press. http://dx.doi.org/10.7208/chicago/9780226062648.001.0001

Borden Colley, S. (2013). When Rocky spoke, people listened and results followed. *Chronicle Herald*, 31 July. Retrieved 5 August 2013, from http://thechronicleherald.ca/opinion/1145332-when-rocky-spoke-people-listened-and-results-followed

Breckenridge, J. (1984). The patience of Shirley Sharzer. *Ryerson Review of Journalism.* Retrieved 10 March 2009, from http://rrj.ca/m3554/

Bryman, A., Teevan, J., & Bell, E. (2009). *Social research methods* (2nd Canadian ed.). Don Mills, ON: Oxford University Press.

Burnard, P. (1991). A method of analyzing interview transcripts in qualitative research. *Nurse Education Today*, 11(6), 461–6. http://dx.doi.org/10.1016/0260-6917(91)90009-Y

Butler, J. (1988). Performative acts and gender constitution: An essay in phenomenology and feminist theory. *Theatre Journal*, 40(4), 519–31. http://dx.doi.org/10.2307/3207893

Byerly, C.M., & Ross, K. (2008). *Women and media: A critical introduction.* Oxford: Blackwell. http://dx.doi.org/10.1002/9780470774908

Cameron, D. (2007). Review of the book *Feminist critical discourse analysis: Gender, power and ideology in discourse* by Lazar, M. (Ed.). [Electronic Edition.] *Language in Society*, 36(1), 112–15.

Canadian Journalism Project. (2012). Katie DeRosa named first James Travers Fellowship recipient. Retrieved 7 April 2014, from http://j-source.ca/article/katie-derosa-named-first-james-travers-fellowship-recipient

Caselman, T., Self, A., & Self, P. (2006). Adolescent attributes contributing to the imposter phenomenon. *Journal of Adolescence, 29*(3), 395–405. http://dx.doi.org/10.1016/j.adolescence.2005.07.003

Chomsky, N., & Herman, E.S. (1988). *Manufacturing consent: The political economy of mass media.* New York: Pantheon Books.

Clandinin, D. (2006). Narrative inquiry: A methodology for studying lived experience. *Research Studies in Music Education, 27*(1), 44–54. http://dx.doi.org/10.1177/1321103X060270010301

Clandinin, D.J., & Connelly, F.M. (2000). *Narrative inquiry: Experience and story in qualitative research.* San Francisco: Jossey-Bass Publishers.

Cobb, C. (2004). *Ego and ink: The inside story of Canada's national newspaper war.* Toronto: McClelland and Stewart.

Coffey, A., & Atkinson, P. (1996). *Making sense of qualitative data: Complementary research strategies.* Thousand Oaks, CA: Sage.

Cohen, N. (2012). How much do freelance journalists make? The Canadian Journalism Project. Retrieved 12 September 2012, from http://j-source.ca/article/how-much-do-freelance-journalists-make?utm_source=CJF+Programs+Newsletters&utm_campaign=1dc58d4b07-2012_09_129_12_2012&

Cole, B.A. (2009). Gender, narratives and intersectionality: Can personal experience approaches to research contribute to "undoing gender"? *International Review of Education, 55,* 561–78. http://dx.doi.org/10.10.007/s11159-009-9140-5

Connell, R.W. (2000). *The men and the boys.* Berkeley: University of California Press.

Connelly, F.M., & Clandinin, D.J. (1990). Stories of experience and narrative inquiry. *Educational Researcher, 19*(5), 2–14. http://dx.doi.org/10.3102/0013189X019005002

Craft, S., & Wanta, W. (2004). Women in the newsroom: Influences of female editors and reporters on the News Agenda. *Journalism & Mass Communication Quarterly, 81*(1), 124–38. http://dx.doi.org/10.1177/107769900408100109

Crenshaw, K. (1990–1). Mapping the margins: Intersectionality, identity politics, and violence against women of color. *Stanford Law Review, 43*(1), 241–300.

Daiute, C., & Lightfoot, C. (Eds.). (2004). *Narrative analysis: Studying the development of individuals in society.* Thousand Oaks, CA: Sage. http://dx.doi.org/10.4135/9781412985246

Daugherty, A. (2013). Women know less about politics than men, study finds (that goes for Canada, too). *Globe and Mail,* 3 July. Retrieved 3 July 2013, from http://www.theglobeandmail.com/life/the-hot-button/women

-know-less-about-politics-than-men-study-finds-that-goes-for-canada-too/
article12947354/

Davis, K. (2008). Intersectionality as buzzword: A sociology of science perspective on what makes a feminist theory successful. *Feminist Theory*, 9(1), 67–85. http://dx.doi.org/10.1177/1464700108086364

de Bruin, M. (2000). Gender, organizational and professional identities in journalism. *Journalism*, 1(2), 217–38. http://dx.doi.org/10.1177/146488490000100205

Dempsey, L. (1976). *No life for a lady*. Don Mills, ON: Musson Books.

Desbarats, P. (1996). *Guide to Canadian news media* (2nd ed.). Toronto: Harcourt Brace.

Deuze, M. (2005). What is journalism? Professional identity and ideology of journalists reconsidered. *Journalism*, 6(4), 442–64. http://dx.doi.org/10.1177/1464884905056815

Dezso, C., & Ross, D. (2012). Does female representation in top management improve firm performance? A panel data investigation. *Strategic Management Journal*, 33(9), 1072–89. http://dx.doi.org/10.1002/smj.1955

Dines, G., & Humez, J. (Eds.). (2003). *Gender, race and class in media: A text reader*. Thousand Oaks, CA: Sage.

Djerf-Pierre, M. (2005). Lonely at the top: Gendered media elites in Sweden. *Journalism*, 6(3), 265–90. http://jou.sagepub.com.ezproxy.library.uvic.ca/content/6/3/265.full.pdf+html

Donsbach, W. (2004). Psychology of news decisions: Factors behind journalists' professional behaviour. *Journalism*, 5(2), 131–57. http://dx.doi.org/10.1177/146488490452002

Durham, M.G. (1998). On the relevance of standpoint epistemology to the practice of journalism: The case for "strong objectivity." *Communication Theory*, 8(2), 117–40. http://dx.doi.org/10.1111/j.1468-2885.1998.tb00213.x

Eichler, L. (2012). Women@Work: The baby bump pushes against the glass ceiling. *Globe and Mail Report on Business*, 20 July, B15.

Elmore, C. (2009). Turning points and turnover among female journalists: Communicating resistance and repression. *Women's Studies in Communication*, 32(2), 232–54.

Ericsson, K.A., Prietula, M., & Cokely, E. (2007). The making of an expert. *Harvard Business Review Reprint* R0707. Cambridge, MA: Harvard Business Review.

Everbach, T., & Flournoy, C. (2007). Women leaving journalism for better pay and working conditions. *Newspaper Research Journal*, 28(3), 52–64.

Fetherling, D. (1990). *The rise of the Canadian newspaper*. Oxford: Oxford University Press.

Fiamengo, J. (2008). *The woman's page: Journalism and rhetoric in early Canada*. Toronto: University of Toronto Press.

Finlayson, J. (1999). *Trailblazers: Women talk about changing Canada*. Toronto: Doubleday Canada.

Fisher, C.D. (1995). *Lotta Dempsey: The lady was a star*. Toronto: Belsten Pub.

Fleras, A. (2003). *Mass media communication in Canada*. Toronto: Nelson.

Fleras, A. (2011). *The media gaze: Representations of diversity in Canada*. Vancouver: UBC Press.

Forrest, A. (1993). Women and industrial relations theory: No room in the discourse. *Industrial Relations*, 3(48), 409–40. http://dx.doi.org/10.7202/050871ar

Fraser, H. (2004). Doing narrative research: Analysing personal stories line by line. *Qualitative Social Work*, 3(2), 179–201. http://qsw.sagepub.com.ezproxy.library.uvic.ca/content/3/2/179.full.pdf+html

Freeman, B. (1989). *Kit's kingdom: The journalism of Kathleen Blake Coleman*. Ottawa: Carleton University Press.

Freeman, B. (2001). *The satellite sex: The media and women's issues in English Canada, 1966–1971*. Waterloo, ON: Wilfrid Laurier University Press.

Freeman, B. (2011). *Beyond bylines: Media workers and women's rights in Canada*. Waterloo, ON: Wilfrid Laurier University Press.

Gerson, C. (2010). *Canadian women in print: 1750–1918*. Waterloo, ON: Wilfrid Laurier University Press.

Gist, M.E. (1993). Through the looking glass· Diversity and reflected appraisals of the self in mass media. In P.M. Creedon (Ed.), *Women in mass communication* (2nd ed., pp. 104–17). Newbury Park, CA: Sage.

Glasser, S. (2014). Editing while female: Field notes from one of journalism's most dangerous jobs. *Politico Magazine* (16 May). Retrieved 24 September 2014, from http://www.politico.com/magazine/story/2014/05/editing-while-female-jill-abramson-106782.html#.vcmd2fldvgz

Globe and Mail. (2010). Editorial, "Leaders must recruit leaders." 9 January, A15.

Grant, J. (1993). *Fundamental feminism: Contesting the core concepts of feminist theory*. New York: Routledge.

Griffin, A. (2014). Where are the women? Why we need more female newsroom leaders. *NiemanReports* (Summer). Retrieved 12 September 2014, from http://niemanreports.org/articles/where-are-the-women/

Gubrium, J., & Holstein, J. (2009). *Analysing narrative reality*. Thousand Oaks, CA: Sage.

Haas, T., & Steiner, L. (2001). Public journalism as a journalism of publics: Implications of the Habermas-Fraser debate for public journalism. *Journalism*, 2(2), 123–47. http://dx.doi.org/10.1177/146488490100200202

Haraway, D. (2004). Situated knowledges: The science question in feminism and the privilege of the partial perspective. In S. Harding (Ed.), *The feminist standpoint theory reader* (pp. 81–101). New York: Routledge.

Hardin, M., & Whiteside, E. (2009). Token responses to gendered newsrooms: Factors in the career-related decisions of female newspaper sports journalists. *Journalism*, *10*(5), 627–46. http://dx.doi.org/10.1177/146488490 90100050501

Harding, S. (1991). *Whose science? Whose knowledge? Thinking from women's lives*. Ithaca, NY: Cornell University Press.

Hayes, D. (2014). Reform spirit drove writer Heather Robertson. *Globe and Mail*, 3 April. Retrieved 4 April 2014, from http://www.theglobeandmail .com/news/reform-spirit-drove-her-work-private-life/article17819966/ #dashboard/follows/

Hess, A. (2014a). Why women aren't welcome on the Internet. *Pacific Standard*, 6 January. Retrieved 19 January 2014, from http://www.psmag.com/ navigation/health-and-behavior/women-arent-welcome-internet-72170/

Hess, A. (2014b). Women at the top of the masthead. *Slate*, 15 May. Retrieved 15 May 2014, from http://www.slate.com/articles/double_x/ doublex/2014/05/jill_abramson_was_everything_to_young_women_at _the_new_york_times.html

Hesse-Biber, S. (Ed.). (2007). *Handbook of feminist research: Theory and praxis*. Thousand Oaks, CA: Sage.

Jones, K. (2014). *The current state of freelance writing 2014*. Tampa, FL: CopyPress Community, 2014. Retrieved 1 May 2014, from http:// community.copypress.com/the-state-of-freelance-writing-2014-white -paper-and-infographic/

Juzwik, M. (2010). Overstating claims for story and for narrative inquiry: A cautionary note. *Narrative Inquiry*, *20*(2), 349–70. http://dx.doi.org/10.1075/ ni.20.2.08juz

Kay, K., & Shipman, C. (2014). The confidence gap. *The Atlantic*, 18 April. Retrieved 20 April 2014, from http://www.theatlantic.com/features/ archive/2014/04/the-confidence-gap/359815/

Kellaway, L. (2012). Jobs, motherhood and varieties of wrong. *Financial Times*, 29 July. Retrieved 2 August 2012, from http://www.ft.com/intl/cms/ s/0/3f1db994-d73b-11e1-8c7d-00144feabdc0.html#axzz3OeGkL55y

Kesterton, W. (1967). *A history of journalism in Canada*. Toronto: McClelland and Stewart.

Lang, M. (1999). *Women who made the news: Female journalists in Canada 1880–1945*. Montreal: McGill-Queen's University Press.

Layton, A., & Shepard, A. (2013). Lack of female sources in NY Times front-page stories highlights need for change. Poynter Institute, 16 July. Retrieved 30 July 2013, from http://www.poynter.org/news/mediawire/217828/ lack-of-female-sources-in-new-york-times-stories-spotlights-need-for-change/

Lazar, M. (2007). Feminist critical discourse analysis: Articulating a feminist discourse praxis. *Critical Discourse Studies, 4*(2), 141–64. http://dx.doi .org/10.1080/17405900701464816

Lieblich, A., Tuval-Mashiach, R., & Zilber, T. (1998). *Narrative research: Reading, analysis and interpretation.* Thousand Oaks, CA: Sage.

Lippmann, W. (1922). *Public opinion.* New York: Harcourt Brace. Retrieved 15 September 2013, from http://www.gutenberg.org/ebooks/6456

Mahtani, M. (2014). Do you see yourself in those who shape the news? *The Broadbent Blog.* Entry posted 17 January. Retrieved 15 September 2014, from https://www.broadbentinstitute.ca/en/blog/do-you-see-yourself -those-who-shape-news

McCall, C. (2008). *My life as a dame: The personal and the political in the writings of Christina McCall.* Toronto: House of Anansi Press.

McCall, L. (1992). Does gender fit? Bourdieu, feminism, and conception of social order. *Theory and Society, 21*(6), 837–67. http://dx.doi.org/10.1007/ BF00992814

McCall, L. (2005). The complexity of intersectionality. *Signs, 30*(3), 1771–99.

McKercher, C. (2002). *Newsworkers unite: Labor, convergence, and North American newspapers.* Boston: Rowman and Littlefield.

McKercher, C. (2009). Commentary. *Feminist Media Studies, 3*(9), 370–4.

McKercher, C., & Cumming, C. (1998). *The Canadian reporter: News writing and reporting.* Toronto: Harcourt Brace.

Media Report to Women. (2009). Industry Statistics. Retrieved 27 April 2009, from http://www.mediareporttowomen.com/statistics.htm

Moosa-Mitha, M. (2005). Situating anti-oppressive theories within critical and difference-centred perspectives. In L. Brown & S. Strega (Eds.), *Research as resistance* (pp. 37–72). Toronto: Women's Press.

Morris, M. (2007). *Using intersectional feminist frameworks in research.* Ottawa: Canadian Research Institute for the Advancement of Women.

Nancoo, R., & Nancoo, S. (Eds.) (1997). *The mass media and Canadian diversity.* Mississauga, ON: Canadian Educators' Press.

Nelson, K. (2004). Construction of the cultural self in early narratives. In C. Daiute & C. Lightfoot (Eds.), *Narrative analysis: Studying the development of individuals in society* (pp. 88–109). Thousand Oaks, CA: Sage. http://dx.doi .org/10.4135/9781412985246.n2.1

Nicodemo, A. (2012). Women's rights, race and reproduction. ASU Research Matters. Retrieved 4 June 2012, from http://researchmatters.asu.edu/ stories/womens-rights-race-and-reproduction-2260/

North, L. (2007). Just a little bit of cheeky ribaldry. *Feminist Media Studies, 7*(1), 81–96. http://dx.doi.org/10.1080/14680770601103738

North, L. (2009a). Gendered experiences of industry change and the effects of neoliberalism. *Journalism Studies, 10*(4), 506–21. http://dx.doi.org/10.1080/14616700902783911

North, L. (2009b). Rejecting the "f" word: How "feminism" and "feminists" are understood in the newsroom. *Journalism, 10*(6), 739–57. http://dx.doi.org/10.1177/1464884909344479

O'Connor, K. (2010). *Gender and women's leadership: A reference handbook*. Thousand Oaks, CA: Sage.

Ojo, T. (2006). Ethnic print media in the multicultural nation of Canada. *Journalism, 7*(3), 343–61. http://jou.sagepub.com/cgi/doi/10.1177/1464884906065517

Ollerenshaw, J.A., & Creswell, J.W. (2002). Narrative research: A comparison of two restorying data analysis approaches. *Qualitative Inquiry, 8*(3), 329–47. http://dx.doi.org/10.1177/10778004008003008

Oputu, E. (2014). Digital media hiring diversity under the microscope. *Columbia Journalism Review: Minority Reports* (14 March). Retrieved 30 April 2014, from http://www.cjr.org/minority_reports/digital_media_hiring_diversity.php

Paustian-Underdahl, S.C., Walker, L.S., & Woehr, D.J. (2014). Gender and perceptions of leadership effectiveness: A meta-analysis of contextual moderators. *Journal of Applied Psychology, 99*(6), 1129–45.

Peiser, W. (2000). Setting the journalist agenda: Influences from journalists' individual characteristics and from media factors. *Journalism & Mass Communication Quarterly, 77*(2), 243–57. http://dx.doi.org/10.1177/107769900007700202

Phoenix, A. (1994). Practising feminist research: The intersection of gender and "race" in the research process. In M. Maynard & J. Purvis (Eds.), *Researching women's lives from a feminist perspective* (pp. 49–71). London: Taylor Francis.

Professional Writers Association of Canada. (2006). Canadian professional writers survey: A profile of the freelance writing sector in Canada. Toronto: PWAC. Retrieved 16 April 2010, from http://pwac.ca/wp-content/uploads/2014/03/PWACsurvey.pdf

Reinardy, S. (2009). Female journalists more likely to leave newspapers. *Newspaper Research Journal, 30*(3), 42–57.

Reinharz, S. (1992). *Feminist methods in social research*. New York: Oxford University Press.

Rex, K. (1995). *No daughter of Mine: The women and history of the Canadian Women's Press Club, 1904–1971*. Toronto: Cedar Cave Books, University of Toronto Press.

Richmond, H.J. (2002). Learners' lives: A narrative analysis. *The Qualitative Report, 7*(3). Retrieved 21 September 2011, from http://www.nova.edu/ssss/QR/QR7-3/richmond.html

Robertson, D. (2014). Surprised? Canadian newspaper columnists are mostly male, middle-aged. Canadian Journalism Project, 14 January. Retrieved 15 January 2014, from http://j-source.ca/article/surprised-canadian-newspaper-columnists-are-mostly-male-middle-agedhttp://j-source.ca/article/surprised-canadian-newspaper-columnists-are-mostly-male-middle-aged

Robinson, G. (1998). Monopolies of knowledge in Canadian communication studies: The case of feminist approaches. *Canadian Journal of Communication*, 23(1), 65–72. http://www.cjc-online.ca/index.php/journal/article/view/1023/929

Robinson, G. (2005). *Gender, journalism and equity*. Cresskill, NJ: Hampton Press.

Rodgers, S., & Thorson, E. (2003). A socialization perspective on male and female reporting. *Journal of Communication*, 53(4), 658–75. http://dx.doi.org/10.1111/j.1460-2466.2003.tb02916.x

Roets, G., & Goedgeluck, M. (2007). Daisies on the toad: Tracing the political potential of our postmodernist, feminist approach to life story research. *Qualitative Inquiry*, 13(1), 85–112. Retrieved 9 October 2012, from http://dx.doi.org/10.1177/1077800406295624

Rosin, H. (2010). The end of men. *The Atlantic* (July/August), 56–72. http://www.theatlantic.com/magazine/archive/2010/07/the-end-of-men/308135/

Ross, K. (2007). The journalist, the housewife, the citizen and the press: Women and men as sources in local news narratives. *Journalism*, 8(4), 449–73.

Ross, K., & Carter, C. (2011). Women and news: A long and winding road. *Media Culture & Society*, 33(8), 1148–65. http://dx.doi.org/10.1177/0163443711418272

Rutherford, P. (1982). *A Victorian authority: The daily press in late nineteenth-century Canada*. Toronto: University of Toronto Press.

Ryfe, D. (2009). Broader and deeper: A study of newsroom culture in a time of change. *Journalism*, 10(2), 197–216. http://dx.doi.org/10.1177/1464884908100601

Sandberg, S. (2013). *Lean in: Women, work and the will to lead*. Toronto: Random House of Canada.

Sangster, J. (2006). Telling our stories: Feminist debates and the use of oral history. In V. Strong-Boag, M.L. Gleeson, & A. Perry (Eds.), *Rethinking Canada: The promise of women's history* (pp. 220–34). Don Mills, ON: Oxford.

Schudson, M. (2000). The domain of journalism studies around the globe. *Journalism*, 1(1), 55–9. http://dx.doi.org/10.1177/146488490000100110

Scott, J. (2007). Experience. In A.M. Jaggar (Ed.), *Just methods: An interdisciplinary feminist reader* (pp. 272–82). Boulder, CO: Paradigm Publishers.

Shermack, K. (2014). Still a man's world: The gender gap is shrinking, but not at the most senior positions. *Convergence* (Spring), 25–7.

Smith, D. (2005). *Institutional ethnography: A sociology for people*. Lanham, MD: AltaMira Press.

Smith, V. (2010). Educating Lotta, Kit and Shirley: How three women journalists responded to the demands of Canadian newspapers to teach the status quo. In D.E. Clover & V. Smith (Eds.), *Connected understandings: Women, gender and education. Proceedings of the 2010 Canadian Society for Study of Women and Education, Concordia University* (pp. 71–6). Ottawa: CASWE. http://www.csse-scee.ca/docs/caswe/cascloverandsmithproceedings2010.pdf

Snyder, R.C. (2008). What is third-wave feminism? A new directions essay. *Signs, 34*(1), 175–96. http://dx.doi.org/10.1086/588436

Sosulski, M., Buchanan, N., & Donnell, C. (2010). Life history and narrative analysis: Feminist methodologies contextualizing black women's experiences with severe mental illness. *Journal of Sociology and Social Welfare, 37*(3), 29–57.

Sotiron, M. (1997). *From politics to profit: The commercialization of daily newspapers, 1890–1920*. Montreal: McGill-Queen's University Press.

Sparks, R., Young, M., & Darnell, S. (2006). Convergence, corporate restructuring, and Canadian online news, 2000–2003. *Canadian Journal of Communication, 31*(2), 391–423.

Speer, S. (2005). *Gender talk: Feminism, discourse and conversation analysis*. London: Routledge. http://dx.doi.org/10.4324/9780203321447

Stabile, C. (2004). Getting what she deserved: The news media, Martha Stewart, and masculine domination. *Feminist Media Studies, 4*(3), 315–32. http://dx.doi.org/10.1080/1468077042000309964

Statistics Canada. (2008). 2006 Census: Ethnic origin, visible minorities, place of work and mode of transportation. *The Daily*, 2 April. Retrieved 7 November 2011, from http://www.statcan.gc.ca/daily-quotidien/080402/dq080402a-eng.htm

Steiner, L. (1998). Stories of quitting: Why did women journalists leave the newsroom? *American Journalism, 15*(3), 89–116. http://dx.doi.org/10.1080/08821127.1998.10731989

Steiner, L. (2009). Gender in the newsroom. In T. Hanitzsch & K. Wahl-Jorgensen (Eds.), *Handbook of journalism studies* (pp. 116–29). New York: Routledge.

Strega, S. (2005). The view from the poststructural margins: Epistemology and methodology reconsidered. In L. Brown & S. Strega (Eds.), *Research as resistance* (pp. 199–235). Toronto: Canadian Scholars' Press.

Strong, C.R. (2011). *Female journalists in New Zealand daily newspapers: From early careers to gender gap in editorship*. (Doctoral dissertation, Massey

University, New Zealand). Retrieved 7 November 2011, from http://mro.
massey.ac.nz/bitstream/handle/10179/2780/02_whole.pdf?sequence=1

Thiel, S. (2004). Shifting identities, creating new paradigms. *Feminist Media Studies, 4*(1), 21–36. http://dx.doi.org/10.1080/14680770410001674626

Timson, J. (2012). Work-life balance: Why it's time to be honest about babies and boardrooms. *Globe and Mail* (National Edition), 20 July, L3.

Trimble, L., Arscott, J., & Tremblay, M. (2013). *Stalled: The representation of women in Canadian governments.* Vancouver: UBC Press.

United Nations. (2006). *Convention on the elimination of all forms of discrimination against women.* New York: United Nations. Retrieved 17 July 2014, from http://www.un.org/womenwatch/daw/cedaw/

Usher, N. (2014). It's not just Jill Abramson: Women everywhere are getting pushed out of journalism. *Washington Post,* 29 May. Retrieved 2 June 2014, from http://www.washingtonpost.com/posteverything/wp/2014/05/28/its-not-just-jill-abramson-women-everywhere-are-getting-pushed-out-of-journalism/

van Dijk, T. (1996). Power and the news media. In D. Paletz (Ed.), *Political communication in action* (pp. 9–36). Creskill, NJ: Hampton Press.

van Dijk, T. (Ed.). (1997). *Discourse as structure and process.* Thousand Oaks, CA: Sage.

van Dijk, T. (2008). News, discourse, and ideology. In T. Hanitzsch & K. Wahl-Jorgensen (Eds.), *Handbook of journalism studies* (pp. 191–204). New York: Routledge.

Vlad, T. (2011). 2010 Annual survey of journalism and mass communication enrollments: Enrollments grow, reversing stagnation of recent years. *Journalism & Mass Communication Educator, 66*(4), 299–324.

Walker, R., Cooke, M., & McAllister, M. (2008). A neophyte's journey through qualitative analysis using Moore's cognitive processes of analysis. *International Journal of Qualitative Methods, 7,* 81–93.

Wallace, A. (2014). Life as a female journalist: Hot or not? *New York Times,* 20 January, A17.

Wente, M. (2011). What glass ceiling? It's the mommy track that's stopping women from reaching the top. *Globe and Mail,* 22 September, A12.

Williams, J., Manvell, J., & Bornstein, S. (2006). "Opt out" or pushed out? How the press covers work/family conflict: The untold story of why women leave the workforce. The Center for Work Life Law, University of California, Hastings College of the Law. Retrieved 27 January 2010, from http://www.worklifelaw.org/pubs/OptOutPushedOut.pdf

Wilmot Voss, K. (2004). Redefining women's news: A case study of three women's page editors and their framing of the women's movement.

(Doctoral Dissertation, University of Maryland). Retrieved 25 April 2010, from http://drum.lib.umd.edu/handle/1903/1955

Wohlbold, E., & Chenier, L. (2011). *Women in senior management: Where are they?* Ottawa: Conference Board of Canada. http://www.conferenceboard.ca/e-library/abstract.aspx?did=4416

Wolf, D. (1996). Situating feminist dilemmas in fieldwork. In D. Wolf (Ed.), *Feminist dilemmas in fieldwork* (pp. 1–27). Boulder, CO: Westview Press.

Woodward, K. (2006). Performing age, performing gender. *National Women's Studies Association Journal, 18*(1), 162–89. http://dx.doi.org/10.2979/NWS.2006.18.1.162

Wong, J. (2012). *Out of the blue: A memoir of workplace depression, recovery, redemption, and yes, happiness.* Toronto: Jan Wong.

Index

Aboriginal people. *See* Indigenous people

Abramson, Jill, 211

advocacy for vulnerable people. *See* social justice issues

ageism: "dinosaur" fears, 36, 44, 63; mid-career journalists, 104; power *vs.* powerlessness, 63; senior journalists, 36, 43–4, 104, 173, 175; theme of, 203. *See also* stereotypes

age of journalist: advantages, 94–5; age and gender *vs.* personality, 99–100; age *vs.* gender gap, 94–6, 129, 132–3, 162–3; hiring decisions, 155–6; humour about, 95, 129; mutual respect, 96; narrative analysis, 29, 33; playing with stereotypes, 117, 142; sexuality, 129

alternative careers: for journalism school grads, 5, 125–6; in PR and communications, 40, 111, 125–6, 140, 165, 198

Ammerata, Carla (mid-career): age and background, 70–1; career vision, 71, 145; city editor, 71, 145; competitiveness *vs.* collaboration, 146; focus group discussion,

144–7; husband, 70; imposter phenomenon, 72, 104; industry upheaval, 70, 104; interview with, 70–3; luck factor, 70, 103–4; male power model, 71, 145–6; mentoring, 146; motherhood, 70; praise for, 120; work/life balance, 70, 205. See also *Hamilton Spectator*

Analysing Narrative Reality (Gubrium and Holstein), 28

Arab, Paula (mid-career): age and background, 194–5, 196–7; columnist and editorial board member, 67, 152, 195–6, 203; diversity, 194, 196; focus group discussion, 151–3; interview with, 165, 194–8; life after daily journalism, 165, 198; single, 91, 197; social justice focus, 194–5, 196, 203; turning-point story, 196. See also *Calgary Herald*

Arenburg, Patricia. *See* Brooks Arenburg, Patricia

arts and culture sections: devaluing of, 38, 63; early career journalists, 138; as gendered section, 155; mid-career journalists, 66, 87;